'These experiences and stories shaped my and my parents' lives, and those of millions of others. Now Taj Ali is recounting and updating them for a new era, one with many would-be Enoch Powells, high on cash and confidence. His book is pacy and imbued with personal commitment. At its heart is an insistence that race and class go together, that we are stronger together and that racism will flourish as long as we live in silos.'

Aditya Chakrabortty, Senior Economics Commentator, the *Guardian*

'A consequential recounting of a long and illustrious history of South Asian resistance and organising in Britain. It reminds us yet again of the vital importance of solidarity and alliances across race, religion and class in changing the world we share.'

Priyamvada Gopal, author of *Insurgent Empire*

'This is forgotten history that needs to be told as a matter of emergency.'

Sathnam Sanghera, author of *Empireland*

'Ali's isn't a nostalgic trip down memory lane but an insightful account of community struggles and solidarities directly relevant to our current conjuncture. This book traces the transnational, class and gender-based nodes through which anti-racist struggles were fought and won, and whilst there is no blueprint that can be lifted from these accounts, there is rich learning to draw.'

Shabna Begum, CEO, The Runnymede Trust

'This is a British history – and one that should be better known across the nation.'

Kavita Puri, *HistoryExtra*

'Like all the great people's historians, Taj Ali has an eye for the past in the present. Cut from the same cloth as the rebels and radicals that inspired him, this fast-moving narrative captures the heartbeat and solidarity rhythms of South Asian working-class struggles across the centuries.'

Liz Fekete, Director, Institute for Race Relations

COME WHAT MAY, WE'RE HERE TO STAY

Manchester University Press

COME WHAT MAY, WE'RE HERE TO STAY

THE STORY OF SOUTH ASIAN RESISTANCE IN BRITAIN

TAJ ALI

MANCHESTER UNIVERSITY PRESS

Published by Manchester University Press
Oxford Road, Manchester, M13 9PL
www.manchesteruniversitypress.co.uk

British Library Cataloguing-in-Publication Data
A catalogue record for this book is available from the British Library

ISBN 978 1 5261 7758 2 hardback

First published 2026

Typeset
by Cheshire Typesetting Ltd, Cuddington, Cheshire

CONTENTS

Preface vi

Prologue 1
1 The Highgate revolutionaries 8
2 Punjabi pioneers 30
3 Seafarer struggles 46
4 Early struggles in post-war Britain 61
5 Black Power 84
6 Finding home 98
7 Fighting back 128
8 A national movement 151
9 Self-defence is no offence 170
10 Solidarity 193
11 Rushdie, rioting and religious divides 219
Epilogue 240

List of interviewees 247
Notes 248
Acknowledgements 266
Index 269

PREFACE

A young South Asian man is walking down a street in Hartlepool when he is punched in the face. Onlookers cheer, laugh and yell racial slurs. 'A Paki got banged', one shouts, as those around him begin to smash the windows of small businesses and kick down the door of a nearby house. Meanwhile, in neighbouring Middlesbrough, a group of white men erect a makeshift checkpoint, halting traffic and interrogating drivers about their ethnicity, demanding to know if they are 'white' or 'English'. In Rotherham and Tamworth, racist mobs try to burn down hotels housing refugees.

These are not stories from the 1970s. They are a snapshot of the horrific scenes we saw in dozens of towns and cities across the UK in summer 2024. Those riots, the worst racist violence in over a century, began following the murder of three young girls at a dance class in Southport, Merseyside, and false claims that the killer was a recently arrived Muslim immigrant, which rapidly spread on social media. The next day Southport's mosque was pelted with bricks and local businesses were targeted. Over the following week the violence spread across England and Northern Ireland.

I barely slept during the riots. My phone buzzed constantly with WhatsApps, Instagram messages and X (formerly known as Twitter) DMs, each reporting a new attack. At the time I was the editor of *Tribune Magazine*, and I was supposed to be on book leave, writing this book on the history of British South Asian political activism. My rationale for this was simple: South Asians have a rich and proud history of political activism; it's important that we record that history and, crucially, learn from it. But history was playing out in front of me, and I couldn't ignore it. It was my community being vilified. My community being attacked. There I was, one of the few Muslim journalists in the British media, being approached by fellow Muslims asking me to report on what was happening around them. I dropped everything and rushed to report on those horrific scenes.

For vulnerable Black and Asian communities, the fear was overwhelming. I recall one particular message that I received at that time. It came from a terrified Muslim man in the north-east of the country after days of violence in Hartlepool, Middlesbrough and Sunderland. 'We're on the outskirts of Bishop Auckland and had to lock the shop up', it said. 'My wife's having panic attacks, terribly upset at the very real threat of violence and property damage. My wife is making non-stop duas [prayers] for our safety and all the Muslims. Just gonna batten down the hatches and pray it's OK, inshallah.'

After a week or so of violence, the riots subsided. Even so, the racist incidents continued, even if few were reported and fewer still made the news. Our political and media class quickly moved on, as if racist rioting was nothing more than a glitch in an otherwise peaceful nation. Few uttered the word Islamophobia, or even acknowledged the fears that communities across Britain faced.

I was angry and frustrated. At politicians and journalists who continued to fan the flames of bigotry. At people who failed to understand the seriousness of what had just happened and what could happen next. And at myself: I hadn't written a page of history that summer. I had quit my job. I couldn't focus. I couldn't write.

But the book wasn't going to write itself. Towards the end of August I headed down to Southall to interview Suresh Grover. An extensive history of Grover's decades-long anti-racist activism would probably require a book in itself, but the man has done more than most and continues to organise. Even so, I didn't get round to interviewing Grover about his life that day. The riots overshadowed everything. We discussed the immediate challenge in front of us and what we could do next. When I began my research for this book years ago, I didn't imagine that I'd be organising alongside many of the people I interviewed. I attended meetings and marches and spoke on stages alongside anti-racist veterans such as Suresh Grover, Mukhtar Dar and Matloub Husayn-Ali-Khan of the Sheffield Asian Youth Movement.

It was quite a common experience for my oral history interviews to turn into conversations about the current challenges we face, from riots to rising hate crime. Everyone I interviewed said that they had seen this before; the parallels to the past were endless. How immigrants were blamed for the violence inflicted on them, how media narratives fanned the flames, and how politicians, both Labour and Tory, engaged in a race to the bottom on anti-migrant hysteria.

As my interviews made clear, the story of that summer of rioting starts long before 2024. In the 1970s and 1980s, front-page headlines about an 'invasion' of immigrants and inflammatory rhetoric from mainstream politicians such as then prime minister Margaret Thatcher, who warned that the UK might be 'swamped by people with a different culture', combined to create a toxic atmosphere in which the far right thrived. And we have seen something similar in recent years: when hundreds of thousands of people began to take to the streets demanding a ceasefire in Gaza in late 2023, a moral panic was whipped up by politicians and journalists about 'Islamists' taking over the UK. Former home secretary Suella Braverman led the charge, labelling peaceful protesters 'hate marchers' in October 2023, while former Tory MP Lee Anderson added that London mayor Sadiq Khan was 'controlled by Islamists'. The leader of Reform UK, Nigel Farage, went further still, stating that British Muslims 'do not subscribe to British values'.

None acknowledged the diversity of the protestors, the thousands of men, women and children from a range of backgrounds. Nor did they acknowledge that the overwhelmingly peaceful marches saw few arrests. Instead, they chose to ramp up an Islamophobic sentiment that had always been there, forcing a narrative of split loyalties and incompatible difference that was, naturally, seized upon by the far right. In November 2023 there was a reported 600 per cent increase in Islamophobic hate crime.

All of this was the precursor to the racist riots of 2024. And the violence did not stop just because the open rioting did. In January 2025 seven London mosques were daubed with anti-Muslim graffiti, while in the months that followed others were attacked in Luton, Aberdeen and Sheffield. In April Muslim graves in Watford were vandalised. In June worshippers were evacuated from the Belfast Islamic Centre when its windows were smashed and a bomb was thrown inside. Then violent protests broke out outside a hotel housing refugees in Epping, an affluent market town in Essex. Bottles and fireworks were thrown at police and two South Asian security guards were attacked in a racist assault. In Ballymena, Northern Ireland, the homes of Filipino workers were firebombed in a campaign of anti-immigrant violence.

As I write this prologue, the UK is facing a surge in racist violence. The Peacehaven mosque in East Sussex was recently set ablaze in a shocking attack. The mosque's manager described a rise in Islamophobic abuse over the previous six months: hijab-wearing mothers harassed as they dropped off their children, Brown and Black pupils bullied in nearby schools and the mosque itself pelted. In Portsmouth, a man wielding a knife recently attacked worshippers at a mosque.

And it's not just Muslims who are impacted. A 9-year-old Black girl in Bristol was shot three times with an airgun in a racist attack, while a Sikh woman in Oldbury was raped as her attackers shouted: 'You don't belong in this country.' Across the United Kingdom, racist graffiti scars walls from Essex to Easington.

We shouldn't, however, be confused about what is causing this new upsurge of race hate. There may be parallels with the past, but there are differences too. Today, we live in the outrage economy, where racist vitriol is rewarded, misinformation is monetised and riots are livestreamed. Minority groups, immigrants and Muslims aren't just the targets any more; we are the content. Without us they would not have their TikTok views, Substack subscribers and YouTube followers. Now is the era of TV channels such as GB News and Talk TV which broadcast hate into the homes of millions. An era when the richest man in the world, Elon Musk, amplifies misinformation on his X platform, regularly retweets far-right accounts such as that of

Tommy Robinson and pours money into right-wing groups around the world.

As these racist narratives continue to shape society, a generation of young South Asians are trying to make sense of their own identities and the world around them.

***

My initial impetus for writing this book was to document the rich and proud tradition of political activism in the British South Asian community. Few of these stories have been documented and some are at risk of being lost. But the events of the last few years have given the book added importance. What lessons can we learn from the past? What are the patterns of history? And why are we in Britain too?

I had initially set out to write the story of the anti-racist movements that had emerged in Britain during the 1970s and 1980s. But many of them had built on an earlier tradition of political organising. Surely the industrial struggles of South Asian workers are worthy of being remembered? And what of the anti-colonial struggles? Through archival research, I've uncovered some fascinating stories: of South Asian students in early twentieth-century Britain fighting for independence; of the global dimensions of the independence movement with their connections with Irish republicans; and of other groups fighting for similar causes and the anti-imperialist attitude that would shape generations to come. All are worth remembering.

Some struggles have been better documented than others. In attempting to capture several early struggles, I have relied heavily on state surveillance files from the India Office Records, as well as newspaper archives. I have also built on the work of incredible historians such as Rozina Visram, who has been so supportive and encouraging throughout this process. If I was to document every single struggle and every single group, this book would never reach publication. It is by no means a comprehensive history. And there are, no doubt, many stories that are yet to be told. But it is my attempt at a snapshot of some important events that have occurred in Britain, that have shaped the Indian subcontinent, shaped Britain and shaped our communities.

There are many themes. Colonialism produced both winners and losers. Some collaborated with the oppressors, while others were co-opted into the system or maintained relentless resistance. The same is true of racism, past and present. And while there are inspiring examples of South Asians putting religious differences aside for anti-colonial and anti-racist struggles, there were always divisions. Between the lascars who toiled on ships and the serangs who served as intermediaries and often exploited them too. Between the Asian youth who fought the fascists on the street, and the self-proclaimed community leaders who condemned their own while enriching themselves. Between the landlords and the tenants. The bosses and the workers. The careerists and the collectivists.

It would be a mistake to treat any one community as a monolith. The biggest lesson from the past is that the struggles are often the same. That there are often struggles waged within communities too, and that the shape they take often varies. This is therefore a book as much about class as it is about race, something that is particularly important due to the erasure of South Asians from many of the wider conversations about class in Britain. We hear a great deal about the white working-class but much less about minority communities that have also been affected by deindustrialisation, cuts to public services and the erosion of social infrastructure. To me, a narrative that obscures the intersection between race and class, and occludes the importance of solidarity, both within and beyond our own specific communities, is a narrative that empowers only those who wish to divide and exploit us.

Recently, I took a guided tour of East India Docks in London. The road names – Clove Crescent, Coriander Avenue, Saffron Avenue – all refer to the spoils of empire. Hundreds of years ago, while colonial powers prospered, lascar seamen lived in squalid conditions on those streets. Today, Tower Hamlets, still one of the poorest boroughs in the capital, is home to the UK's largest Bangladeshi community. There, in the shadow of Canary Wharf and the towers of the financial district, I couldn't help thinking how little has changed and how much work there remains to do.

There is much work to do in tackling street-level racism too. Inspired by many of the individuals I interviewed for this book, in the summer of 2025 I set up an independent monitoring and support service named Radar – Reporting and Documenting Acts of Racism. My goal is to produce regular detailed reports mapping where racist attacks have risen, how the media has covered them and whether authorities have taken meaningful action.

The writer James Baldwin once said, 'You think your pain and your heartbreak is unprecedented in the history of the world, but then you read. It was books that taught me that the things that tormented me most were the very things that connected me with all the people who were alive, who had ever been alive.'[1] The history of South Asians in Britain is a history of struggle. But it is also a history of resistance. Far from being passive victims, South Asians organised against racism, colonialism and everyday exploitation. They stood on the shoulders of those who came before them and, in turn, laid foundations for those who would follow.

This book is my attempt to record some of that resistance. So that we can honour it, learn from it, and, above all, ensure that it endures. I offer it in the hope that it might help inspire a new generation in the struggles we continue to face in Britain and across the world today.

PROLOGUE

> We're here because you were there.
>
> A. Sivanandan[1]

> The orders went out to shoot every soul ... It was literally murder ... I have seen many bloody and awful sights lately but such a one as I witnessed yesterday, I pray I never see again. The women were all spared but their screams on seeing their husbands and sons butchered, were most painful ... Heaven knows I feel no pity, but when some old grey bearded man is brought and shot before your very eyes, hard must be that man's heart I think who can look on with indifference.[2]

Those were the recollections of one British army officer in the aftermath of the rebellion of 1857, when thousands rose up in central India against exorbitant taxes, repressive rule and outright disregard for religious customs. The rebellion was soon violently put down by the colonisers, with some who took part hanged, while others were strapped to cannons and blown to pieces. This was the reality of the British Empire.

At its height, the British Empire ruled a quarter of the world, some 400 million people. India was the pinnacle of its riches. From spices to silk, tea to textiles, the subcontinent was a cash-cow for the British East India Company.

It was never going to give it up easily. Founded in 1600, by the mid-eighteenth century the East India Company had established a firm foothold in the region, and controlled vast swathes of territory. Dissent from the natives would not be tolerated. There was an army of 260,000 to say so. It was this army that allowed the British East India Company to quickly transition from a trading body to a political power, eventually culminating in direct rule of India by the British Crown.

In English literature, control of India was portrayed as a burdensome civilisational mission, a noble pursuit required to enlighten the 'savages'. But the events of 1857, and the true South Asian experience under British rule more generally, tell a different story. When the colonised fought back, they were met with barbarity – and it would change them and India forever.

Thousands of years earlier, long before British colonial rule, the Indian subcontinent had been home to a rich tapestry of cultures and civilisations. Among the most prominent was the Indus Valley civilisation, which was known for its sophisticated urban planning, including the world's first known sanitation systems. Its cities were made up of baked-brick homes and the similarity in size among the buildings demonstrated a remarkable degree of egalitarianism and wealth distribution. It was in India, during the third millennium BCE, that the first accurate system of standardised weights and measures was developed. Trade links with ancient Mesopotamia were probably maintained for hundreds of years during this period too.

In the centuries that followed, numerous kingdoms ruled the Indian subcontinent. Many were key participants in the Indian Ocean trading network, alongside Arab, African and Malay kingdoms, which saw the exchange of both commodities and ideas. By the seventeenth century Mughal India was one of the manufacturing marvels of the world, known for its agriculture, textiles, shipbuilding and steel industries.

Of course, pre-British India was not without its problems. Mughal power was waning before the British arrived, and the kingdoms that comprised the Indian subcontinent were increasingly fragmented. It was British rule that ushered in the end of India's economic dominance. At the beginning of the eighteenth century, India's share of the world economy was 23 per cent – as large as all of Europe put together. By the time of India's independence in 1947, this had dropped to 3 per cent. Drawing on detailed data on tax and trade, economist Utsa Patnaik estimates that Britain drained nearly $45 trillion from India between 1765 and 1938.[3]

It was in this context that the 1857 uprising took place. Often referred to as the Indian Mutiny or the First War of Independence, the uprising was a response to long-standing grievances among Indian soldiers, or sepoys as they were known, serving in the East India Company's Bengal Army. Poor pay, limited opportunities for promotion, cultural insensitivity and growing fears of religious interference all contributed to widespread discontent. But the immediate catalyst was the introduction of the new Enfield rifle. Rumours that its cartridges were greased with cow and pig fat – offensive to both Hindus and Muslims – led to widespread alarm and reinforced existing concerns about forced conversion to Christianity.

On 29 March 1857 a sepoy named Mangal Pandey attacked his officers at Barrackpore in northern Calcutta and was quickly arrested and later executed. Tensions continued to rise, and on 10 May the rebellion truly began in the city of Meerut near Delhi. Eighty-five sepoys refused to accept their cartridges and were court-martialled, humiliated and imprisoned. Their comrades, incensed by the punishment, mutinied, freeing the prisoners, killing British officers and civilians, and marching on Delhi. There they were joined by the local garrison, and the ageing Mughal emperor Bahādur Shah II was proclaimed the symbolic leader of the revolt.

The fall of Delhi gave the rebellion momentum. It soon spread across northern and central India. Despite the serious threat it posed, the British eventually regained control, and the aftermath was brutal. Thousands of sepoys and civilians were executed. The East India Company's rule came to an end, with the British Crown assuming direct control of India in 1858. The British response – the enactment of horrific violence – stayed with those who witnessed it and survived. The scenes were described to future generations. The British thought they had buried the revolution in 1857, but they had merely planted its seeds.

The decades that followed, with India now under direct British rule, proved particularly difficult for rural farmers. Land was taken away from the families of individuals involved in the uprising and punitive taxes were imposed on villages believed to have lent the rebels support. Some villages were burnt to the ground entirely.[4] Further challenges came in the form of droughts, food shortages and the colonial land tenure system for small landowners, which uprooted the subsistence farmers who had once dominated village life and placed over them a class of landlords, known as zamindars, who were given the right to collect taxes. As a result, many peasants were force to become landless labourers, while many up and down the country found themselves trapped in a cycle of indebtedness to moneylenders from whom they borrowed in order to pay exorbitant taxes. Countless numbers of peasants could no longer sustain themselves through agriculture, which exacerbated rural poverty and vulnerability to famines. Between 1850 and 1899 India suffered 24 major famines, leading to an estimated 15 million deaths.[5]

These conditions, alongside the exploitation and entrenchment of existing caste divisions on the Indian subcontinent, gave rise to large-scale migration across the British Empire. And this migration was of huge benefit to the imperialists. The abolition of the transatlantic slave trade meant that there was demand for cheap labour on plantations; significant numbers of Indians were in this way absorbed into the indentured servitude system in Mauritius, British Guiana, Trinidad, Fiji, Natal (South Africa) and other colonies. Hundreds of thousands migrated to East Africa to work on railway construction. Between 1834 and 1960 thirty million South Asian migrants left the Indian subcontinent, spreading the diaspora far and wide. Many would go on to play a pivotal role in later struggles for independence across the Empire.

***

One force that was significant in shaping the Indian independence movement emerged on the subcontinent itself: the Bengal Renaissance. From 1772 to 1911 Calcutta served as the capital of British India, and as the colonial metropolis of western Bengal it became the first city in Asia to adopt a European-style education system. In 1817 the Hindu College was founded, marking a pivotal moment in the history of Indian education. For the first time, higher education in English became available, and a new generation of intellectuals were nurtured, many of whom began to challenge traditional norms in Indian society. The efforts of the reformers were assisted by the wide availability of books in both English and Bengali in Calcutta, the epicentre of the printing press on the subcontinent.

One young professor, Henry Louis Vivian Derozio, was particularly influential. While teaching at the Hindu College, he introduced his students to the ideas of Francis Bacon, David Hume and Thomas Paine, encouraging them to question the rules of the society around them. British officials had assumed that an English-style education would serve their imperial ambitions by cultivating a class of subjects loyal to the Crown. Instead, the liberal principles embedded within that education, such as ideas about just rule, the social contract and individual rights, resonated with a population increasingly resentful of British rule. For a growing generation of Indian intellectuals, loyalty to the Crown came to represent a direct contradiction of the very values they had been taught to admire. Ironically, it was the English education system itself that furnished the emerging Indian nationalist movement with its most powerful intellectual foundations.

Raja Ram Mohan Roy, often referred to as the father of the Indian Renaissance, started Atmiya Sabha (Society of Friends), a philosophical discussion circle which played an influential role in propagating reformist ideas such as questioning established practices in Indian culture such as idolatry, caste rigidities, child marriages and sati (self-immolation by widows). Around the same time, accounts of English radicalism and the French Revolution began entering public consciousness, sparking the imagination of Indian nationalists who sought an alternative to oppressive British rule.

In 1903 the British government announced its intention to partition Bengal into two. The western half was to be a Hindu-majority state, while the eastern half was to be a

Muslim-majority state. This partition was necessary, the government claimed, because of the enormous size and diversity of Bengal. Lord Curzon, the Viceroy of India, thought that it was so big as to be impossible to govern effectively. But the local population resented the plans, believing it was an attempt to divide and rule. Curzon pressed ahead regardless, and in 1905 unrest broke out across Bengal. Opponents employed a range of tactics including appeals, petitions and press campaigns, as well as more radical methods including strikes, boycotts and even assassinations.

On 7 August 1905, as part of the campaign against Bengal's partition, the Swadeshi movement was launched at Calcutta Town Hall. The movement advocated the boycott of foreign goods and the promotion of Indian-made alternatives. Cloth from Manchester and salt from Liverpool were boycotted, while British-run schools and courts were shunned. Instead, Indians began to set up their own institutions, such as the Bengal National College. Shops selling foreign goods were picketed and individuals who sold such goods were ostracised.

The movements created by the British plan to partition Bengal only added to the intellectual tumult created by the Bengal Renaissance. From this emerged a new motto, the clarion call for a new Indian society: swaraj, or self-rule. A growing number of Indians were explicitly questioning the legitimacy of British rule in India and calling for self-government. Calls for swaraj would soon begin to ring out among the growing South Asian diaspora too.

1
THE HIGHGATE REVOLUTIONARIES

The leafy North London suburb of Highgate, home to ancient woodlands and associated with numerous English literary icons from T. S. Eliot to Samuel Taylor Coleridge, isn't the first place that springs to mind when one thinks of the Indian independence struggle. But the epicentre of Indian revolutionary activity in Britain was once a Victorian mansion on one of its tranquil streets. From 1905 to 1910, within this seemingly unremarkable student residence, bomb-making workshops were conducted, assassination plots were hatched, and gun-smuggling was organised.

India House, as it became known, was founded in July 1905 by Krishna Varma, a lawyer who had made a fortune investing in cotton presses, and was an ardent supporter of the Hindu reform movement. But its true origins lie further back, in the India of 1897, which was then suffering from an outbreak of bubonic plague. To deal with the outbreak, the British Raj set up a special committee, with Walter Charles Rand, a civil service officer, acting as a commissioner in Pune, an area with a significant population of European soldiers and their families. Under Rand, British soldiers took a heavy-handed approach to the plague, entering private homes and stripping and examining women in public. There were even accusations that the British vandalised property and religious symbols.

Bal Tilak, a schoolteacher, Sanskrit scholar and one of India's most prominent nationalists at the time, who was based in Pune, had railed against these tactics in his newspapers. In doing so, he quoted the Hindu scripture, the Bhagavad Gita. No one, it said, attached blame to anyone who killed an oppressor without thought of reward. On 22 June 1897, on the day of Queen Victoria's Diamond Jubilee celebrations, three brothers – Damodar, Balkrishna and Vasudeo Chapekar – shot Rand along with his lieutenant, Charles Egerton Ayerst. The brothers were charged with murder and hanged, and Tilak was arrested for incitement. This created problems for Varma. He was a friend and political associate of Tilak, whose papers had done so much to fan the flames of discontent. The growing threat of censorship and the breadth of sedition laws made advocating for revolution on the Indian subcontinent increasingly difficult. In March 1897 the decision was made to continue to advocate for revolution in Britain, where conditions were more favourable and repression less likely.

After arriving in Britain in March 1897, Varma turned his attention to the ways in which he could aid his compatriots in their struggle for independence. He would soon focus his attention on the small number of Indian students residing in Britain. The reasons for Indian students to come to Britain were many: the examinations for the Indian Civil Service were only held in London, and the bar in Calcutta and Bombay was confined to barristers trained in the colonial metropole. For Indian students, then, Britain was their passport to power.

An earlier generation of students included Mohandas K. Gandhi, who studied law in London from 1888 to 1891, as well as Muhammad Ali Jinnah, a prominent member of the All-India Muslim League and later founder of Pakistan, who had done the same between 1892 and 1895. But their number was always small, and mostly confined to male migrants from the upper echelons of Indian society, with most others prevented from studying due to the steep cost of university education, as well as the cost of travel and accommodation once in London. To assist others, in 1904 Varma announced a series of fellowships for Indian students which would allow them to study in Britain on the condition that they would refuse employment with the British government upon completion of their studies. These students, Varma believed, would then come to play a vital role in propagating the cause of Indian independence.

The following year, Varma would further his advocacy for independence by launching a monthly periodical committed to India's freedom, the *Indian Sociologist*. In it, Varma went further than earlier reformers, who had called for a more just British rule in India, arguing that foreign rule itself was the problem. He castigated the Congress Party, a more moderate nationalist party, for what he saw as its timid advocacy, and criticised Gandhi for siding with the British against the Boers in South Africa. The solution instead, he wrote, was revolution, and the masthead of his journal bore Herbert Spencer's words: 'Resistance to aggression is not simply justifiable but imperative.'

The journal was soon branded a 'seditious rag' by the British government, and it was later banned in India. Its first editorial set out its purpose plainly:

> The political relations between England and India urgently require a genuine Indian interpreter in the United Kingdom to show, on behalf of India, how Indians really fare and feel

> under British rule. No systematic attempt has, so far as our knowledge goes, ever been made in this country by Indians themselves to enlighten the British public with regard to the grievances, demands, and aspirations of the people of India and its unrepresented millions before the bar of public opinion in Great Britain and Ireland.[1]

Varma insisted that the publication would remain unaffiliated to any political party and would be guided by rationalism. During his time in Britain, Varma had come under the influence of Spencer, the English philosopher better known for his association with Darwinism and libertarianism, but who remained an ardent opponent of British colonial rule. The magazine's first editorial referenced Spencer twice: first to emphasise individual liberty: 'every man has freedom to do all that he wills, provided he infringes not the equal freedom of any other man'; and second to express his opposition to authoritarianism, in all forms: 'all despotisms, whether political or religious, whether of sex, of caste, or of custom, may be generalised as limitations to individuality, which it is the nature of civilisation to remove'.

But publishing alone was not enough. On 18 February 1905, inspired by Irish republicans, Varma founded the Indian Home Rule Society from his home in Muswell Hill.[2] Around twenty Indians attended its inaugural meeting, which resolved to secure Home Rule for India, promote propaganda in Britain towards this goal and spread unity among Indian people. Varma became its president. He saw the society as a bolder alternative to the Congress Party's cautious politics, and it kept close ties with revolutionaries in India. This was important to radicals in both countries; as Tilak wrote to Varma in 1905, 'The freer atmosphere of England gives you scope which we can never hope to get here.'[3]

Unlike other Indian associations of the time, membership was restricted to Indian people. On 9 May 1905, the eve of the anniversary of the 1857 uprising, Varma and others celebrated the occasion at an Indian restaurant on Shaftesbury Avenue, in London's West End. Alongside commemorating the historic uprising, the group discussed the ongoing famine and the next steps in the freedom struggle. By then it had become clear that one of the most pressing issues would be housing for Indian students in London. With more arriving on Varma's scholarships, this problem would only get worse. White landlords often refused to let rooms to Asian tenants, deepening the students' isolation. Determined to cultivate a community of committed nationalists, Varma purchased a second property at 65 Cromwell Avenue in July 1905. This was to be India House, and it could accommodate 25 residents.

What began as a student lodging soon transformed into a centre of revolutionary activity, with communal life and regular discussions shaping radical thought. India House was inaugurated by Henry Hyndman, the leader of the left-wing Social Democratic Federation, and among the guests at its opening event were Punjabi nationalist Lala Lajpat Rai, Irish republican Charlotte Despard and Liberal MP Dadabhai Naoroji. Each of these figures loomed large in radical circles at the time. Naoroji had made history in 1892, becoming the first Indian to be elected to the British Parliament after winning the Finsbury Central constituency for the Liberal Party. He had been involved in several organisations promoting Indian rights and had been one of the co-founders of the Indian National Congress in 1885. Yet his most important contribution, one which figures such as Varma would frequently cite in their writings, was the 'drain theory', a detailed economic analysis of how Britain had drained India's wealth.

'As things stand', Hyndman announced that day, 'loyalty to Great Britain means treachery to India. The institution of this India house means a great step in that direction of Indian growth and Indian emancipation, and some of those who are here this afternoon may live to witness the fruits of its triumphant success.'[4] India House would soon live up to Hyndman's words, earning a formidable reputation. Among its rooms were a lecture hall and library, and it became the headquarters of the Indian Home Rule Society, which held weekly meetings there.

One of the things that Varma and his colleagues at India House valued most was international alliances. In July 1906 he and Abdullah al-Mamun Suhrawardy, vice president of the Indian Home Rule Society, attended a Pan-Islamic Society event honouring Mustafa Kamel Pasha of Egypt. Suhrawardy gave a welcome address on behalf of the Indian Home Rule Society in Arabic. 'From the capital of this great empire', he said, 'your cry will reach not only your brethren in faith in the farthest corners of the globe, but you will also find an echo in the heats of patriots of other countries, your partners in suffering.'[5] Varma then followed, congratulating the Pan-Islamic Society and praising Pasha's efforts as editor of the *Al-Liwa* nationalist newspaper, the first mass circulation newspaper in Egypt. He assured Pasha that Indians sympathised with both Muslims at home and in Egypt. Kamel Pasha, in turn, would give extensive coverage to the struggles of Indians.

Varma's vision of religious plurality was further demonstrated by his decision to introduce scholarships in the names of several Muslim rulers such as Akbar, Bahadur Shah Zafar and Tipu Sultan. Muslim students received fellowships too – most notably Abdul Aziz, Khuda Baksh and Haider Raza, who were all associated with India House. When, in October 1906, Gandhi arrived in London to lobby on behalf of Indians in South Africa, he spent his first two nights at India House, taking the opportunity to engage in discussion with Varma and other radicals about India's future.[6] From the outset, it was clear that there was much disagreement on tactics, methods and rhetoric, with Varma criticising Gandhi in particular for his position on the Zulu revolt, where he had initially supported the British because he believed it would prove Indian loyalty and earn rights within the Empire.

Links were also made with the struggle for Irish independence, with the *Indian Sociologist* republishing articles from the New York-based *Gaelic American* newspaper, which did the same with essays on the Indian struggle from the *Indian Sociologist*. Such was the internationalist atmosphere at India House that on 22 September 1906, when it hosted the first Edmund Burke lecture, delivered by Indian nationalist R. G. Pradhan, who argued that India had fared better before British rule,[7] the evening concluded with the singing of Bande Mataram in Sanskrit, with a piano accompaniment to the tune of the French national anthem 'La Marseillaise'. In a later issue of the *Indian Sociologist*, Varma would translate 'La Marseillaise' into several Indian languages.

Word of the organising efforts in London soon spread, and before long an Indian Home Rule Society was set up in Paris, modelled on the London organisation and maintaining frequent contact with it. It was established by a founding member of the Indian Home Rule Society, Sardar Singh Rana, and Bhikhaji Cama, a social reformer associated with the India House radicals who had earlier lived in London. Cama maintained extensive connections with European socialists, and her home in Paris was a hub for Indian revolutionaries. She would later find fame when, in August 1907, at the Second Socialist Congress in Stuttgart, she unfurled what might have been the first flag of Indian independence. Addressing delegates, she described the devastation of famine and called for support. The tricolour flag, inscribed with Vande Mataram, symbolised religious unity.

Yet while Cama and others were committed to pluralism and equality, not all India House alumni would follow her example. In July 1906 a young firebrand arrived in Hampstead. Born on 28 May 1883, in western Maharashtra, Western India, Vinayak Damodar Savarkar had always been drawn to the tales of Maratha warriors who had fought back against the Mughal Empire. As a child, he had immersed himself in Maratha poetry, inspired by what he considered to be courageous rulers who had fought to protect their land. By the time he was a teenager, Savarkar was an enthusiastic nationalist, quickly earning the mentorship of Bal Gangadhar Tilak, and in 1899 he was one of the founders of the Mitra Mela, a secret revolutionary society devoted to the armed overthrow of British rule. By 1904, inspired by the Italian unification leader Giuseppe Mazzini's Young Italy movement, it had been renamed Abhinav Bharat (Young India Society). In 1905 Savarkar participated in the symbolic burning of foreign cloth to protest the partition of Bengal.

Recognising the young man's promise, and his passion for freedom, Tilak sent a letter of recommendation to Varma, securing Savarkar a scholarship to study law in London. Once there, it didn't take Savarkar long to make a name for himself. Every Sunday, India House's lecture hall would be packed, as Savarkar and his comrades from the Free India Society he founded in London spoke about revolution and lectured on Indian history and politics.[8] Students from Oxford, Cambridge, Manchester and Edinburgh would make their way to Highgate to hear the young revolutionary speak.[9] At times, around a hundred people could be in attendance – a sizeable number given how small the Indian population was at the time. His lectures ranged across the world, covering the revolutions in Italy, France and America, yet while he drew inspiration from European revolutionaries and nationalists, he was keen to emphasise India's rich history and culture. Members of the Free India Society swore secret oaths of initiation and sang patriotic songs, reminiscing about Mother India's glorious past.

With all this revolutionary agitation, it's no surprise that the activities of India House soon came to the attention of the British authorities. In 1907, concerned by its influence upon a growing number of students, the Secretary of State for India, Lord Morley, set up the Lee-Warner Committee of Inquiry to investigate the experience of Indian students in Britain. The committee examined a hundred witnesses, both Indian and English students and tutors, and uncovered widespread racism in the universities. Students, it found, were lonely and isolated, while as historian Rozina Visram notes, 'diet, religious and cultural conventions would have further restricted their lives'.[10] It was virtually impossible for those who fell on hard times to find work, and racist abuse was rife. The inquiry noted that all of this led many in the direction of the India House revolutionaries. Fearful that the unrest in Bengal could have implications closer to home, the Lee-Warner report suggested greater social opportunities for Indian students in order to limit the influence of the radicals.

The *Indian Sociologist* also began to attract scrutiny. On 17 May 1907 Francis F. Skrine, a retired member of the Indian Civil Service, wrote in *The Times*:

> For several years past Indian students, who flock in crowds to London and the Universities, have been exposed to influences calculated to fill them with unreasoning hatred of Europeans. They are attacked by persons who have plenty of money at their command, and are able to assist their young compatriots in finding tuition and lodgings ... Several young fellows, whose relatives commended to my care, have been ruined by these scoundrels.

Skrine singled out Varma for criticism:

> Even in England exists an ardent Indian rebel, a Mr. Shayamji Krishnavarma, M.A (Oxon.), President of the Indian Home Rule Society, numbering 150 members, whose influence over the young Indians who come to England for legal or other education can scarcely be very good from the British Government's point of view.

The press campaign didn't stop there. A *Times* editorial on 19 June 1907 accused the India House radicals of advocating armed rebellion. In June 1907, under growing pressure as the public face of India House, Varma decided to leave London for Paris.

For those left behind, the pressure didn't abate. Just a month later, the *Indian Sociologist* revealed that a man who went by the name of O'Brien, and who claimed to be representing the *Gaelic American* of New York and Dublin's Sinn Féin, was caught lurking on the doorstep of India House. He told those inside that 'he desired to write articles for those papers supporting our views'. The man, who the students soon suspected of being a detective, was keen to rub those present for information on the movement in India, taking 'copious notes' throughout. The residents of India House never saw the man again, seeming to confirm their worst suspicions. In a demonstration of how seriously the British authorities were taking the agitation of the Indian students, a short while later an officer from Scotland Yard called the magazine's printer, 'demanding a copy of the then current number of the *Indian Sociologist*'. 'There have been', the journal noted, 'several such visits since then. All this shows the seriousness of the unrest which the British Government has to face in India and elsewhere.'[11]

We can now see, thanks to the archival record, how right the suspicions of Varma and the others were. The earliest record of Special Branch activity in connection with India House comes from 11 May 1907, when officers attended a meeting at which 'seditious' pamphlets were distributed,[12] while just a few months later, in October, the importing and sale of the *Indian Sociologist* was officially banned in India.

Varma continued to publish the *Indian Sociologist* from Paris, but his influence at India House was significantly diminished in his absence, which was much to the advantage of Savarkar. A prolific writer, Savarkar translated a biography of the Italian nationalist hero Mazzini into Marathi, and throughout this period he was in contact with his supporters in India. In 1909 he published a book on the Indian War of Independence, which spoke of Muslim–Hindu unity against a common oppressor and which praised the revolt's Muslim leaders. Unsurprisingly, the book was soon banned in India, although his supporters found ways to smuggle it across the border.

Many of Savarkar's letters home referenced King Shivaji of the Maratha kingdom, invoking the glorious past that he sought to revive. He was also intrigued by the history of the Sikhs, learning Gurumukhi script and publishing a pamphlet called *Khalsa* in which he called on Sikh soldiers in the British army to revolt.

Indian students were growing in number. They were becoming more assertive too. On 10 May 1908 the India House radicals marked the 51st anniversary of the 1857 uprising with a special celebration. This was seen as an incendiary thing to celebrate in the heart of the colonial metropole. India House was decorated for the occasion with red banners, and, according to Savarkar's report, 'beautiful floral arrangements',[13] while framed photos of the heroes of the uprising were displayed. They included Bahādur Shah, the symbolic leader of the rebellion; Shreemant Nana Saheb Peshwa, who led rebel forces in the Cawnpore area during the uprising; Rani Laxmibai of Jhansi, who famously fought against the British on horseback with her young son strapped to her back; Maulvi Ahmadullah Shah, a Sufi scholar who used religion to inspire people against British rule; and Babu Kunwar Singh, who despite being 80 years old, was the chief organiser against British forces in the state of Bihar. So many people attended, with people travelling from Cambridge, Oxford, Cirencester and Reading, Savarkar reports, 'that many had to stand on the street outside ... There were many women too.'[14] In another sign of growing assertiveness, a pamphlet entitled *Oh Martyrs!*, which glorified those who had fought against the British, was printed and circulated among Indian students at Oxford and Cambridge as well as at the Inns of Court in London. Many students even wore badges with the slogan 'Honour to the Martyrs of 1857'; two students at Cirencester Agricultural College, Harnam Singh and Rafiq Muhammad Khan, were expelled for refusing to remove them.

Savarkar's influence at India House was growing too. One account comes to us from English writer David Garnett.

At 17, Garnett had met a young Bengali by the name of Sukhsagar Dutt at the London Tutorial College, and he in turn introduced Garnett to several of his Indian friends in London, one of whom was Niranjan Pal, who was the son of the famed Indian revolutionary and leading member of the Swadeshi movement, Bipin Chandra Pal. Many of these young Indians lived together in Bayswater, in West London, which gained the nickname 'Asia minor' for the concentration of Indian students there. On one occasion, Garnett joined his friend Dutt on a visit to India House, where he met Savarkar and other Indian students. 'Inside the building', Garnett notes, 'were about thirty Indians, almost all very young men, for the most part students, who, like Dutt, had been sent to study law and had made about as much progress in it as he had.'

> Soon after my arrival we trooped into the dining-room and Savarkar, after addressing the company in Hindi, stood up and began to read aloud. I could not understand what he was saying, I looked about the room without paying much attention to him. The sight of those brown men, some sitting round a long table, others leaning against the walls, all listening intently to the staccato voice of the speaker, was very strange to me. When I was with Dutt or Mitter I could forget they were Hindus and I was an Englishman, but at this meeting I felt alone. My race and colour did indeed create a gulf between me and those brown men.[15]

The stirring speeches were just the start. Under Savarkar's leadership, Free Indian Society members embarked upon physical training, preparing for the coming revolution, and even going so far as to join rifle clubs to hone their skills. Lectures were given on bomb-making, with another lecturer proposing that the students infiltrate the Indian army.[16] Such was the feverish activity that on 14 January 1909 the British authorities were alarmed to hear that permission had been granted for the construction of a mini rifle range at India House, while another British state surveillance report referred to a 'war workshop' in the backyard of India House, with bomb-making tutorials taking place in the garden.[17]

The year before, two individuals associated with India House, Hemchandra Das and Pandurang Mahadev Bapat, popularly known as Senapati Bapat, had travelled to Paris to learn the art of bomb-making from exiled Russian revolutionaries. Later, they would smuggle cyclostyled copies of a manual on bomb-making into India; the manual was discovered in police raids on bomb factories in Bengal in 1908, and was used in an attempt to assassinate an unpopular magistrate in Alipore.[18] One member of India House, Koregaonkar, would later confess to their activities, confirming Savarkar's intention to send arms and seditious literature into the country.[19] Savarkar planned, he admitted, to encourage military training and to stir up the Indian army to revolt. One of the allegations was that seditious pamphlets, wrapped in English newspapers, had been sent to India, sometimes being sent first to New York and Germany to prevent interception. Koregaonkar also detailed the radicals' physical training: 'Dhingra, J.D.N. Dass and myself and several others started a "Shakti Puja Samiti" for teaching Ju-Jitsu, boxing and wrestling ... There was an air gun in India House and amateur shooting was in progress.'[20] Others went further still, such as India House's cook Chaturbhuj Amin, who was encouraged to smuggle 20 Browning pistols into India.[21]

There were even attempts to further international struggles against colonialism. At the time Spain was occupying part of the Moroccan coast, and war had broken out with Berber tribes in the mountainous Rif region in the north. Savarkar persuaded Dutt and another India House resident, M. P. T. Acharya, to join Abdul Krim's forces and fight against the Spanish. As Garnett recounted, the events soon descended into farce:

> It seemed to them that they had better go armed, since the Riffs had probably no rifles to spare. I therefore lent Dutt the Winchester rifle ... It was, as I had proved, inaccurate at any range over forty yards and ammunition for it was almost unobtainable in Europe. Nevertheless, Dutt was glad to set off with it to Gibraltar on his way to join Abdul Krim. When the two volunteers reached Gibraltar the customs detained my rifle. The two imitators of Garibaldi went on to Algiers, but found it impossible to reach the Riff and, becoming quickly discouraged, returned to London.[22]

***

The suspicions of the radicals were increasing, too. One day a new resident, a man named Kirtikar from Maharashtra, arrived. He had previously worked as a translator at the Bombay High Court and knew several languages, and he told the India House radicals that he was in London to study dental surgery. Soon he became a resident, and he quickly grew close to Savarkar.[23] On waking, Kirtikar would share his breakfast with another resident, T. S. S. Rajan, before they left together for their respective hospitals. But his actions quickly began to arouse suspicions; after only a few months, Kirtikar began to laze in bed, arriving late for breakfast and not turning up to hospital. Soon after, he began a relationship with India House's English maid. Rajan raised his concerns with Savarkar, who dismissed it as the behaviour of a young aristocrat, but Kirtikar's odd behaviour continued. After several months, Rajan inquired about Kirtikar at the hospital, only to be told that he had attended for just one week before disappearing.

One evening, while Kirtikar was out attending a play with his English girlfriend, V. V. S. Aiyar, a Tamil resident and a close associate of Savarkar who Rajan had confided his suspicions to, saw an opportunity. Using a duplicate key to gain entry into Kirtikar's room, he found a report that he had written for the Metropolitan Police. The document revealed details of a meeting held at India House, confirming that Kirtikar was, in fact, an undercover informant, tasked with gathering and passing along secrets. That night, when Kirtikar returned to India House, Aiyar was waiting for him. With a loaded revolver concealed in his pocket, he confronted Kirtikar and questioned him about his activities. Aiyar bolted the door, pulled out the revolver and aimed it at Kirtikar, warning him that he would shoot if he did not confess to his activities. Aiyar produced the report. Kirtikar collapsed at Aiyar's feet, pleading for his life. Rather than alert the others, Aiyar and Rajan decided to keep Kirtikar under surveillance at India House, forcing him to submit his reports to Aiyar for review and revision before they were passed along to Scotland Yard. The radical now controlled the flow of information. Kirtikar would also have to donate two pounds every month to the Free India Society – a substantial amount at the time.[24]

The discovery left the India House radicals increasingly paranoid. Could there be more informants in their midst? Plainclothes detectives were loitering near the house, following anyone who walked out. Members of India House often jumped into taxis to escape their pursuers. When M. P. T. Acharya, a young Tamil from Madras, arrived a few months later desperate for a job, the India House radicals were deeply suspicious. Acharya was able to prove his innocence and win their trust. He even went a step further, with Aiyar convincing him to go and see the high-ups in Scotland Yard, encouraging them to pay him for information.[25] The issue of India House residents being tailed by detectives was even raised in the House of Commons by an MP in March 1909.[26]

On 30 April 1909 Varma was disbarred for writing a letter in *The Times* advocating Indian Home Rule. Growing hostility to India House from politicians and the press as well as the threat of further disbarments led to a decline in attendance. Intelligence reports described a 'marked abatement of activity', 'growing distrust and disunion', with meetings 'very poorly attended' and 'very quiet'.[27] India House's days were clearly numbered. A surveillance report in May 1909 revealed that only Aiyar and Rajan, as well as two others, M. P. T. Acharya and Govind Amin, were left as residents.[28]

On 9 June 1909 news reached London that Savarkar's older brother, Ganesh, had been sentenced to transportation for life, and at a public meeting in India House, Savarkar swore vengeance on the British.[29] Two days later he was told that his call to the bar would be postponed because of his 'seditious activities'.[30] The radical was fuming.

Savarkar's book on the 1857 uprising ends with a rather prophetic poem from the Mughal emperor Bahadur Shah. 'As long as there remains the least trace of love of faith in the hearts of our heroes, so long the sword of Hindustan shall remain sharp and one day shall flash even at the gates of London.'[31] On 1 July 1909 the sword would strike at the very heart of the Empire.

***

On a warm July evening in 1909, Madan Lal Dhingra left his Bayswater residence with deliberate purpose. The young Indian, dressed in a plain brown suit and a sky-blue turban, was armed with two Colt revolvers and a dagger. Earlier in the afternoon he had practised his shooting at a range on

Tottenham Court Road located above a penny arcade. He'd been attending two or three times a week for the previous few months, honing his craft: now he was ready to carry out the deed. Dhingra caught a cab to the Imperial Institute in South Kensington.[32]

The National Indian Association had organised an evening gathering and Dhingra's presence was hardly cause for commotion. He had been a member for a year, and he had conversed with many other members. On arrival Dhingra exchanged pleasantries with the other guests, but as the clock struck 11 and guests started to leave, he grew increasingly agitated. On the steps of the Imperial Institute, he pulled out his revolver and shot Sir William Curzon Wyllie, aide-de-camp to the Secretary of State for India, five times in the face. Cawas Lalcaca, a Parsi doctor, attempted to intervene. Dhingra shot him twice, killing him too. Then he turned the gun on himself, but he had accidentally put the gun's safety catch on and couldn't fire. He was pushed to the ground.

What had compelled this 25-year-old to carry out this deed, people asked? Born in Amritsar, the sixth of seven children fathered by a civil surgeon who remained loyal to the British, Dhingra had left his native Punjab to study engineering at University College London in 1906. He soon became a regular attendee at India House, embracing their radical politics and coming under the spell of Savarkar. He'd also experienced racism and hostility from English people, which only solidified his nationalist politics.

At trial, Dhingra refused to recognise the authority of the British courts. He was not represented by counsel and called no defence. The trial was brief, lasting less than an hour and a half. Dhingra did, however, request that a statement be read out on his behalf. In it, he highlighted the violence of colonial rule, referring to the 'murder of 80 million Indian people in the last 50 years', and the economic exploitation of Britain, which he said was taking £100 million from India every year. The assassination was justified, he claimed, as a response to the British who were responsible for 'terrible oppression and horrible atrocities' and the 'outraging of our women'.[33] Dhingra was found guilty and sentenced to death.[34]

David Garnett recalled meeting Savarkar in the aftermath of the assassination:

> He gave me a copy of Dhingra's statement and asked me if I could get it published. That was easy. I took my first and only journalistic scoop to Robert Lynd, then on the staff of the *Daily News*, and it appeared in that paper next morning. Savarkar was extremely pleased. Curiously enough, after being deprived of his statement, Dhingra had been unable to express himself nearly so well or quite to the same effect. It occurred to me that someone might have written it for him and that he had not bothered to learn it by heart. If so, I guessed who the author of it was and realised that he was an accessory.[35]

Earlier that month, five days after the assassination, a condolence meeting at Caxton Hall had been called, presided over by Sir Aga Khan, one of the most influential Indian Muslims of all time and a founder of the All-India Muslim League, who would later play a pivotal role in the founding of the state of Pakistan. A resolution was passed in which Khan declared, 'The meeting unanimously condemns Madan Lal Dhingra.' Yet one hand was raised in objection: Savarkar's. Furious at this intervention, an Englishman by the name of Edward Palmer sprang up and struck Savarkar's forehead. M. P. T. Acharya, a fellow India House radical, flashed out his pistol ready to shoot Palmer. Savarkar stopped him.

That same night, Savarkar penned a letter to *The Times*. No one should condemn the act of Dhingra, he wrote, unless he was found guilty by the court.[36] Magazines and newspapers, including the *Gaelic American*, *Bande Mataram* and Varma's *Indian Sociologist* all proclaimed Dhingra a martyr, while *The Times* reported that a placard in support of Dhingra had been seen in Dublin, where a freedom struggle akin to India's was gaining traction.

A few days after the assassination, Gandhi was back in London. He condemned Dhingra as a dishonourable coward, describing his actions as motivated by 'ill digested reading of worthless writings' and the 'cowardly promptings' of Shayamji Krishna Varma.[37] Despite these criticisms, he was willing to meet Savarkar and others associated with India House at a dinner. Though critical of their methods, Gandhi praised their 'high degree of morality, great intellectual ability and lofty self-sacrifice'.[38]

But the radicals could no longer sustain themselves in the face of state and public opposition. Soon, India House was sold off, and Savarkar began living at a small Indian restaurant in Red Lion Passage near Westminster. He later moved to Paris, just as Varma had done several years earlier. In his absence, the authorities moved against him, framing him on charges of 'waging war against His Majesty the King Emperor of India' for speeches that he had delivered in India several years previously. When, rather unwisely, he returned to London, he was arrested and taken to Brixton jail, where he was held before being returned to India to stand trial. Yet Savarkar's life of resistance wasn't over yet: when the ship taking him back docked at Marseilles, he escaped and swam to shore. But British officials were quick to pursue him and he was taken back into British custody.

Finally imprisoned on the Andaman Islands, Savarkar signed mercy petitions pledging to abandon his agitation against the British. In the years that followed, his politics shifted decisively. Anti-imperialism gave way to exclusionary Hindu nationalism, which increasingly defined India not against colonial rule but against its Muslim population who, he argued, belonged to a separate nation. In 1923 he published *Essentials of Hindutva*, his most influential work, which articulated this vision and legitimised violence against Muslims. His ideas would go on to inspire the formation of the Rashtriya Swayamsevak Sangh (RSS), the parent organisation of the Bharatiya Janata Party (BJP), today the largest far-right party in the world.

In government, the BJP has presided over a sharp escalation in anti-Muslim violence, an authoritarian crackdown on opposition parties, and widening inequality. In 2019 it introduced the Citizenship Amendment Act – a bigoted law that legitimises discrimination on the basis of religion and disenfranchises Muslims. And beyond discriminatory laws, Islamophobia remains deeply embedded in public life, with mob lynchings increasingly common.

Savarkar undeniably played a role in India's freedom struggle, but over time his vision of India diverged starkly from that of many of his contemporaries. Today, countless Indian Muslims live with the weight of his legacy, and for many, freedom feels more distant than ever.

I visited India House in May 2024 with my friend and fellow journalist Reha Kansara. The first time we'd met, we'd bonded on the Bakerloo Line over our shared interest in Savarkar and Hindu nationalism. Reha, a British Hindu, had reported for the BBC on the influence of Hindutva in India and Britain, including the Hindu–Muslim unrest in Leicester in 2022. While researching at the British Library,

I would regularly send her photographs of British state surveillance files on India House. 'They even spied on the table tennis', I remember texting, half-amused, half-alarmed.

It was a bright, sunny afternoon when we finally stood outside India House at 65 Cromwell Avenue. We were struck by the affluence of the surrounding streets and by the sheer scale of the building itself. A blue plaque commemorating Savarkar was unveiled there on 8 June 1985 by Lord Fenner Brockway. Brockway – a British socialist and committed anti-racist and anti-imperialist – would, I imagine, be deeply troubled by the contemporary power of Hindutva. The Indian subcontinent today is more divided than at any point in recent history, and those religious tensions have increasingly spilled across the global diaspora. Yet that afternoon I was simply standing beside a British Hindu friend, joking about my poor photography skills and fantasising about acquiring enough wealthy acquaintances to buy India House ourselves. We were walking the same streets as Savarkar had more than a century earlier, conscious of the contradictions he left behind, but also of a shared history that is too often forgotten.

2
PUNJABI PIONEERS

Wanted: Brave soldiers to stir up Ghadar in India
Pay: Death
Prize: Martyrdom
Pension: Liberty
Field of Battle: India

The inaugural issue of the *Ghadar* newspaper, published in November 1913, was blunt about the organisation's aims: only through armed insurrection would India achieve its independence. The newspaper was published by Lala Har Dayal, an intellectual who had studied at Oxford between 1905 and 1907 and had come under the influence of the India House radicals. Dayal took these radicals' ideals with him, first to Paris in 1908 where he worked alongside Madame Cama on the *Bande Mataram* newspaper, before moving to the United States in 1910 to take up a position as a lecturer.

There, Har Dayal cut his teeth in the trade union movement, and he joined the Industrial Workers of the World union, rising to become the secretary of its Oakland branch. The IWW had been established in Chicago in 1905, and it was unique in its internationalism and anti-racism, accepting members from all walks of life. Many of its members were loggers and seamen, workers who were geographically mobile. This was particularly true for seamen who had frequently encountered foreigners, connecting their own struggles with those overseas.

In the US, Har Dayal came across a small but tight-knit Punjabi community, consisting mainly of young men seeking economic opportunities in a country with widespread labour shortages. Many of the Punjabi immigrants worked in America's lumber mills, on its railroads and on its farms. Like the communities of Chinese and Japanese migrants, who were treated as a suspect community due to the 'yellow peril' moral panic at the time, Punjabis faced widespread racism – often with violent consequences. In 1907 a 600-strong mob of white lumberjacks in Washington launched a violent assault on the homes of some 250 Punjabi mill workers. The workers were viciously beaten, with their belongings thrown on the streets. In March 1910 another mob attacked Indian workers in Oregon. This time though, Indian workers, far more assertive and growing in number, beat them back with sticks and clubs.

With the threat of racist violence constantly looming, being apolitical was a luxury few could afford. Back in Punjab, there was growing unrest over land seizures by the government. Sensing their growing frustration with injustice at home and abroad, Har Dayal sought to build a cadre of committed revolutionaries among the diaspora. Sure enough, Punjabi farmworkers, mill labourers, seamen and students eagerly joined the Ghadar Party. They gathered on farms and ranches to listen to Har Dayal and other firebrands preach about the horrors of colonial rule and the need to revolt. The *Ghadar* newspaper was published in both Urdu and Gurmukhi, and it circulated widely among the South Asian diaspora in America, even reaching as far afield as Canada, Shanghai, Hong Kong, Malaysia and Singapore. It was an effective piece of propaganda, winning many converts to the cause. In North America alone at one point, the Ghadar movement had over 5,000 members gathered into 72 branches.[1]

The movement's most influential publication by far was the *Ghadar di Goonj*, a weekly poetry collection focused on the revolt of warriors standing up against tyranny. Many poems recalled the epic battles and sacrifices of Punjabi heroes, calling on Indian soldiers to reclaim the pride and dignity which had been lost serving the British.[2]

Many Ghadarites embraced class politics too. This was particularly true of those who came under the influence of the IWW. As one influential Ghadarite, Pandurang Khankhoje, who hailed from Maharashtra, later said: 'We stayed in log cabins and every night after work we sat around a campfire and listened to the lectures of the old labour leader who had got me my job. This was the first time I had heard of the labour movement in America and it was my first introduction to socialist thought.'[3] The Ghadar movement was explicitly secular, embracing people of all religious backgrounds.

When, on 4 August 1914, Britain declared war on Germany, the Ghadar movement, aware of the large number of Punjabi soldiers in the British army, sensed an opportunity to strike. In an article entitled 'The Trumpet of War', the movement gave a call to arms: 'O warriors! the opportunity that you have been looking for has come ... Don't delay a moment ... This is the right moment to start a war of independence. You can very soon expel the British from India.'[4] Yet these ambitious revolutionaries were no match for a well-armed nation that would soon exercise control over a quarter of the planet. A mere 150 Ghadarites set sail for India, hoping to stage an uprising. Given no clear instructions, aside from inciting native troops and killing English soldiers, they were arrested on arrival.

One of those arrested, Kartar Singh Sarabha, a farm labourer in California, was just 17 years old when he joined the Ghadar Party, and he had assisted with the movement's newspaper. At trial, he averred that every 'slave' had a right to revolt, and that it could never be a crime to fight in defence of his rights. In view of his age, the judge pleaded with him to adjust his incriminating statement and appeal. 'Why should I?' he responded. 'If I had more lives than one, it would have been a great honour to me to sacrifice each of them for my country.' He was executed at the age of 19, and most of his Ghadarite comrades suffered a similar fate. Further plots in 1915 and 1917, in collaboration with the Germans, also failed.

The movement was short-lived and ultimately unsuccessful, owing to a sophisticated surveillance operation by the British as well as a lack of strategy among those involved. Despite these failures, the movement's global reach and legacy would influence South Asians for generations to come.

***

They had gathered to celebrate Vaisakhi – the harvest festival in Punjab that marks the birth of Sikhism. After offering their prayers, thousands of people flocked to Jallianwala Bagh in Amritsar, a popular park close to the city's iconic Golden Temple.

Then the bullets came. Guns were fired indiscriminately on the crowd, and men, women and children ran in terror. But there was nowhere to escape. The park could only be exited on one side, and General Dyer, the brigadier-general in charge of the British troops that day, had blocked the route. The firing did not stop until each soldier had exhausted his ammunition. The ordeal continued for ten minutes: 1,650 rounds. It was a bloodbath.

Many of those in the crowd were unaware of a new order preventing mass gatherings. A month previously the Rowlatt Act had been passed, extending the use of measures introduced during the First World War to clamp down on political activity. The act was enforced heavily in Punjab. A protest against it had indeed been organised at Jallianwala Bagh, but many caught up in the massacre on 13 April 1919 were there to celebrate a holy festival, unaware of the restrictions. Hundreds were killed; thousands were injured. There was no medical aid from the soldiers, and no mercy whatsoever.

Dyer showed no remorse for his actions. A day after the massacre, he received a telegram from Sir Michael O'Dwyer, Lieutenant Governor of Punjab: 'Your action correct. Lieutenant Governor approves.'

O'Dwyer's words would come back to haunt him.

***

Udham Singh grabbed his revolver. It was 13 March 1940, a day he had long awaited. Earlier that morning he had visited the India Office in London to obtain a travel endorsement for his passport, and on his way out he caught sight of a notice announcing a meeting of the East India Association later that day at Caxton Hall. This would be his chance to avenge the massacre. He made his way to the venue and sat patiently through the proceedings. When the event ended, Singh rose, walked steadily to the stage, and drew his .44 calibre Smith & Wesson. He fired six shots in quick succession, killing Sir Michael O'Dwyer instantly, and wounding two others, Lord Lamington and Sir Louis Dane.

A second assassination in the name of the Indian freedom struggle had now taken place on British soil. But who was the man behind the gun, and what had led him to London?

Udham Singh was a young orphan when the Jallianwala Bagh massacre took place. He grew up at a time when Punjab was a hotbed of anti-colonial activity and soon fell under the influence of the Ghadar movement. As a teenager, he carried their pamphlets from village to village, spreading their message.

Looking for work, Singh turned first to Uganda, where he briefly laboured on the railways alongside other Punjabis, including many fellow Ghadarites, before entering the United States via Mexico in 1924. He settled in San Francisco, the Ghadar Party's stronghold, and he soon met its leading members. In total, Singh lived in the United States for three years, spending time in Detroit, New York and Chicago, and during this time he married a Mexican woman, Lupe Hernandez, and together they had two children.

In 1927 he returned to India, where he was swiftly arrested. Charged with possessing both a firearm and seditious literature (Ghadar pamphlets), he was sentenced to five years' imprisonment. In Multan jail he spoke openly to his fellow inmates about the evils of British rule, urging them to take up the struggle for freedom. For his defiance, he was thrown into solitary confinement and flogged repeatedly. Later, after he was transferred to Mianwali prison, he encountered the young revolutionary Bhagat Singh, who had been jailed for the killing of a British police officer. Singh revered him, and would later speak of Bhagat Singh as his guru.[5]

By 1934 Udham Singh had reached London, where he lived a nomadic existence, frequently changing addresses and adopting numerous aliases. Records suggest he lived in Southampton, Canterbury and London. He was known to have a pedlar's licence, allowing him to trade goods door-to-door, and, on occasion, he found work as an extra in crowd scenes at a film studio in Denham, Buckinghamshire.

When he was brought to trial for the Caxton Hall shooting, Singh declared his name as Muhammad Singh Azad, a deliberate fusion of identities, expressing his belief in unity across faiths and his commitment to freedom (Azad in Hindi). Asked by the Chief Constable why he had killed O'Dwyer, Singh was defiant. 'He deserved it', Singh said.

> He was the real culprit, he wanted to crush the spirit of my people, so I have crushed him ... For a full 21 years, I have been trying to wreak vengeance. I am happy to have done the job. I am not scared of death. I am dying for my country. I have seen my people starving in India under British rule. I have protested against this, it was my duty.[6]

On 31 July 1940 Udham Singh was hanged at Pentonville prison. Just as Madan Lal Dhingra's actions in 1909 had struck terror into the British establishment, Singh's deed sent ripples of fear through Whitehall. Soon, old fears about Indian revolutionaries at large in Britain were to return.

***

Udham Singh was not alone in carrying the politics of Punjab to Britain. In the 1920s and 1930s rural agitation in Punjab led a growing number of young men from the region to migrate to Britain in search of work, and according to an Indian National Congress survey, by 1932 there were some 7,128 Indians residing there.[7] Many came from the Doaba region in central Punjab, hailing from cities such as Hoshiarpur, Jalandhar and Ludhiana, hotbeds of anti-colonial political activism. The men who left often carried that spirit with them. Such journeys were not unusual. Punjabis had long sought livelihoods overseas, whether on the Pacific coast of America, in East Africa, or in other corners of the Empire. For those who arrived in Britain, however, opportunities were limited. Industrial jobs were typically closed to migrants, and racism was widespread. White workers regarded migrants as competitors for scarce employment and housing, and many of the new arrivals were forced into the peddling trade, going door-to-door selling ready-made clothes and small goods.

Such was the atmosphere of hate in interwar Britain that racist riots broke out in 1919 across Britain's port cities. Though most Punjabi migrants were not caught up in these, all were forced to deal with the aftermath: racist discrimination intensified, and Indian workers were left feeling isolated and unwelcome. In response, they banded together, with shared lodgings, communal kitchens and village networks providing both safety and companionship.

The Ghadar Party drew much of its support from the Punjabi diaspora; even so, it made few inroads in Britain, while other organisations active in Britain and advocating for independence did. The India League, founded in 1926 by the lawyer and editor Krishna Menon to champion the cause of independence among progressives in Britain, drew from a different constituency. Menon maintained close ties with socialists and regularly wrote for the left-wing paper *Tribune*, and the League established branches across Britain, and was increasingly radical in its demands, unlike other organisations such as the Indian National Congress that merely called for a more just British rule. But its membership was largely comprised of the British elite, with few Indian members.

The Punjabi migrants who faced discrimination in the workplace and exclusion from the trade union movement soon recognised the necessity of establishing their own organisations, and in 1938, in a modest terraced house in Coventry, the Indian Workers' Association (IWA) was founded with the declared aim of campaigning for Indian independence and offering support to comrades abroad. From contemporary surveillance reports, we can see that there were four men behind its founding: Charan Singh Cheema, Thakur Singh Basra, Ujagar Singh Basra and Kartar Singh Cheema.[8] Many were radicals, sympathetic to the Ghadar Party. Thakur Singh Basra was by then one of the most prominent Sikh figures in the Midlands, and he would come to play a prominent role in raising funds for Udham Singh's defence after the assassination of O'Dwyer. Charan Singh Cheema was from Coventry where he had attended local communist gatherings. He would provide links to Ghadar through his uncle, Karam Singh Chima, a notable Ghadar leader involved in the abortive 1914 rising who later became vice president of the Desh Bhagat Parivar Sahaik Committee, an organisation established to support the families of imprisoned, deported or executed revolutionaries.[9]

The IWA grew partly through kinship and communal ties. Punjabi migrants tended to cluster together with those from their own villages or extended families, making recruitment easier. But there were practical incentives too. The IWA offered real, tangible support: help with writing letters, filling forms, finding lodgings, or evading conscription in wartime Britain. Branches soon sprang up in Birmingham and Bradford, where on 31 July 1941, the first anniversary of Udham Singh's execution, the IWA organised a commemoration meeting. These activities soon began to alarm the authorities, even if intelligence reports suggest that in its earliest years the IWA was not especially effective: wartime conditions hindered its work, and German air raids during the winter of 1940–41 disrupted activity in the Midlands. The association's membership, drawn largely from industrial workers toiling for long hours on low wages, had little time for sustained political organising.

Momentum increased, however, in 1942 with the arrival of Vellala Srikantaya Sastrya, an educated Indian from Madras, who became secretary of the Birmingham branch. Sastrya, a Trotskyist, urged his compatriots to forge closer ties with the labour movement, and he determined that the IWA should not remain merely a welfare body, but that it should become a political organisation with real teeth. Fluent in English, surveillance records note that Sastrya had first come to Britain in 1936 to train as a journalist, before eventually securing the rare position of shop steward at Daimler in Coventry, where he helped spread his socialist views among his fellow workers. Later he was employed in Birmingham, where he was labelled 'the most dangerous Indian in the Midlands' by the British authorities, with one report claiming that 'He is dangerous not because of the views he holds but because of his organising ability.'[10] As general secretary, Sastrya pursued workplace grievances, investigating accidents and injuries and pressing claims for compensation. Under his leadership, the IWA ran classes in English and Hindi, while offering assistance with housing and employment.[11]

Its expansion was also aided by the wartime demand for labour. By April 1943 between 1,500 and 2,000 Indians were living in the cities of Coventry and Birmingham, many working in aerodromes, ammunition dumps and militia camps.[12] Branches of the IWA also began to appear in Huddersfield, Wolverhampton, Newcastle, Manchester,

Dundee, Liverpool and London. Glasgow, meanwhile, where there was a wartime influx of seafarers, labourers and pedlars, saw the creation of the Hindustani Majlis, an organisation with aims similar to the IWA. Its outlook was strongly anti-colonial, and it too commemorated the Jallianwala Bagh massacre, while its Sikh members ensured close ties to the IWA. Although mainly a Sikh organisation, it wasn't exclusively so. A surveillance report on a Bradford meeting of 22 February 1942 recorded the presence of '17 Sikhs and 12 Mohammedans', while Choudhury Akbar Ali Khan, a Muslim who had once shared a house in Coventry with one of the IWA's founders, Thakur Singh Basra, served as chairman of the central organisation.

Despite persistent hostility to migrants from much of the British labour movement, the IWA and others like it continued to see themselves as part of a broader working-class struggle. Many of its members were also communists, while there were reports that members of both the Trotskyist Fourth International and the Independent Labour Party attended IWA gatherings.[13] We can see these links in striking detail at the 1942 May Day march in Coventry, where over a hundred IWA members paraded with banners, even winning the prize for the most striking display. The IWA was also active in its attempts to forge links with British workers: 'We who are staying in this country must appeal to the English working class', declared Jan Mohammed at a meeting in Birmingham in 1944 held to commemorate Jallianwala Bagh, 'and those of you who are in India will be fighting actively against British Imperialism. With the help of the British working-class organisations we can have a movement here in regard to India, similar to the "Hands off Russia".'[14] The 'Hands off Russia' campaign was an international political initiative first launched by British socialists in opposition to British intervention on the side of the White armies against the communists in the Russian civil war.

The IWA's links to both communists and the Ghadar movement soon saw it drawing intense scrutiny from the state. There were reports that its meetings in both Bradford and Birmingham featured frequent 'subversive speeches', and on 10 February 1942 a state surveillance file described a joint meeting between the IWA and the India League in Birmingham which, despite the poor grasp of Hindustani of the spies sent to attend, concluded that 'some of the protagonists are known to have relations with the Ghadar Party'.[15] In response, the IWA was not shy in taking its protests directly to the British government. On 15 October 1943 it targeted L. S. Amery, Secretary of State for India, at a Conservative Party meeting in Birmingham. Around thirty Indians, joined by a larger contingent of communists, disrupted the proceedings, and distributed a pamphlet demanding an end to the famine in India, immediate food shipments, the release of political prisoners and independence. There was widespread anger over the Bengal Famine of 1943, which, according to some estimates, resulted in the deaths of up to three million Indians.[16] The crisis was intensified by Britain's wartime financing of the military, which triggered severe inflation and drove food prices beyond the reach of much of the population. Many critics argued that the British government failed to take adequate measures to relieve the famine, deepening resentment towards colonial rule. The meeting descended into uproar. A banner was unfurled that declared: 'Churchill and Amery are killing men, women and children.'

In October 1944 the IWA coordinated a wave of 'Quit India' demonstrations in Birmingham, Coventry, Bradford, Leeds, Manchester and Newcastle. Sastrya was said to have toured these cities personally, with a Scotland Yard report claiming that his purpose was to mobilise Indians to disrupt any meeting addressed by Amery. There were, it warned, 'about 50 Indian volunteers who are ready to give Mr Amery a hostile reception'.[17] Sastrya, meanwhile, was also identified as the ringleader of hecklers at a Conservative meeting in Sparkbrook.

By September 1943 British officials reported that some Indian migrants were contributing as much as a tenth of their income to the IWA's funds. The IWA was also producing its own publications, including the bi-monthly bulletin, the *Indian Worker*, which was edited in English and Hindustani by Mohammed Fazal Hussein, though wartime paper shortages hampered regular circulation. Later it was replaced by *Azad Hind* ('Free India'), a newsletter published by the Coventry branch and edited by Kartar Singh Nagra and Vidya Parkash Hansrani, and modelled on the old *Hindustani Ghadar* paper. Its line was militantly anti-colonial, with its first issue commemorating Jallianwala Bagh and praising Udham Singh and Bhagat Singh. When news of it reached Whitehall, the authorities were alarmed. Officials described it as 'as extreme as anything which has yet appeared in this country in any Indian language'.[18] The fear was that it might inspire 'a second Udham Singh'. It was, they warned, 'insidious and poisonous propaganda which aims at corrupting the political views of the working-class Indian in this country and at instilling revolutionary and terrorist ideas'.[19] Hansrani went further still. In 1945 he published a pamphlet entitled *The Blessings of the British Raj*, systematically dismantling the apologist arguments for empire such as narratives about Britain building the railways (Hansrani maintained that this was to assist the looting of Indian resources, not a benevolent gift for the natives).

The IWA's associations with both communists and Ghadarites, and above all its reverence for Udham Singh, provoked serious concern in the India Office. Of particular concern was the activity of those such as Choudhury Akbar Ali Khan, from Coventry, who they described as an ardent nationalist, and a person who was seen as exerting a strong influence among Muslims, encouraging Indians to resist conscription. 'Whenever the British have wanted to make other countries slaves', he was quoted as saying, 'they have used Indians to do so. When Indians can fight for another nation to make others slaves, then they can fight for themselves.'[20] In the event of a German invasion, six members of the movement were to be interned: Khan himself, alongside four Sikhs (Thakur Singh Basra, Charan Singh Cheema, Karam Singh Overseer and Kartar Singh Nagra), and Sastrya in Birmingham. Officials feared that these radicals would exploit British vulnerability and ally themselves with the Germans in pursuit of independence. Such was the path pursued by Indian nationalist Subhas Chandra Bose who, in 1941, arrived in Germany to make alliances with the Nazis.

The authorities attempted to weaken the IWA by relocating its key leaders for employment in other parts of the country. A March 1944 report described Sastrya as a 'political menace',[21] and the Ministry of Labour considered transferring him to the north-east to blunt his influence.

The IWA was not without its limitations, however. Meetings conducted in Hindustani excluded many Bengali-speaking lascars, while the group's membership fees, though modest, were supplemented by constant appeals for donations to support the families of martyrs or revolutionary causes in India. Members in Coventry, struggling, resented this focus on overseas work and pressed the leadership to give greater priority to local welfare.[22]

By the end of 1944 the organisation had split. Choudhury Akbar Khan was elected president and moved to wrest control of branches from Sastrya and Surat Ali of the Federation of Indian Associations in Great Britain. His faction, known as the Mazdoor Majlis, aligned itself with the Committee of Indian Congressmen, a group of Indians in Britain loosely affiliated with the Indian National Congress. In April 1945 it hosted screenings of *Padosi* ('Neighbour'), a classic Indian social drama film which made a strong plea for Hindu–Muslim unity against a backdrop of growing communal tensions in India. The film was shown at London's Mayfair cinema and later in Coventry, attracting large audiences of seamen and factory workers, with 500 attending in the capital and 300 in Coventry. Khan used the events to recruit members and raise donations. The group published its own Urdu newsletter, *Mazdoor*, with Khan as editor.

By 1946 Khan's organisation had active branches in Coventry, London and Birmingham, with members scattered as far as Doncaster, Peterborough, Reading, Maidenhead and Luton. Scotland Yard labelled it the 'Heterodox IWA', distinguishing it from the 'Orthodox' group led by Hansrani in Coventry. Surveillance suggested Khan's faction was the larger, claiming several hundred members. A year later, a new branch opened in Nottingham, with its membership largely Muslim. It too aligned with Congress and Indian socialist parties, and that summer IWA branches in Coventry and Birmingham organised meetings opposing partition and calling for a united India. Khan and other leaders made clear their vision: a socialist republic of India, free not only from British rule but also from the communal divisions fostered by the Muslim League, Hindu Mahasabha and others.

In August 1947 India was to get its independence. In the aftermath, the country was partitioned, with a population transfer of unprecedented magnitude, accompanied by devastating communal violence. Some 15 million Hindus, Sikhs and Muslims rushed to cross the hastily demarcated borders before the partition would be complete, while up to two million South Asians died in the process. Many were unaware of what partition meant until they were in the middle of it. Independence was won but it came at great cost. There was little to celebrate and a lot to mourn.

Many IWA members had returned to the subcontinent by this point. With wartime restrictions on travel lifted and its central purpose achieved, the organisation began to unravel. By 1950 it had all but disappeared. The lull, however, proved temporary. In the decades that followed, fresh waves of migrants breathed new life into the IWA. Divisions and factional rivalries persisted, but those who rallied beneath its banner remained committed to the socialist and anti-imperialist ideals on which it had been founded. From Dorset to Edinburgh, new branches continued to emerge. What began in a modest terraced house in Coventry nearly a century ago endures to this very day.

3

SEAFARER STRUGGLES

Canary Wharf, the sleek, skyscraper-filled financial district of East London, is known today for its gleaming glass and steel towers. Beneath these monuments to modern capitalism, however, lies a much older story.

Two centuries ago it was the West India Dock, a fortress of commerce built in 1802 by Robert Milligan, a slave trader whose wealth flowed from Jamaican sugar plantations. The East India Dock was opened four years later to handle the ships of the East India Company, whose wealth was derived from the looting of India (the word 'loot', Hindustani slang for plunder, was one of the first Indian words to enter the English language). Together, they formed the Empire's front door, allowing sugar, spices, tea and other commodities to be funnelled from the colonies to the capital. The past still whispers in the street names: Clove Crescent, Coriander Avenue, Saffron Avenue and Nutmeg Lane.

Britain's trade relied not only on the riches of India and other colonies, but also on their labour. With high sickness and mortality rates among white sailors on India-bound ships, British shipping companies came to rely heavily on lascar labour, especially for return voyages to the subcontinent. The word 'lascar' was used to describe sailors from the Indian subcontinent and other colonies who worked on European ships. As early as the seventeenth century, these South Asian seafarers, mainly from Bengal, Gujarat and other coastal regions, were recruited by British shipping companies. Their experience on board was far from smooth sailing: stormy winds, inadequate food and water, and rampant disease took their toll on the sailors. Worse still, English captains regularly mistreated lascars. Many were beaten or flogged. Some died during the voyage; others disembarked at the other end severely ill or injured. In one account from Christian missionary Joseph Salter, an entire lascar crew of Muslims deserted a ship when it docked in the Thames, accusing the captain and his second-in-command of torture. They 'had been hung up with weights tied to their feet', he wrote, flogged with a rope and forced to eat pork. 'The insult carried further by violently ramming the tail of a pig into their mouths and twisting the entrails of the pig round their necks.'[1] One lascar jumped overboard, trying to escape his tormenter, and drowned. Another account describes nine lascars dying because of wounds inflicted by their captain, with their bodies thrown overboard.[2]

Many sailors, of course, resisted this mistreatment on board ship. Some refused to work unless their pay and conditions were improved; others, once on land, refused to return to their ships. And it wasn't only against their English captains that they struggled; many did so against some of their fellow countrymen, intermediaries known as serangs. These intermediaries controlled the recruitment of lascars, and often accepted bribes in return for jobs, many being known to cheat lascars of their wages and to mistreat those inferior to them in the labour hierarchy.

In the early days, most lascars spent only brief spells in Britain, returning to India aboard another vessel soon after embarking. That pattern began to change, however, in the seventeenth century with the introduction of the Navigation Acts. Designed to protect British seafaring jobs, these laws required three-quarters of a ship's crew to be British. In practice, they had the unintended consequence of producing an oversupply of lascars stranded in British ports. Captains, obliged to meet the new crew ratios yet reliant on skilled seamen from the subcontinent for the return voyage, often brought them to Britain with no plans for their onward employment.

In times of war the demand for lascar labour rose sharply. With British sailors pressed into naval service, merchant ships increasingly turned to South Asian crews. Between 1803 and 1813 – during the Napoleonic Wars – over 10,000 lascars arrived in Britain, many working alongside Chinese, Arab, African and West Indian seamen, and often ending up in the same lodging houses once there. The 1830s brought the advent of steamships, transforming the nature of work at sea. For many lascars, the change meant gruelling stints in sweltering engine rooms, shovelling coal into boilers to power ships in temperatures exceeding 60°C. Exhaustion was so severe that there were reports of men leaping overboard simply to escape the unbearable heat.

Life ashore offered little relief. After long voyages, many arrived in Britain in poor health. Accommodation, whether in barracks or boarding houses, was overcrowded and insanitary. Those abandoned by their captains or fleeing ill-treatment were left to fend for themselves in unfamiliar port cities. Indian servants, some similarly stranded when their employers died or deserted them, joined their ranks, forming the earliest South Asian communities in

Britain. Some found work sweeping the streets. Others begged to survive.

The newspapers of the day painted a bleak picture. In 1850 *The Times* reported that forty 'sons of India' had died of starvation in London. Six years later, fearing for the reputation of Christianity abroad, Joseph Salter founded the Strangers' Home for Asiatics, Africans, and South Sea Islanders in Limehouse, East London, then known as the 'oriental quarter' for its diverse population. As word spread about the mistreatment and poverty of lascars in Britain, Salter believed that this could have an adverse impact on the work of Christian missionaries on the Indian subcontinent.

Some ex-seafarers set up cafés and lodging houses in port cities such as Glasgow, Cardiff and Liverpool, laying the foundations for Britain's first multicultural neighbourhoods. These areas soon became notorious, with Salter describing the opium dens, gambling houses and sex workers in these dockside communities. It was his moral duty, he believed, to preach the word of Christ while steering residents away from vice.[3]

As the number of lascars employed on British ships grew, they became more assertive in protesting their ill-treatment. In 1901 a crew of lascars aboard a ship sailing from Calcutta to Dundee went on strike to protest the actions of a physically abusive junior officer; their refusal to work brought the vessel to a standstill mid-ocean. Several English engineers attempted to coax the men back to duty, but without success. The captain personally intervened, placing some of the crew in irons and detaining them for several days. At the chief engineer's request, they were released and returned briefly to work. The breaking point came when an engineer struck a lascar in the face multiple times. Upon reaching Dundee, the lascars refused to return to the ship, and the following day twenty-nine lascars marched into the city centre to lodge complaints at the post office. As the *Dundee Courier* reported,

> They invaded the Post Office, and put the officials in a state of alarm by their incessant jabber of unintelligible voices. The post officials telephoned the police office, and a force of constables had to be despatched to raise the siege. The motley crew were conveyed to the police office, and an attempt was made to ascertain the cause of the trouble.[4]

The case soon went to trial. The lascars waited outside the courthouse, attracting crowds of curious locals. In the end, the engineer received a warning, and the men were advised to return to their ship.

The lascars recruited to work on British ships were all men; South Asian women in Britain during this period were few and far between. There were some ayahs, women recruited to work as servants in the homes of wealthy aristocratic families, but they were isolated in individual homes, and dispersed throughout the country. Lascars by contrast had the advantage of living with their countrymen in boarding homes and sailors' houses, their collectivity giving them the opportunity to resist their exploitation. Britain did, however, have some prominent South Asian women from wealthy backgrounds who championed their compatriots. Many helped to shape British democracy, too.

One early champion was Sophia Duleep Singh, the daughter of the deposed Maharajah Duleep Singh. Born into wealth, Singh is best known today as a suffragette who used her social status to advocate for the rights of women. A member of the Women's Social and Political Union, Singh was often seen selling *The Suffragette* newspaper outside Hampton Court Palace.[5] She was among more than 300 suffragettes who marched from Caxton Hall to Parliament Square on 18

November 1910, demanding to see the prime minister. He declined to meet them, and when they refused to disperse, they were physically and sexually assaulted by the police.[6] After the events of 'Black Friday', as it came to be known, Singh continued her advocacy for women, participating in the mass boycott of the 1911 census. 'No Vote, No Census', she told the press. 'As women do not count, they refuse to be counted. I have a conscientious objection to filling up this form.'[7]

Singh also supported her fellow Indians in Britain, forming ties with the Sikh community, and frequently visiting the Shepherd's Bush gurdwara. And in 1909 she helped raise crucial funds to set up the lascars' club near the Victoria Dock which supported stranded lascars struggling to make ends meet in London – from January to June 1910 alone, 4,180 lascars made use of the club.[8]

By the end of the First World War Indian seamen made up around a fifth of the British merchant navy, transporting food, troops and munitions under severe German U-boat attacks.[9] More than 1,200 lascars were imprisoned by the German army during the conflict. It was not just lascars who served during the war. Around 1.4 million Indians served in the British army, with soldiers fighting across major fronts such as the Western Front in Belgium and France, Gallipoli in Turkey and Iraq. Yet those who returned to Britain found the same meagre wages, punishing conditions and entrenched racial prejudice that had defined their working lives before the war.

The climate in interwar Britain was volatile. Economic decline, mass unemployment and appalling housing drove a wave of industrial militancy, with railway workers, miners and even police officers and soldiers going on strike. During 1919 alone, Britain saw 34 million days lost to strike action – a staggering leap from just 6 million the year before. Alongside this, there was growing resentment at the employment of Black, Arab and Asian seafarers in the port cities. This turbulent atmosphere soon turned violent. In towns and cities such as Glasgow, Cardiff, Liverpool, South Shields, Salford, Hull, Barry and Newport, as well as in London's East End that year, racist riots erupted. Black, Arab and Asian sailors were assaulted in the streets, blamed by white workers for mass unemployment and inadequate housing. Some attackers targeted interracial relationships, going after those who had white partners.

The Black and Asian communities had few allies in the labour movement. In September 1919 the Trades Union Congress passed a motion condemning Asiatic labour, claiming it undermined the pay and conditions of European sailors. Many unions actively campaigned to exclude lascars, fearing competition for jobs. Others, however, took a different view, and chose to see lascars not as rivals but fellow members of an exploited global working class. In 1920 in the newly founded Communist Party of Great Britain (CPGB), inspired by the Russian Revolution, anti-racist and anti-imperialist ideas took root. The CPGB worked to build solidarity between British and colonial workers, opposing both imperialism abroad and discrimination at home.

In India, meanwhile, similar tensions were boiling over. The interwar years brought rapid industrialisation, with the textile mills of Bombay, Calcutta and Madras swelling the ranks of the working class. Drawing on earlier traditions of organisation, pioneered by leaders such as Narayan Meghaji Lokhande in the late nineteenth century, workers staged a wave of strikes. Between 1920 and 1924 over a thousand took place in industries including railways, textiles, the postal service and printing presses. The colonial authorities, fearful of Bolshevik influence, responded with repression. The Kanpur Conspiracy Case of 1924 saw leading trade unionists arrested and accused of plotting a communist uprising. Later, the much larger Meerut Conspiracy Case, which ran from 1929 to 1933, resulted in 27 convictions. One of those was Shaukat Usmani who, from prison, was nominated as a CPGB parliamentary candidate in Yorkshire in an act of protest.

For the British communists of this era, a transnational approach was needed. Members and organisers even crossed the Empire's borders themselves to support the movement; two leading members, Philip Spratt and Ben Bradley, travelled to India in 1926 and 1927 respectively, to assist union organisers, where they soon found themselves behind bars.[10]

***

It was in this turbulent context that Shapurji Saklatvala – the Labour Party's first MP of colour – rose to prominence. Born in Bombay in 1874, the son of a Parsi merchant and nephew of an industrial magnate and the owner of India's largest commercial and industrial empire, Jamsetji Tata, Saklatvala arrived in England in 1905. Initially a Liberal, he soon gravitated towards socialism, and he joined the Independent Labour Party in 1909 before switching his allegiance to the CPGB after the Russian Revolution. A year before that, he founded the Workers' Welfare League of India (WWLI) which sought to promote workers' rights across the Empire.[11]

Elected Labour MP for Battersea North in 1922, Saklatvala drew on the constituency's radical history and diverse working-class community, which included a strong Irish presence and figures such as John Archer, Britain's first Black mayor. He built alliances across ethnic and political lines, forging links with pan-Africanists, Muslims and anti-colonialists. The recognition he received for his work was international: African-American newspapers celebrated his parliamentary victories,[12] and at the 1925 American Negro Labor Congress, a portrait of Saklatvala hung from the walls of the hall alongside prominent Black revolutionaries. When he was denied a visa to the United States, a multiracial coalition rallied in his support.[13]

During these years Saklatvala dedicated considerable time to the wider trade union movement. At the 1921 Trades Union Congress in Cardiff, delegates received copies of the WWLI manifesto,[14] while two years later, during a strike in the jute mills of Dundee, he organised meetings urging British workers to demand that Indian labourers in Bengal's jute plantations receive the same pay and conditions.[15] His persistence soon paid off, and the National Union of Boot and Shoe Operatives, Leicester Trades Council and the Iron and Steel Workers Confederation all affiliated to the WWLI.[16]

The WWLI also defended Indian trade unionists facing repression for strike action under British rule, and it became the British representative for the All India Trades Union Congress, the oldest trade union federation in India, which has over 14 million members today. Saklatvala maintained close ties with its leaders, once sharing a house in Manchester with Diwan Chaman Lall, the AITUC's first general secretary.[17]

By 1923 Saklatvala's attention had turned to the plight of the lascars. Through the newly formed Lascars' Welfare League he held meetings in Birmingham, Cardiff and London, and he sent several of his associates to Liverpool that same year to meet the striking workers so that he could raise their concerns in the Commons.[18] By the mid-1920s the lascars' struggles had intensified. The 1925 Coloured Alien Seamen Order required them to register with the police, leading to increased harassment, and an ongoing shipping slump exacerbated job competition in the industry. With most factories operating a colour bar, forbidding the employment of non-white workers, many lascars were forced into precarious work such as door-to-door selling.

Yet in Britain's port cities, small pockets of community solidarity emerged. In London's East End, a small but growing Bengali community, mainly hailing from Sylhet, banded together to survive the difficult times. In 1923 ex-seafarer Ayub Ali set up the Shah Jalal restaurant on Commercial Street, which became a focus of South Asian life in the East End, and his house at 13 Sandys Row became famous with Sylheti sailors from around the world, doubling as both a shelter and an informal support hub for lascars. Ali, affectionately referred to as Ayub Ali Master, had jumped ship at Tilbury in 1919. He could read and write, and he assisted lascars who had abandoned ship, providing them with rooms and translating letters and forms for them.[19]

From these grassroots networks emerged ever more radical organising. One avenue for this during the 1920s was the Indian Seamen's Union (ISU), for which Saklatvala served as president, with other prominent communists such as Clemens Palme Dutt (an activist and the brother of the leading member of the CPGB, the Indian-Swedish activist and theorist Rajani Palme Dutt) as its coordinator, and Nathalal Jagjivan Upadhyaya its organising secretary.[20] The latter was tasked with the bulk of the organising. Known to friends as Paddy, Upadhyaya was born into a Gujarati family in 1895, and arrived in England in 1922. An ardent communist, in his ISU role he devoted himself to unionising lascars, distributing literature in multiple Indian languages, and holding meetings at London docks and in boarding houses.[21] Thanks to his ceaseless activity and that of other members, by 1926 the ISU had over 300 members, a figure which would rise to 1,500 a year later, and it had an office at 88 East India Dock Road in the East End. Soon it also had its own paper, the *Seaman's Bulletin*, available in both Urdu and Bengali, and its presence had spread to other port cities.

With union membership growing, Upadhyaya began to face relentless state obstruction. In July 1925 he was accused of trespassing on private property, with port police shutting down his meeting. On another occasion, he was 'forcibly ejected' from the Strangers' Home (a residence for lascars) and by December 1926 he was barred altogether. In 1928, while addressing lascars at Tilbury docks, he was thrown out for not having a dock permit.[22]

At one point, Upadhyaya was interrogated by the police while leaving the Communist Party headquarters. In Parliament, Labour MP Frederick Hall accused him of 'fomenting revolutionary plots among coolie seamen' and behaving in an 'undesirable manner', encouraging the home secretary to deport him.[23] Despite these difficulties, Upadhyaya continued his organising, even at one point going as far as posing as a missionary on the docks and concealing communist leaflets in religious tracts.

By 1930 ISU membership had reached 6,000. Yet despite Upadhyaya's efforts, there was no major improvement in pay and conditions for lascars. Without wider trade union support, Indian seamen had little leverage, and over the next few years the ISU's influence would wane.

In East London during this period, there was a small community of former seafarers from Sylhet (Bangladesh) who had settled there after their service in the First World War.

When lascar ships were docked, they would often call in to the homes of these early settlers for a meal and an exchange of news. Some would seek to supplement their income by selling exotic goods at the Club Row open air street market in Bethnal Green. A growing number of lascars began jumping ship in the 1930s, with most heading to Aldgate, where they were able to access support and guidance.

Shah Abdul Majid Qureshi, one of the first Sylhetis to own a restaurant in Britain, recalled his own experience of jumping ship in London in 1936:

> I had one or two addresses, but they were wrongly written, they were not correct, and when I showed them to anyone, they didn't know. I was very much disappointed, didn't know what to do. At that time I cannot go back to my ship, because I have to come here to stay ... I suddenly saw a young man, about twenty-five, very dark looking ... I thought probably he is from Madras ... he spoke to me in Sylhet dialect ... I was so very glad, I held him, embraced him. I said 'by good luck, at last I have found someone who can help me.' He said, 'you have come from the boat?' I said 'yes'. He said, 'come with me, I will give you shelter, I live in Mr. Munshi's house.'[24]

The early pioneers who jumped ship in the 1920s were often the first point of contact for new arrivals. As well as Mr Munshi's lodging house, Ayub Ali's Shah Jalal restaurant at 76 Commercial Street was another magnet for new arrivals. The restaurant provided a much-desired curry for lascars who would have missed home-cooked meals in Britain. As one lascar, Haji Kona Miah, remembered fondly: 'He was a very good man, he helped a lot of people, no take money, nothing. When people couldn't speak English, he helped them. There were plenty of others after him, but nobody like him.'[25]

***

In 1935 the British Shipping Act was passed, which gave preference to the employment of white seamen over lascars, further compounding their difficulties in finding work. At the same time a new organisation was set up to advocate on their behalf, the Colonial Seamen's Union, another initiative backed by the Communist Party. At its first conference, held the next year, the union condemned the Act, and demanded that all seafarers be given full democratic rights when it came to trade union organisation, as well as in freedom of assembly and freedom of speech. Unlike the ISU, however, the Colonial Seamen's Union was much broader in its membership, recruiting Chinese, African, Arab and West Indian seafarers as well as Indian ones.

Yet despite numerous public meetings and the recruitment work of former seafarer Surat Ali, there was no major improvement in pay and conditions for Indian workers. Some Indian communists, including Rajani Palme Dutt, as well as pivotal figures such as M. N. Roy and Shapurji Saklatvala, felt that the Party had not done enough to support the plight of the lascars, criticising the lack of financial support for such work. As Saklatvala wrote in 1934 after returning from a tour of the Soviet Union:

> There is a tendency to treat the colonial problem as a mere side issue and as nobody's business in particular. There are no special funds allocated for expenditure for work among colonial students or workers in Great Britain ... [The] condition of indifference and suspicion between the British Party and their colonial nationals is deplorable.[26]

Lascars increasingly looked for allies across the Empire, and in 1937 the All-India Seamen's Federation (AISF) was formed, which brought together a number of lascar unions around the world, including the Indian Seamen's Union, the Indian Quartermasters' Union, the Bengal Mariners' Union and the Karachi Seamen's Union. Drawing its strength from the growing nationalist movement in India, as well as the increasingly politicisation of lascars in their struggle, the federation sought an end not just to their unjust exploitation but to the unjust British rule that it was tied to. Among its activities was an All-India-Seamen's Day called in 1939, held in every port of India as well as in many ports across the UK, with demands including a 50 per cent increase in wages and the appointment of a recruitment committee to check against bribery and corruption.[27]

In London the day was marked by a meeting of lascars chaired by Aftab Ali, held at the United Ladies Tailors' Union Hall in Whitechapel. Like many who came before him, Ali sought allies from across the British labour movement, and in August 1939 he spoke at a Glasgow Trades Council meeting, highlighting the plight of the lascars and the widespread bribery embedded in recruitment practices.[28] By then, however, the situation of lascars had changed significantly. Britain was on the brink of entering the Second World War and white seafarers were once again being recruited into the British navy; shipping companies were more desperate for lascar labour than ever before. By this point there were over 50,000 lascars in the British merchant navy, around 26 per cent of the total labour force. Now, with the ability to paralyse Britain's maritime operations, the lascars had leverage, and they were not afraid to use it. The All-India Seamen's Federation, led by Surat Ali and Aftab Ali, was ready to lead global strikes in ports across the British Empire, demanding a pay rise and a war risk bonus.

In autumn 1939 strikes took place aboard ships in British, South African, Burmese and Australian ports, attracting worldwide attention. Shipping companies were under pressure, and questions about the treatment of lascars were raised in the House of Commons. Four days before the outbreak of war, employers in London agreed to pay a 50 per cent bonus on existing rates in a bid to prevent further action. Yet for some, lacking legal protections, it was a pyrrhic victory; by December 1939 hundreds had been charged with breaking their contracts and imprisoned.

As war began, Surat Ali continued to play a leading role in the struggle, publishing an article in the *East London Advertiser* in 1941 calling for fixed working hours, overtime pay, compensation for illness and a welfare fund for retired sailors. Ayub Ali Master, meanwhile, set up the Indian Seamen's Welfare League in 1943, which formalised the work already being done in the East End to support the welfare of South Asian sailors, including by helping them to read and write letters.[29]

Like the Punjabi pedlars we met earlier, these seafarers were responsible for establishing some of the earliest South Asian communities in Britain. After the Second World War, many would return to their newly independent countries; some, though, stayed in Britain, finding jobs in industries that were now struggling with post-war labour shortages. They were soon to be joined by many more of their countrymen as Britain looked to its former colonies for labour as part of its post-war rebuilding.

4

EARLY STRUGGLES IN POST-WAR BRITAIN

> There are many Southalls. Black communities built on the rubble of the decaying inner cities ... they were the aid, the Marshall plan, on which Britain's immediate post-war prosperity was founded. And yet they themselves were kept from that prosperity, from a stake in that society and, by virtue of their colour, condemned to live amidst the detritus of inner cities.
>
> A. Sivanandan[1]

In one pocket of West London, Punjabi script adorns the tube station's signage, welcoming you to the district. On the High Street, Punjabi music blares from row after row of shops selling Indian clothes, while the aroma of Punjabi and North Indian food dresses the air with its scent. It's no wonder this corner of West London is called Little Punjab.

My earliest memory of Southall is tied to The Broadway, the main commercial thoroughfare, where I begrudgingly followed my family through a maze of fabric shops in preparation for a grand wedding celebration. The air was filled with the rich aroma of samosas, jalebi and other mouth-watering Indian street foods. It felt as though the High Street went on forever. I'd never seen so many South Asian shops in my life. And footfall was high. Sikh men with their turbans, women with their dupattas. Our equivalent in Luton was Bury Park, full of Pakistani and Bangladeshi shops, but Southall felt enormous. 'It's Bury Park on steds', we'd joke. Across Britain today there are many equivalents, from Wilmslow Road in Manchester, affectionally known as the Curry Mile, to Ladypool Road in Birmingham and Ealing Road in Wembley. Inner-city areas full of independent businesses. Today, they are hubs of South Asian life.

Across the country today, South Asians number in the millions, making up 7.5 per cent of the UK population. Behind the colourful storefronts and the aroma of freshly fried samosas is a story of post-war migrants who endured numerous struggles from racist violence on the streets to exploitation at work. They endured, they resisted and they fought to build the diverse working-class communities that many of us reside in today.

***

In the aftermath of the Second World War many of Britain's industries experienced severe labour shortages. This was particularly acute on the transport network and in the newly established National Health Service, but factories, mills and foundries across Britain were struggling for workers too. So acute was demand for labour that, assisted by the Nationality Act of 1948 which granted British citizenship to all citizens of Britain's colonies and former colonies and gave them the right to live and work in Britain, many companies even recruited workers directly from their home countries. In April 1956, for instance, London Transport began recruiting staff in Barbados, supplying their fares to travel to Britain as loans which were then repaid from their wages.[2]

Life was often difficult for those who arrived, with migrant populations experiencing severe discrimination throughout this period. This was felt particularly acutely in housing and work, with discrimination rife and many white workers agitating in favour of colour bars for their industries. On a number of occasions these resentments broke out into open confrontation: between 1946 and 1949 disturbances erupted at hostels housing West Indian workers in West Bromwich, Hertfordshire, Leeds, Derbyshire, Nottingham and Birmingham, many sparked by Polish or Irish migrants who resented Black men associating with white women. The authorities regularly responded by suggesting that Black men be transferred elsewhere and that their numbers be capped.[3] In the summer of 1948 there were anti-Black riots in Liverpool fuelled by hostility towards Black seafarers, who were seen as competition for jobs. Further disturbances occurred in July 1949 in Deptford, south-east London, followed by attacks on the homes of Indian workers near Birmingham that August,[4] while in 1954 there were racist riots in Camden Town prompted by a white mob attacking Black residents with bottles.[5]

Perhaps the most infamous post-war riots took place in 1958. In August that year Nottingham was engulfed in anti-Black rioting, once again triggered by an interracial relationship, and when Black and Asian residents fought back, sensationalist reporting incited even larger crowds, with up to a thousand people shouting, 'Let's get the Blacks' and 'Let's lynch them.' The city's two MPs, one Labour and one Tory, showed no sympathy for the victims. Instead, they demanded that no further Black people be allowed into Britain and called for new deportation laws.[6]

That same month there was further racist rioting in Notting Hill, West London, an area then home to one of Britain's largest West Indian communities. Composed of overcrowded and squalid slums where both Black and white working-class families suffered exploitation at the hands of racketeering landlords, the West Indian community had long been subjected to harassment by Teddy boys (young men immersed in the rock and roll subculture). Throughout August Black and Asian residents faced intensified attacks, with homes, cafés and restaurants vandalised by mobs.

We can get a sense of the hostility many immigrant communities faced at the time from the results of a Gallup poll conducted immediately after the riots. It showed that 71 per cent of Britons opposed mixed marriages, while 61 per cent said they might move if Black families settled near their homes. Yet, though often isolated and vulnerable, West Indians refused to remain passive, with many organising to defend their homes and their social spaces in the wake of the rioting. Even so, life for immigrant communities in post-war Britain was fraught. This was a world of suffocating racism in every aspect of their lives.

STRIKING BACK IN SOUTHALL

Also arriving in the post-war years were a growing number of South Asians. By the end of 1958 the South Asian community in Britain numbered 55,000, a significant increase from the 7,000 present in Britain in 1932.[7] Of those, many moved to industrial centres in the Midlands and the North, forming strong communities and working in textile and manufacturing industries.

But it was in Southall, in the West London borough of Ealing, that the fightback against racism was to prove particularly significant. In 1951 the number of South Asians stood at just 350, with many former army officers from Punjab.[8] That would change after the general manager of the Woolfs rubber factory, a veteran who had served alongside Punjabis during the Second World War, began actively recruiting from the region. Punjabis were seen as a reliable and, importantly, a cheap source of labour, willing to take on the work that white workers increasingly rejected: the often dirty, gruelling and poorly paid jobs on the factory floor.

Many of the initial arrivals found lodgings in Aldgate, far away in East London, where there was an already-established South Asian community that had been in place since the interwar years. But long hours made the daily commute unsustainable. Southall, with its proximity to Woolfs (on the border of Hayes and Southall) and cheaper rents, soon became the preferred place to settle. However, while their labour was desired, they quickly found out that, much like other post-war immigrant communities, their presence was despised.

By the mid-1960s the South Asian population had grown to such an extent that they formed 12 per cent of Southall's population.[9] Most were young men from Punjab's Jalandhar and Hoshiarpur regions, and like those who came before them, they practised communal living, residing in overcrowded terraced houses and taking turns to sleep on the few mattresses they were able to fit inside them. The local white population soon came to resent their presence, leading to the formation of the Southall Residents Association in 1963, which demanded segregated schools, put pressure on estate agents not to sell to Black and Asian families, and called for a halt to Commonwealth migration.[10]

But many of the new arrivals, like the Punjabis who came before, brought with them traditions of militancy. Some families had Ghadar connections; others counted members of the Communist Party of India as kin. They brought their politics with them, giving new life to the Indian Workers' Associations that had existed before the war.

One such arrival was Vishnu Dutt Sharma. Born in Punjab in 1921, Sharma had developed his politics in the Indian trade union movement, rising to become assistant general secretary of the Punjab Provincial TUC; his militancy earned him six arrests. He had also been a committed communist since the late 1930s, and when he arrived in Britain in 1957, with his self-taught English and just three pounds in his pocket, he quickly joined the local Communist Party. He would also help to establish Southall's IWA branch. Like the IWAs of earlier decades, it combined politics with practical support, running English classes, offering housing and immigration advice, and creating social spaces for a community finding its feet in a foreign land. In Southall, the IWA worked with the Indo-Pakistan Cultural Society to host Sunday film screenings to raise funds to print Indian newspapers. In 1957 the group established a welfare service for new arrivals at the Southall Community Centre, and by 1962 it had opened a full-time welfare centre on Featherstone Road, which doubled as the nerve centre of its political activity. The IWAs also promoted working-class unity, extending associate membership to Pakistani workers and encouraging South Asians to join trade unions. Though more South Asians were able to access industrial employment than in previous generations, little had changed in the attitudes of trade unions: the struggle was often against both the bosses and the trade union officials who left them out to dry.

In the factories, conditions were bleak. South Asians were often placed in the dirtiest, lowest-paid jobs, segregated from white workers and supervised by white chargehands. These foremen wielded enormous power, sometimes demanding bribes for overtime, or even so that a worker could keep his job. 'Asian labour was hired in gangs', the

Race Today Collective (an anti-racist group formed in 1973 that championed and reported on many anti-racist struggles) later observed, 'and put under the control of one white charge-hand who would allocate the work, dispense overtime, recommend the hire and fire of workers and, in many cases, take bribes for doing or not doing something for, or to, the workers under his charge.'[11]

By the early 1960s these new arrivals had begun to flex their industrial muscle. In 1962 Vishnu Dutt Sharma led 165 workers in a walkout at the Rockware Glass factory in Greenford, a few miles away from Southall. Three years later a two-week strike broke out at Duratube and Wire Ltd, five miles away in North Feltham. The action, driven by concerns over low pay, cost-cutting measures and demands for union recognition, was led by IWA activists including Gurdial Dhami and Darshan Singh Giani, both of whom would go on to serve as president of the association. It was at Woolfs rubber factory, though, Southall's largest employer of Punjabis, that the most seismic industrial disputes would occur.

Woolfs had always relied on cheap labour, first employing poor white workers from depressed coalmining communities in Wales and the north-east during the 1930s, and then in the immediate post-war period a number of Polish workers. But by 1965 Punjabis made up 90 per cent of its workforce. The work, making rubber components for cars, was difficult and dirty, and like other factories that relied on Asian labour, Woolfs used antiquated and inefficient machinery, adopting labour-intensive processes to cut costs rather than investing in new machinery. For many of its Punjabi workers, it was not uncommon to work a seven-day, 75-hour week, while many were forced to bribe white foremen to get overtime or even to keep their jobs at all.

For the work they did they were paid a mere £11 a week as a basic rate (the average wage was £12–13 a week).

The first attempt by the Punjabi workers to exercise their collective strength occurred in 1960, when Gurdev Singh, a prominent member of the IWA, recruited 400 Asian workers at the factory into the Transport and General Workers Union. When the union asked for official recognition, Woolfs' management refused. Even the intervention of the Ministry of Labour in Harold Macmillan's Tory government, which recommended recognition, wasn't enough for the intransigent management.[12] Three years later another attempt was made. By this point several IWA executive members were working on the shop floor, and they had recruited fellow members into the TGWU too. As Vishnu Sharma, who worked on the production line, recalled, to recruit members to the union they went

> secretly, going house to house in the community, so management could not know the people who were actively behind this. After two, three months a majority of the workers in the production department had become members of the union and the matter was handed over to the union officials to negotiate with factory management.[13]

At the secret meetings, Hindus, Sikhs and Muslims all swore on their holy books not to bribe white foremen for overtime.[14]

From these efforts a total of 452 workers were recruited into the union, marking a turning point in their collective struggle. The following year their efforts paid off when management formally recognised the union, putting an end to the corrupt practice of white supervisors demanding bribes from South Asian workers in exchange for shifts. Yet management continued to resist broader calls for fair pay and improved working conditions, including a higher base wage and guaranteed tea breaks. The workers then imposed an overtime ban, finally forcing management to give in to their demands.

Throughout, the union and the IWA continued their struggle against the pervasive racism of the shop floor. In a sign of the growing tension, in October 1964 an IWA member was suspended for allegedly insulting a white foreman. Events quickly escalated, and after the worker claimed that the foreman had demanded a bribe, the workers went on strike, leading to their dismissed colleague's reinstatement. This was a sign that the workforce's power was growing, and keen to avoid further disruptions, management worked with the TGWU to establish a formal disputes procedure. That deal would soon be broken, however; a year later management dismissed ten active union members. The workers demanded immediate industrial action, but the TGWU refused to intervene, so once more the Woolfs workers launched an overtime ban, with many withholding their union dues in protest while denouncing Danny Evans, the TGWU's local officer tasked with negotiating, as a racist. Eventually, thanks to the pressure exerted from within the Punjabi community, the union replaced Evans with Fred Howell, a tough, left-wing negotiator known for his commitment to organising Black and Asian workers, and he successfully secured the reinstatement of seven of the dismissed workers (two others had taken up other jobs and chose not to return).

Tensions were to flare again soon after. In November 1965 Mukhtiar Singh, a Punjabi worker, reported a chargehand for stealing materials from the factory. Instead of addressing the complaint, management retaliated by firing Singh – citing his lateness by just ten minutes. That evening the Asian shop stewards called for an all-out strike and by the following morning over 600 Asian workers were picketing outside the factory gates.

With no strike pay available, the striking workers relied heavily on support from the IWA and the wider South Asian community. Despite a lack of support from the union leadership, the community rallied behind the workers: landlords waived rent, local shops offered goods on credit, and around £1,500 was raised to support the strike. The IWA also opened its offices to the workers, providing them with a vital base of operations. Other unions tried to help the striking workers, too. Roger Cox, a former shop steward at the ENV engineering works in Willesden, which had a reputation as a hotbed of militant union activity at the time, sought to raise funds to support the strikers: 'You have to understand that the level of racism against immigrants was terrible, far worse than today', he remembered in 2016. 'Raising support for an Asian strike meant having an argument – even in a factory with a lot of Irish workers, many of whom had come to Britain after the war.'[15]

Despite these difficulties, the ENV did organise a levy of all workers – 1,100 at the time.

> There was resistance to the levy among some workers, despite ENV being known for its solidarity with other workers on strike. Sometimes stewards were able to enforce it because people respected them. But there were tensions. At the time our arguments against racism were a bit crude. We'd talk about the need for working-class unity and make humanistic appeals. But remember, we hadn't had the big outbreak of Asian struggles or a big anti-racist movement to lean on; all of that was to come later. So we were just learning about how to take on racial prejudice in our own class.[16]

The leading shop stewards went the extra mile, including a member from the Trotskyist International Socialists.

> They kept a close relationship with the Woolfs strikers and advised them on how to operate in the union. IS [International Socialist] member Geoff Carlsson was particularly important. He was absolutely clear on the need to oppose racism. I remember him having a big row with a fellow member who thought we should soften our opposition to immigration controls. The whole episode reminds me of just how important even a small number of committed revolutionaries can be, and how precious that tradition is.[17]

One of the tactics used by Woolfs management was an attempt to hire Pakistani workers from Luton, High Wycombe and Bradford as 'scab labour'. As one personnel officer admitted, the company was trying to divide the workforce along 'ethnic lines'.[18] This tactic strained relationships, and at one point a fight between Indian and Pakistani workers broke out outside the factory gate. To calm the febrile mood, the IWA worked with the Pakistani Welfare Association to calm the situation, even writing an appeal in Urdu for Pakistanis to support the strike.

After six weeks of industrial action, the strike ended in defeat, with most of the workforce returning to the factory. Despite extensive lobbying by IWA members, the TGWU said that the union would only give the strike 'industrial' not 'official' support, leading to lorry drivers crossing the picket lines due to the strike not being officially supported. Management, meanwhile, issued dismissal notices to the entire striking workforce, sending out letters offering to re-employ them on new contracts. Those seen as militant or as leading the strike received no such offer. It's little wonder, under such intense pressure, that the striking workers were unsuccessful.

THE RED SCAR MILL STRIKE

Industrial militancy was not confined to Southall, however. From Bradford to Blackburn, Burnley to Batley, in the post-war period South Asians were the saving grace for the British textile industry, preserving the Lancashire and Yorkshire mills that were then hampered by severe labour shortages. They also provided a cheap solution to the old and inefficient mills dotting the British mill towns, outcompeted by overseas firms equipped with new automatic looms and spinning machinery. Instead of updating their antiquated machinery, British firms sought to make the industry more labour-intensive, taking advantage of new arrivals desperate to earn a living. One tactic employed by many mills was the introduction of production-boosting night shifts to boost output, which came to be dominated by migrants from the Indian subcontinent, as they were mostly men without the same family commitments as white workers with families in Britain.

As elsewhere, the new arrivals refused to remain silent in the face of exploitation. Yet while the struggles in London have been well documented, thanks in part to organisations such as the Institute of Race Relations, which reported on numerous strikes in places such as Southall and Newham, similar conflicts elsewhere in Britain have received far less attention. Even so, a number of disputes involving South Asian workers did break through to the national press.

One such moment came in May 1965, when South Asian workers in Preston found themselves at the centre of a major industrial confrontation. At Courtaulds' Red Scar mill, which produced rayon fabric, management sought to require Black and Asian workers to operate more machines while paying them proportionately less. Management and the union officials had struck up a deal behind their backs, telling the shop stewards (only one of whom was Asian) to convene a meeting to accept the supervision of one-and-a-half machines instead of the existing one. For this, they would receive a ten-shilling bonus; in effect a 50 per cent increase in output for just 3 per cent increase in wages. Workers were outraged, and they hastily arranged a meeting with the union's regional organiser, asking him to explain the deal. The official was attempting to defend the indefensible, and he was jeered by the workers who rejected the proposals. The plan was soon shelved – or so the workers thought.

A month later, workers on the afternoon shift had new work allocations forced on them, and line managers moved in with red paint and brushes, drawing boundary lines on machines, dividing them into halves. Workers would now be forced to man one-and-a-half machines. The result was an impromptu sit-in. Machines were clogged for 17 hours; other workers, predominantly Indian and Pakistani, walked out. The TGWU chairman at the factory, Richard Roberts, urged workers to return before any negotiations, telling the press that the strike was 'unofficial' and 'racial'. But the workers remained resolute. In the end they stayed out on strike until mid-June. They organised autonomously, in a self-styled action committee, from a base of operations at the Continental cinema on Tunbridge Street, even threatening to withdraw from the TGWU and 'fight the case on our own shoulders'.[19]

Malik Khaliq, the Commonwealth Citizens UK Association (CCUKA) chairman and an experienced shop steward from Bradford, implored workers to reject the offers of union officials who wanted to mediate. Despite the efforts of the workers, which included an eclectic range of tactics such as inviting an American lawyer to seek an injunction against management and asking Labour's Minister of Technology to advocate on their behalf, the striking workers faced a number of difficulties throughout the action. They were isolated from the rest of the workforce – around 2,000 white workers continued working, mitigating the strike's impact on the mill's productivity. There was racial segregation on the shop floor, and the TGWU rejected calls from the strikers for a mass meeting of all Courtaulds workers. In early June 120 West Indians involved in the action returned to work after a 'pep talk' about 'responsible behaviour' from representatives of the West Indian High Commission. Unlike in Southall, there was no equivalent to the IWA rooted in the community and able to mobilise in support of the workers. The Racial Adjustment Action Society led by Roy Sawh and Michael de Freitas (Michael X), a radical anti-racist organisation inspired by Malcolm X and the Black Power movement in the United States, attempted to support the workers. But aside from letters of support and some coverage in the Sunday papers, RAAS, a relatively small organisation with limited resources, was unable to help build the industrial dispute more broadly – the group had no real experience in trade union organising, and was unable to mobilise mass support for the workers.

In the third week of the strike, with 250 workers back at work, Khaliq and the leader of the strike committee, A. A. Chaudhry, announced that they would travel to Downing Street and commence a hunger strike; 110 workers pledged to join them.[20] Despite this, the strike came to an abrupt end after just three weeks. On 10 June TGWU officials secretly intervened with Courtaulds bosses. The next day the strike committee reluctantly agreed to a settlement.

With numbers dwindling and strike fatigue settling in, the remaining strikers, 240 in total, met at the Continental cinema, where the vast majority voted to return to work.

Once again, South Asian workers were struggling to fight a battle on two fronts against racist trade union officials and greedy bosses. Another strike had ended in defeat.

THE INDIAN WORKERS' ASSOCIATION(S)

By the mid-1960s the Indian Workers' Association was at the heart of community life in Southall. Such was its influence that, in 1965, it was able to purchase the Dominion cinema, and in doing so, increased its organisational and financial capacity. At weekends the cinema thrummed with crowds queuing to watch the latest Bollywood films, while during the week it became a base for political organising. The purchase gave the IWA both prestige and resources: thousands of locals attended screenings, and the profits poured back into welfare programmes, advice services and campaigning. Such influence meant that control of the IWA was worth fighting for. Elections were not sleepy affairs but full-blown contests, shaped as much by kinship networks as by ideology. Voting loyalties often stretched back to villages in Punjab: a man might still feel bound to support the same elder who had helped him find his first job or a bed when he landed in Britain. But there were deeper rifts too. The scale of these contests astonished outsiders. Researcher DeWitt John observed of the 1965 internal IWA election in Southall that 'For months before the election, rival groups manoeuvred and tried to negotiate alliances ... Perhaps a hundred men took time off from work to visit Indian homes and drum up support.' In total, John estimated that around '3,000 Indians voted in the election – 75 per cent of the

IWA members and perhaps half of the adult Indian males in Southall and surrounding towns.'[21]

While most IWAs across the country leaned heavily towards communism, Southall was different. Its membership was broader, with the centre-left Indian National Congress Party increasingly ascendant. In response, the local IWA's leadership took a more conciliatory line – especially in its dealings with the Labour Party. According to the journalist Cyril Dunn, in 1968 five parties contested the 21 executive committee posts in the IWA internal elections, and that year's election was such a large affair that polling booths were set up in two local schools.[22]

Yet the more powerful the IWAs became, the sharper the internal divisions grew. Since the late 1950s local IWAs had been structured as branches of a central body – the IWA (GB) – with office holders from each branch forming a general council. National leaders were elected from this council, and a third of all branch income was channelled upwards to sustain the centre. In practice, not everyone accepted the arrangement: Southall, with the deep pockets of the Dominion cinema behind it, bristled at surrendering its income. These splits were further deepened by ideology. Midlands branches, strongly tied to the Communist Party, distrusted Southall's growing Congress Party influence and its willingness to cooperate with Labour, and the conflict came to a head in 1962, when Southall withdrew from the main national body. As Vishnu Sharma, himself a communist, complained, the national body had become too sectarian, shutting out Indians who did not share their politics.[23]

Race relations were another flashpoint. The Race Relations Act of 1965 marked the state's first serious attempt to legislate against discrimination. Most IWAs dismissed it as window-dressing, refusing to collaborate with government bodies they viewed as complicit in racism. But Southall took a different path. It joined the newly formed Campaign Against Racial Discrimination (CARD) and later accepted state funding to run its programmes – a move strongly opposed by other branches who believed in the importance of autonomy.

There were other reasons behind the splits. According to sociologist Sasha Josephides, some critics picked up on 'the petty, the ridiculous and the corrupt reasons for schisms', such as 'fights over Bhangra outfits, a particular leader's tendency to make foolish comments to the press to gain cheap personal publicity, and various forms of fraud'.[24] Sometimes the schisms reached all the way back to India itself: in 1967 the Naxalbari uprising in West Bengal, a peasant revolt, sparked one such split; supporters of the Communist Party of India, led by Prem Singh, denounced the rebellion and sided with Moscow in the Sino-Soviet split, while others, led by figures such as Jagmohan Joshi in the West Midlands, threw their weight behind the insurgents and aligned with the Chinese Communist Party. As a result, two rival IWAs sprang up in many cities, one loyal to Joshi and the other to Prem Singh.

Joshi was born in Hoshiarpur, Punjab, and embodied that region's long association with Communist Party activity, rooted in the peasant uprisings of the early twentieth century, the Ghadar movement and the legacies of folk heroes such as Lala Lajpat Rai and Bhagat Singh. After arriving in the UK in 1958 at the age of 21, he quickly immersed himself in the political activity of the Birmingham Indian Workers' Association. Just three years later he launched the Coordinating Campaign Against Racial Discrimination (CCARD) alongside Maurice Ludmer, a

Jewish ex-serviceman. Ludmer's anti-racist convictions were deeply influenced by his visit to the Belsen concentration camp. CCARD would come to play a pivotal role in the campaign against the 1962 Commonwealth Immigrants Act which sought to restrict 'coloured' migration, and it became a radical counterweight to Campaign Against Racial Discrimination (CARD), an anti-racist organisation founded in 1964 which it criticised for its timidity and its dependence on the state.

CCARD brought together a wide range of organisations, including the Pakistani Workers' Association, the West Indian Standing Conference, the *West Indian Gazette*, the Movement for Colonial Freedom, the National Council for Civil Liberties and the Methodist Mission. It also forged connections with the US civil rights movement and hosted members of the Black Panther Party. Such was Joshi's commitment to Black Power politics that CCARD, under his leadership, refused to accept state funding or to collaborate with state institutions, viewing the state as an integral part of the problem. Indeed, much of its campaigning focused on state racism, from policing to immigration policy.

Instead, Joshi advocated for autonomous self-organisation. For Joshi the more establishment CARD was little more than a front for the Labour Party, dominated by careerists and middle-class elements. 'We knew from the United States that such a movement could only pacify people', he later said. 'We must do all that we can to make sure that the resentment among our people is not repressed. We must channel it into the proper forms of commitment.'[25] He also criticised its failure to engage the masses, arguing that 'CARD is a political pressure group at the top, without having its feet on the earth. It has not reached the hearts of the people.'[26]

By 1964 Joshi had become president of the IWA (GB), a role he held until his death in 1979. Yet while Joshi's faction drew inspiration from the Black Power movement in the United States, he was no separatist. He consistently stressed the primacy of class struggle and coalition-building. 'There can be no question of black power outside of the class struggle', he declared in his 1970 general secretary's report. It was this class-consciousness that underpinned serious efforts to organise trade union activity across the Midlands.

MILITANT TRADE UNIONISM IN THE MIDLANDS

The foreman told us to push the barrows faster,
But pushing harder was breaking our legs,
But there was no-one to tell my sorrow to,
As I struggled to push the barrow on.
When I came to England I was overjoyed,
I didn't know how hard life would be,
Who shall I sing my sorrow to,
As I struggle to push the barrow.

These were the words of one foundry worker, Balbir Bhujangy, who turned his pain into poetry.[27] After long gruelling shifts in the Midlands foundries, Punjabi workers took to the few pubs that would allow them entry and often sang about poor conditions in the workplace. According to the Bhangra historian Narinderjit Singh Winnie, the workers 'would reminisce about their life in Punjab, village life, farmers and markets. They would tap their hands on the tables and make rhythmic sounds singing about village life. Boliyan are short ballads of happiness and this is where folk music originated from, the factory workers.'[28]

Like the textile mills of Yorkshire and Lancashire, the foundries of the Midlands drew large numbers of South

Asian workers. Conditions were often brutal, with labourers toiling in intense heat, handling molten metal without adequate protection. Injuries were frequent, and few workers were provided with safety goggles or helmets. The work was shunned by many white workers, but for migrants seeking employment it was often the only option. To make matters worse, racial discrimination was also entrenched: even the toilets were segregated.

Yet because trade union presence was weak in these foundries, the 'gentlemen's agreements' that often restricted the hiring of Black and Asian workers elsewhere did not take hold. This allowed for a significant concentration of South Asian workers, and it was here that the IWA began building some of its strongest trade union branches.

One of the most influential IWA organisers in the Midlands was Avtar Singh Jouhl. Born in Jandiala, Punjab, he came from a political family and grew up under the influence of the Communist Party, even helping to organise school strikes, before being arrested in India for his activism. He arrived in Smethwick in 1958, and after a leaflet in a food parcel introduced him to the IWA, he joined soon after.

Jouhl found work at the Shotton brothers' foundry, where inequalities were laid bare. White moulders earned twice the wages of Indian labourers despite doing lighter work. 'One day I happened to read the payslip of the moulder – his salary was about £17 and my wages were about £7.50', he recalled.[29] Outraged, Jouhl began recruiting his fellow Indians into both the IWA and the union to challenge these injustices. His efforts, and those of other IWA members, were strengthened by the solidarity of fellow Communist Party members who had a strong presence in British trade unions at the time. When one worker lost an eye in a foundry accident, the union secured £2,000 in compensation – a substantial sum. Victories such as this persuaded more Asian workers to join the union.

At the Midland Motor Cylinder Company's Birmid works, Jouhl also led a campaign against segregated toilets, encouraging IWA members to defy the 'whites only' signs. The strategy of confrontation and collective action soon became a hallmark of Midlands IWA organising.

By the mid-1960s South Asian workers in the Midlands were at the forefront of some of the most militant trade union struggles in Britain. In April 1967 350 Indian and Pakistani workers at the Coneygre foundry in Tipton struck against the sacking of 21 men. The workers had proposed an alternative work-sharing arrangement whereby they would work a three- or four-day week to avoid redundancies, but management had rejected it.[30] Just one white worker joined the strikers; the remaining 150 members of the Amalgamated Union of Foundry Workers (AUFW) continued working, with a local AUFW official stating that his members 'were not involved in the redundancies and therefore not in the strike'.[31] The strike lasted ten weeks and saw the employer bring in scab labour from elsewhere. Heavy picketing from disciplined IWA members prevented strike breakers from crossing the picket line. In the end, the workers were victorious, with ten workers given their jobs back (the other 11 did not wish to return).

There were other disputes too. In Wolverhampton in 1964, a strike led mainly by Asian workers at a foundry revealed the deep corruption of a foreman who had been extorting money and gifts from employees in exchange for promotions. Journalist Robert Leeson later recorded the events through the recollections of Brian Mathers, the Midlands regional secretary of the Transport and General Workers'

Union, who maintained that the strike changed industrial relations in the Midlands.

> One day in Wolverhampton a Jamaican chap came to me and said, 'Look I was in the union back home. But in this factory, where it is mostly Indian labour, there is no union and the foreman rules with a rod of iron.' I gave him some forms and he came back to me with an Indian whom he introduced as a community leader. We chatted and he asked for 500 application forms. Now I had heard such stories before, but I was astounded when two days later, all the forms were filled in, signed and one week's subscription paid.[32]

A meeting was held and shop stewards were elected. Since the firm worked under national agreements, gaining union recognition was not difficult. But a fortnight later the same Jamaican worker informed Mathers that he had been sacked. The foreman had falsely accused him of threatening him with a hammer over a piecework price. Mathers believed this was a case of victimisation for organising a union and told the worker to encourage his colleagues to stand by him.

> The next thing I heard was that the factory was at a standstill and the employers' association was complaining of an unofficial strike. Meetings were held in a Sikh Temple where I had to remove my shoes, cover my head with a handkerchief and speak through an interpreter.[33]

After three weeks of strike action, the strike was paused with both the shop steward and the foreman suspended with pay while the case went through procedure.

But the suspension of the foreman raised questions for Mathers.

> I asked one of the leaders of the men to tell me what was going on. After talking to some of his friends he told me a fantastic story. For a long time the foreman had been extracting money from them. If there was a vacancy for a fork-truck driver he would offer it to a labourer on the basis of £5 now

> and so much a week. There were plenty of examples, and with the help of the Birmingham Community Relations Officer, statements were drafted and signed … There were hair-raising stories of people taking gifts, bottles of brandy, shoes for his wife, to the foreman's house. I presented the statements to the Chief Constable of Wolverhampton.[34]

The shop steward was eventually reinstated, while the foreman attempted suicide.

Reflecting on the strike, Mathers said:

> It was one of the first such successful actions by immigrant workers and its example spread through their community to other factories. It brought other immigrant workers into union activity and the Indian shop stewards later on played a big part in demonstrations against the Industrial Relations Bill.[35]

South Asians in the Midlands quickly gained a reputation as formidable trade unionists.

5
BLACK POWER

The 1964 general election was one of the most racist campaigns in the nation's history. The result produced a victory for Harold Wilson's Labour Party on 15 October, but it was overshadowed by the notorious Conservative candidate, Peter Griffiths, who unseated shadow foreign secretary Patrick Gordon Walker in the West Midlands town of Smethwick; one of Griffiths's most memorable slogans was 'If you want a n***** for a neighbour, vote Labour.' As the defeated Walker left Smethwick Town Hall after the count, local Tories yelled after him: 'Where are your n****** now, Walker?' and 'Take your n****** away!' 'I would not condemn anyone who said that', Griffiths told *The Times*. 'I regard it as a manifestation of popular feeling.'[1]

That 'popular feeling' often found its outlet in racist violence, outright discrimination and colour bars enforcing segregation. Soon a campaign was set up by white residents in Smethwick, calling on the local council to buy up empty houses and make them available exclusively to white families. 'This is worse than America. This is worse than Harlem', said Malcolm X, the American anti-racist activist as he walked down Marshall Street, a Smethwick road lined with rundown housing the following year. As he passed the red brick terraces, he was heckled. 'We don't want any more Black people here. What's your business here?" asked one white resident.[2]

Malcolm X's trip to Smethwick was not his first time in the UK. A few months earlier, in December 1964, he was invited to address the Oxford Union, where he met Tariq Ali, then a British-Pakistani student, who would become a leading figure on the international left. 'His speech was, by common agreement, the most brilliant to have been heard in that hall for many decades', Ali later recalled.[3] Malcolm also spoke in Sheffield, Manchester, Birmingham and London.

A towering figure in the civil rights movement and, at one point, a leading member of the Black nationalist Nation of Islam, Malcolm X had once preached racial separatism as the only viable solution to racism. But his visit to Britain came at a pivotal moment in his life. He had broken away from the Nation of Islam, become a mainstream Sunni Muslim, and had performed hajj and travelled extensively across the Middle East, Africa and Europe. A skilled orator, he captivated audiences from Boston to Beirut with his powerful and unapologetic advocacy for racial justice.

His later 1965 visit to Britain was coordinated by Claudia Jones, a Trinidadian Marxist, alongside members of the Indian Workers' Association, and the invitation had been sent by Shirley Joshi, the wife of the leading member of the IWA from the West Midlands, Jagmohan Joshi. This was the era of political blackness, when being 'Black' was about more than just skin colour; political blackness was a broader strategic term that sought to unite all people of colour in a collective struggle against racism. Members of the IWA under Joshi's leadership had embraced Black Power politics and taken on Malcolm X's assertive stance on racism, advocating self-defence.

'I was in Birmingham, Alabama, the other day. This will give me a chance to see if Birmingham, England, is any different', said Malcolm X to the press on 12 February 1965. The US city, once described by Martin Luther King Jr as 'probably the most thoroughly segregated city in the United States',[4] took centre stage during a hard-won campaign of non-violent direct action during the civil rights struggle.

During his visit to Smethwick, he visited a local school and walked through the town, witnessing first-hand the colour bars enforced by many businesses. Among the starkest examples were the signs hanging outside numerous drinking establishments, stipulating that 'No Blacks' were allowed in. 'You know we don't serve Blacks', said a barmaid at the Blue Gates pub on Smethwick High Street, refusing his entourage entry. Even Smethwick Labour Club operated a colour bar. In contrast, members of the local South Asian and Black communities greeted him with enthusiasm, viewing him as a man who not only understood their situation but articulated their desire for a better and more equitable life with passion and clarity. Malcolm X's visit was later described by the IWA as a 'shot in the arm for the anti-racist struggle in Britain'.[5]

In the years that followed, the IWA continued its campaigning. Alongside fighting discrimination in the workplace, it was pivotal in the campaign against the colour bar in pubs and clubs. IWA members organised pub crawls with white university students, who were able to buy pints where IWA members could not, and the organisation's leaders such as Avtar Singh Jouhl would also collate evidence of discrimination in pubs, causing racist landlords to lose their licences.

The IWA also played a crucial role in the campaign for the dismissed Wolverhampton bus driver Tarsem Singh Sandhu, who after returning from sick leave in 1967 wearing a turban was dismissed for breaching the company's dress code.[6] The IWA rallied to him and pressurised the TGWU into seeking a renegotiation on uniform rules. The case also drew in Sikh religious organisations, and gained international attention; at one point the president of the UK branch of the Shiromani Akali Dal, Sohan Singh Jolly, threatened self-immolation if the ban remained. Fourteen others vowed to follow suit. The campaign culminated a year later, in 1968, when 6,000 Sikhs marched through Wolverhampton demanding a lifting of the ban on the wearing of turbans.

Throughout the late 1960s industrial unrest in Wolverhampton was building. The following year, in February, there was broader industrial unrest throughout the city with strikes by teachers, Ford workers and bus workers, among others.[7] This was primarily in response to the Labour's government's deeply unpopular proposals to curb trade union powers, *In Place of Strife*. The volatile atmosphere put the bus company under further pressure. Meanwhile, most neighbouring transport committees had allowed turbans to be worn, and calls for Wolverhampton's transport committee to reconsider its ban were coming from multiple quarters. Jagmohan Joshi, addressing a mass meeting of Indians in Wolverhampton, drew up a plan of action, which would include a protest march through the town linking the turban ban with issues such as housing, education and jobs.[8] Meanwhile, the local paper reported that more than 600 members of the Wolverhampton IWA had backed a call for the setting up of a united action committee to coordinate and plan the fight against racial discrimination.[9] 'One of the first targets will be the transport committee', it stated. There was even a large protest against events in Wolverhampton in New Delhi.[10]

Two years of pressure finally came to a close in 1969, when the Wolverhampton transport committee finally scrapped the ban. It was a landmark victory: in the early post-war years, many Sikhs had felt compelled to abandon their turbans and beards to secure employment. Now, backed by numbers and organisation, they asserted their right to religious identity in Britain – a trend that would grow stronger in the decades to follow.

RIVERS OF BLOOD

One of those who backed the employers in this dispute was Wolverhampton's sitting MP, Enoch Powell. In 1968, while the dispute was running, he would deliver his infamous 'Rivers of Blood' speech, in which he quoted John Stonehouse, a Labour MP and government minister. 'The Sikh communities' campaign to maintain customs inappropriate in Britain is much to be regretted', Powell quoted Stonehouse as saying.

> Working in Britain, particularly in the public services, they should be prepared to accept the terms and conditions of their employment. To claim special communal rights ... leads to a dangerous fragmentation within society. This communalism is a canker; whether practised by one colour or another it is to be strongly condemned.[11]

Powell had been empowered by the divisive rhetoric of the then governing Labour Party. He would take it a step further. In fifteen to twenty years, he said, 'the black man would have the whip hand over the white man'. White Britons, claimed Powell, had become 'strangers in their own land'. Such was the divisiveness of his rhetoric that he was promptly dismissed from the shadow cabinet by the Tory leader Edward Heath, but not before igniting a political firestorm. Nor did his views make him a pariah in society more generally. Shortly after the speech, a poll revealed that some 74 per cent of the British public sympathised with Powell's views, while dockers and meat porters marched through the East End of London in support of his statements.[12]

For many South Asians, Powell's words marked a turning point. Balwinder Rana, one of only five Asian students studying at Gravesend College in Kent at the time, remembered the impact of Powell's speech. 'I was in the common room talking, and a student came round and threw a newspaper in front of me with the headline "Send them back, says Enoch Powell". He smirked and laughed at me with others.' There was, Rana remembered, a sudden shift in atmosphere: 'There were, of course, racist students, but before then they kept quiet. This rhetoric suddenly gave them some confidence. I remember standing in the queue for lunch – they were sniggering at me and shouting "Enoch Powell is right."'[13]

The following year, Rana and other young Indians in Gravesend felt compelled to set up the Kent Asian Youth Federation to fight back against the rising tide of racism. 'We had heard all the stories about Indian anti-colonial revolutionaries who fought for Indian independence. We knew our history was a history of struggle.' Reaching out through local hockey and football clubs, the group mobilised South Asians into collective action and talked to them about the necessity for self-defence.

Their public launch came during the 1969 Indian Independence Day celebrations. They booked a hall, invited the local MP, mayor and councillors, and made a deliberate effort to include professionals from sectors where racism was rife, such as bank managers, many of whom who had refused to give Asians mortgages, as well as headteachers and railway staff. 'We had live entertainment, and we did a lot of publicity to get a big audience', said Rana. 'We wanted to let them know that we were united: we were an organisation, and we were going to demand to be treated equally.' Over a hundred people signed up on the day.

The group quickly turned words into action. At one of their first meetings, a member mentioned a nearby pub that refused to serve Indians. They decided to confront the ban head-on. As Rana remembered:

> There were very few people inside. I went up to the bartender [with the rest of the organisation behind me] and asked for fifty pints of lager. They had the shock of their lives. In the past, if anyone went, they'd say 'We don't serve Indians'. Now, they were running around like headless chickens. Eventually, we were served.

Meanwhile, in the Midlands, Joshi also recognised the urgent need for collective defence. A group of self-styled British Klansmen had been targeting the homes of Black and Asian people, sending threatening letters and staging cross burnings. The Ku Klux Klan, notorious for its campaign of terror against African-Americans, had supporters in the Midlands, and a number of racist incidents linked to the group had caused alarm. In April 1968, at a house in Leamington Spa that had recently been attacked by the KKK, Joshi co-founded the Black People's Alliance (BPA). Like many Midlands towns, Leamington Spa had a growing Asian community, many of whom had faced racist violence. In 1966, for example, Punjabi Sikh businesses in the town had their windows smashed, while racist graffiti was daubed on walls and railway bridges. Shop owners, fearful for their safety, armed themselves.

At the BPA's inaugural meeting, more than fifty delegates representing twenty immigrant organisations met for six hours, committing themselves to organising community self-defence. Joshi told the press that it was 'the first time in the history of race relations in this country that black people had decided to unite forces to combat discrimination and the onslaught of fascism'.[14] Soon after, the group began to stage demonstrations, including one outside the US embassy in 1970 to protest the repression of the Black Panther Party, and it rose to become 'potentially the most powerful coloured organisation to emerge in Britain', according to the journalist Malcolm Southan, with fifty-five affiliates representing some 700,000 people. Joshi, Southan said, was pivotal in this: committed to Marxist principles, well-organised, and backed by 'a huge and loyal power base in Birmingham'.[15]

The organisation refused to admit groups that had 'compromised with government policy ... fallen prey to government hand-outs ... or looked to the Labour party for redress'.[16] Those present at the inaugural meeting also pledged to make 'preparations for protection and security' and acknowledged the need to form 'vigilante patrols'.[17]

The BPA's success, however, was short-lived, soon undone by factionalism and internal disagreements. Yet its very formation demonstrated how many organisations at the time were trying to transcend narrow nationalism, building alliances across diverse communities.

PAKI-BASHING

> The name of the game is Pakky bashing. In London's East End, the skinheads might have learned the rules from the Hitler youth. Any Asian careless enough to be walking the streets alone at night is a fool.

So began an *Observer* piece on 5 April 1970. The next day Tosir Ali, a 50-year-old kitchen porter and father of four, was murdered on his way home from work in East London. A gang of skinheads had attacked him, slitting his throat before leaving him for dead in the St Leonard Street area of Tower Hamlets.

This was no one-off. One year earlier, in a BBC documentary broadcast to millions of households, a group of skinheads spoke candidly about their visceral hatred of Pakistanis. 'Who's your natural enemy?' asked the reporter. 'Pakis, Grease', said one skinhead. 'Pakis ain't so much your natural enemy. They're just like a pastime aren't they?' said another. The others chuckled.

> 'What do you do about it when you dislike the Pakistanis?'
>
> 'Beat em up. You call it rolling Pakis, Paki bashing. Roll a Paki, you know, when you've nicked his money and that … just lay in. You boot them. You pick up anything you can use … Hit em over the head anything like that … Running to get a better run-up. Just jump them.'[18]

London's East End was then still scarred by the Blitz, its devastating effects visible two decades on. Kids played on bomb sites, while slum housing notorious for disease and overcrowding was a serious issue. The docks, which once provided abundant employment, were beginning to fall into decline.

Among the youth, a subculture influenced by the West Indian 'rudeboys' was gaining traction. These 'skinheads', as they came to be known, were defined by their close-cropped or shaven heads and their choice of clothing: Dr Martens and steel toe-capped work boots. For many, Paki-bashing soon became common; it was just another sport. A popular pastime. A bit of fun. Yet for South Asians, it was hell.

The victims were often recent arrivals from the Indian subcontinent, a significant number of whom had arrived from what is now Bangladesh. Most worked in the rag trade and lived in slum housing in the poorest parts of Tower Hamlets. Many had no intention of settling in Britain, hoping to make enough money to be able to support their families back home.

For this population, the period between 1969 and 1970 was particularly difficult. Bernard Weinraub, a foreign correspondent for the *New York Times*, reported on the atmosphere in the East End in 1970: 'In the twilight gloom along Commercial Road', he wrote,

> the dull red brick homes are locked and silent. The Pakistani children peer wide-eyed through white window curtains, gazing nervously at the strangers passing on the street. 'I am so terrified', said Vijay Chandekar, a social worker who sat this afternoon in the chilly East London Mosque. 'There is a viciousness now in the streets.'[19]

The scale of the violence was so severe that Pakistan's High Commissioner, Salman Ali, would visit the East End of London to provide reassurances, and he raised his concerns with the Home Office. Local MP Peter Shore, meanwhile, wrote to Home Secretary James Callaghan to inform him that between February and April of 1970 there had been at least twenty racist attacks in Tower Hamlets alone. Yet despite assurances from the government and the authorities, the violence continued. In the East End, Weinraub reported on a puzzled and frightened mood, with Pakistanis beaten up on their own doorsteps and hit with bottles, sticks and iron bars.

> One evening several weeks ago, a Pakistani doctor was beaten up in the Bethnal Green subway station five blocks from the hospital by a gang of 'skinheads' who broke his nose and fled. Recently, a 25-year-old telephone operator was attacked as he walked to the subway station. The 'skin heads' – shouting

> 'here comes old Hare Krishna' – kicked the operator in the face and stomach. He is still receiving treatment for an injury to one eye, though doctors say the damage will probably not be permanent.[20]

But the recent arrivals were not passive victims of racist attacks, and they soon began to fight back: 'Even before the death' of Tosir Ali, Weinraub wrote, 'the East End Pakistani community of 4,500 had slowly and uneasily begun to organize. Monday evening, the Pakistani Workers Union – which claims more than 4,000 members – announced "citizens defense patrols" to protect Pakistani families.' In the article, he quotes Abul Ishaque, chairman of the union: '"The police are not doing anything for us", Ishaque said, "we will be our own police."'[21]

Like Jagmohan Joshi's IWA in the Midlands, the Pakistani Workers' Union (PWU) and the Pakistani Progressive Party (PPP), another militant anti-racist group, were influenced by the Black Power movement in the United States, and they, too, advocated self-defence in the face of vicious racist attacks, with Pakistani, West Indian and English people setting up patrols to provide self-defence for people in the area.[22] This was in contrast to the Pakistani Welfare Association, another group campaigning on behalf of the local Pakistani population, which favoured a much more 'integrationalist' approach to the problem of racism, deferring to the authorities and working with institutions. Neither the PWU nor the PPP had any trust in the authorities.[23]

Following the murder of Tosir Ali, the PPP, alongside the Universal Coloured People's Association, a prominent Black Power organisation set up in 1967, distributed leaflets highlighting the lack of support from local MP Peter Shore despite 16 complaints of assaults and robbery on Pakistani people in Aldgate. 'If the law cannot protect us, then we have the right to defend ourselves', they wrote.[24] Another leaflet from the same organisations declared: 'Self-defence = No other Choice ... We therefore have no choice but to organise ourselves to prevent further racist violence. Our policy will be tit for tat. There will be a tooth for a tooth. Criminal assaults will be met by just retaliation. Racists beware!'[25]

The groups were soon gaining momentum, and when on Sunday 19 April the Pakistani Workers' Union called a meeting in East London, up to a thousand people attended. The meeting was so big, in fact, that it had to spill over into two halls. There, the PWU announced that it would organise a march from Speakers' Corner in Hyde Park to Downing Street.[26] As the socialist paper *Red Mole* reported, those at the meeting 'pointed out that the East Londoners themselves, not the police, stopped the fascists coming through in Cable Street in the '30s'. 'The Pakistanis would not allow themselves to be massacred like the Jews in Germany; they would fight back.'[27] At the end of the meeting around thirty to forty men volunteered to take part in self-defence patrols. Sibghat Kadri, chairman of the PWU's legal committee, told the meeting: 'Peaceful we may be, but cowards we are not ... Pakistanis will not take the law into their own hands, but will adopt self-defence ... Even if you kill in self-defence, it will not be murder ... Enoch Powell is the godfather of what is happening here.'[28]

Throughout April 1970 there were self-defence patrols across the borough, with around 200 people taking part according to local vicar Kenneth Leech.[29] A month later around 2,000 people marched to Downing Street under the banner: 'Stop skinhead hooliganism, demand effective measures, support multiracial defence.' In these actions, the Pakistani population were supported by other local groups, including the Black Panther movement, the Black People's Alliance, the Irish National Liberation Solidarity Front (INLSF) and the Working People's Party of England (a group that had splintered off from the Communist Party of Great Britain). As Edward Davoren of the INLSF told the press, 'the Pakistani cause was the same as the Irish cause'. He hoped, he said, to form 'Irish-Pakistani defence groups in East London'.[30] This sense of internationalism was made clear when demonstrators chanted 'British Imperialism – Out, People's War – Yes' as they passed by the Irish embassy. Chants of 'Black Power' were also heard.

At the time, the PPP claimed to have 275 members, and it announced that it would be setting up karate and judo classes so that local Pakistanis would be able to defend themselves;[31] as one member, Abdul Hyem, told the press, the PPP 'is a defensive organisation. We have no intention of fighting or killing anyone, but if it comes to us, we will hit back.'[32] Hyem made clear that the PPP had spent a considerable amount of time contacting the local MP and pleading with the government to take action. 'If the authorities still fail to act, we will organise street patrols ... We shall have no choice but to organise self-defence.'[33]

We can get a sense of the scale of the activities of the Pakistani Workers' Union and the Working People's Party of England from a pamphlet the groups put out around this time. 'On June 2nd 1968 a street patrol arrested two white thugs who had just attacked Mr. Nazir Uddin', it said. 'One thug escaped but the other was handed over to police officers from Tottenham Court Road Police Station.' The case was then dismissed at the Old Bailey due to an apparent lack of evidence, but the actions of the local community led to an increase in police patrols in the area. The leaflet continued:

> The June 2nd arrest by our own patrol also had a good effect on the morale of the Pakistani community. On June 9th, when an African school-teacher and a Pakistani worker were attacked near the Middlesex hospital by a score of white hooligans chanting 'Enoch Enoch!', some local Pakistanis and an Englishman went to their assistance and helped drive the thugs off.[34]

Just three of the nine white thugs were charged, while the police also arrested two Pakistanis several streets away who had not even seen the fight, let alone taken part in it. One of the Pakistanis was accused of carrying an offensive weapon: he had a spoon in his hand with which he had been eating his dinner. The hearing at the Old Bailey ended with the three Englishmen apologising and shaking hands with the Pakistanis.[35]

Despite these efforts, racist attacks grew in ferocity in the years that followed. It was into this climate of hostility that Bangladeshis, scarred by the brutalities they had witnessed back home, began to arrive in growing numbers.

6
FINDING HOME

A decorative arch in English and Sylheti greets visitors to Brick Lane. To its right is a colourful mural celebrating rural life in Bangladesh. It shouts loud and proud about Bangladeshi identity in an area where Bangladeshis have overcome many challenges to call it home. Up the road is the iconic Brick Lane Jamee Masjid. This Grade II listed building was first established in 1743 as a Protestant chapel by the French Huguenot community. They had escaped persecution in France and many had settled in Spitalfields, gaining a reputation for their silk-weaving and textile skills. In 1891 it was adopted by the Jewish community as a synagogue; they too had escaped persecution, this time in Russia and Central Europe, and they called Brick Lane home.

Today the area is home to the largest Bangladeshi community in Britain. Its roots are firmly planted, with street signage and tube signs and the abundant curry houses reflecting their presence. But there are many challenges. According to the Runnymede Trust, between 2010 and 2016 Tower Hamlets saw the fastest rate of gentrification in London.[1] Soaring rents have begun to drive out long-term residents, many from the Bangladeshi community, while the curry houses and cash-and-carries that once defined

Brick Lane have given way to fancy cafés and vegan eateries catering to a wealthier, whiter crowd.

This isn't the first time that the borough's South Asian population has faced intense struggles over housing and resources. In fact, the story of the Bangladeshi residents of East London has been shaped over generations by a series of struggles.

***

> Abdul Bari had run out of luck. Like thousands of other people in East Bengal, he had made the mistake – the fatal mistake – of running within sight of a Pakistani patrol. He was 24 years old, a slight man surrounded by soldiers. He was trembling because he was about to be shot.

So began an article in the *Sunday Times* on 13 June 1971. The two-page story by Pakistani journalist Anthony Mascarenhas, titled simply 'GENOCIDE', stunned the world. It documented the atrocities being carried out by the Pakistani army in Bangladesh, highlighting the brutality of 'kill and burn missions' as the army units, after clearing out the rebels, carried out pogroms in towns and villages.

Just a few months earlier, on 26 March 1971, Bangladesh's war of independence from Pakistan had begun, and it was marked by the mass killing, rape and torture of Bengalis by Pakistan's armed forces. The number of civilians killed is disputed, but estimates range from 300,000 to 3,000,000. 'I was personally subjected to an attack by the Pakistani armed forces', recalled Rajon Uddin Jalal. 'They came to our village and burned down our house because my uncle was an independence activist. They had beaten up my brother and many neighbours.'[2] The war ended in December that same year. Bangladesh won its independence, but it did so at great cost.

Like many Bangladeshis, Jalal found few opportunities in his newly independent country, deeply scarred by the intensity of the conflict. Just a year later he would arrive in Britain, one of the tens of thousands of Bangladeshis who made their way there in the 1970s, with many settling in towns and cities such as Birmingham, Oldham and Luton. Many also arrived in London's East End, which had an existing Bengali community that dated back to the 1920s. Most of these new arrivals were men who hoped to return to their country after earning an income in Britain. Soon, however, after the British government introduced further restrictions limiting the entry of migrants into the country, there was a significant increase in chain migration, with women and children joining them in great numbers.

'We were told that Britain was the land of opportunity. That it was the best place in the world', Jalal recalled. 'But when we arrived in the East End of London, the reality was very different. We witnessed a lot of poverty, lack of employment opportunities, rundown housing.' This struggle for housing would become one of the first significant campaigns for the new arrivals.

Prior to the arrival of their wider families, many young men opted for cheap, rundown, hostel-style accommodation, where they would take shifts on mattresses. Yet as the number of families with young children grew, this ceased to be appropriate. Since Tower Hamlets' waiting list rules stipulated that new arrivals did not qualify for council housing, and with institutional racism rife, families often found themselves sharing overcrowded flats.[3] Those Bengali families that did manage to secure tenancies often only did so in poor-quality accommodation, generally in predominantly white housing estates where they were isolated and subjected to frequent racist attacks. In inner-city areas of London, such as Spitalfields, Hackney, Islington and Brixton, these frustrations formed one part of a glaring contradiction: widespread homelessness amid abundant empty property. During these years, many middle-class families had moved out of the inner cities to the suburbs and the new towns of post-war Britain. The housing they left behind awaited demolition, but that process was slow, and desperate Londoners, including many new arrivals, would take matters into their own hands. Soon, thousands of houses were reclaimed and repaired by squatters.

Shabna Begum, CEO of the Runnymede Trust, herself the child of squatters, documents the stories of these squatters in her book, *From Sylhet to Spitalfields*. One of the families she writes about is that of Abdul Kadir, who with four other family members, before they moved into squatted properties, were stuck in a small one-bedroom flat at the mercy of an indifferent local housing officer. Squatting, for them as for many others, emerged out of necessity; though vital, it was not without its difficulties: many of the buildings were in abysmal condition and required a great deal of repair work.

With husbands often working long hours, many in the local garment factories, it was women who were the day-to-day guardians of the squats, taking on caring responsibilities while also fighting back against racist street thugs and hostile officials. Abdul Kadir's wife, Sufia Begum, recalled a council worker regularly banging on her front door. 'He would come and give me trouble', she said, 'and he would threaten me and I would just threaten him back – he was a bad sort.'[4]

Abdul Kadir and Sufia's daughter Halima Begum grew up in this squat. From an early age her life was intensely political, and not out of choice. 'Our very first home was on Goulston Street, which is off Petticoat Lane Market. And that's where the National Front used to have a newspaper stand.'[5] She recalled excrement being regularly posted through their letterbox and bricks being put through the window, and a daily act of defiance by her mother:

> My mother used to suffer racist abuse on the school run but she would always stand up to them. She'd wear her sari and her big winter coat and she'd have to rush past the racist thugs. They'd push her, sometimes spat at us. And I used to see my mum show resilience and courage to get about our everyday business. We didn't have the choice to run away and find sanctuary elsewhere. Our life was in Spitalfields. Hate was quite literally on our doorstep.

Begum's mother went further still. 'She even patrolled the streets to ensure safe passage for some of the other kids at the first Bengali language school set up on Goulston Street – this was the East End Community School which was one of the first Bengali language mother tongue schools.'

Beyond facing up to street thugs and other everyday acts of resistance, Begum's mother also played a pivotal role in building vital social infrastructure for new arrivals from Bangladesh and helping to stitch community bonds. 'She fed all the single men who worked with my Dad.' In many ways, said Begum, 'it mirrored how the miners' wives kept the home and the protest movement going during the coal strike in the 80s'.

While families like Begum's were forced to squat out of necessity, for others it was an active political choice. Squats could function as social and activist spaces, housing radical magazines, artist collectives and political groups, including anti-racist organisations. Olive Morris, a founding member of the Organisation of Women of Asian and African Descent (OWAAD), was one of the founders of a social centre, the

121 Social Centre, in a squat in Brixton. The centre served the local community as a bookshop, café, gig and rehearsal space, printing facility, office and meeting space. Many involved in the British Black Panther movement and the Race Today Collective, two groups that would come to play a leading role in the fightback against racism throughout this period, also made use of squatting, giving them the opportunity to dedicate their lives to unremunerative activist work that otherwise would not have been an option.

Race Today would be a particularly significant force throughout this period. A monthly journal under the editorship of Darcus Howe, a well-known Black Power activist, it lent a voice to anti-racist campaigns and industrial struggles involving Black and Asian workers. It was also based, for much of this period, in a number of squatted buildings in Brixton, South London. The magazine would prove significant for generations of Black and Asian activists. As Mukhtar Dar, a founding member of the influential Sheffield Asian Youth Movement, later recalled, 'We all read *Race Today*. We didn't have any money so we would share them between our members. It was a way for us to get a picture of what was happening nationally at the time.'[6]

Members of the collective also intervened in more direct ways. In 1976 the *Race Today* offices received a call from a Bangladeshi textile worker in Brick Lane. He said he lived in a house with 11 other Bangladeshi men, four to a room. They believed they had bought the house; in reality, they had been swindled. The house and street belonged to the Greater London Council, which was now coming to evict them as the street was marked for demolition. That evening three member of the collective, Mala Sen, Farrukh Dhondy and Leila Hassan, went to the address they had been given. The house, off Whitehorse Road, was boarded up, with the windows and doors barred with plywood. When the GLC eviction squad arrived, they were confronted by the collective, and a back and forth argument protesting the eviction ensued. When a burly Irishman passed on the opposite pavement, he was told what was going on, and he confronted the GLC officials. The occupants, he explained, were squatting and were the legal occupants of the house. As Farrukh Dhondy recalled,

> We were struck by this. He went on to explain as much to us as to the GLC bods, 'If you are caught breaking in, that's illegal, but once you are in an unoccupied property and have changed the locks and possess the key, the law says you are a legal squatter and can't be evicted.'[7]

The man's name was Terry Fitzpatrick, an Irish former soldier who was also squatting in a house not far away, and he had been helping Bangladeshi workers move to empty houses in the area, working with them to break the locks and replace the toilets and basins, which the council would often destroy to discourage squatters moving in, and offering legal advice.

Though none of the collective were from the Bangladeshi community, Mala Sen, from West Bengal, was fluent in Bengali, and was able to build up rapport and trust with the local community, helping to report on Bengali squatters. By 1976 the collective was also involved in on-the-ground activity, providing lawyers for the squatters to advise on their rights, and assisting families moving into properties.

With numbers growing, the squatters, with the assistance of the Race Today Collective and other groups such as the Tower Hamlets Squatters Union, soon formalised their activity, and on Friday 6 February 1976 they formed the Bengali Housing Action Group (BHAG) – a name with additional significance: bhag is the Bengali word for tiger. Soon, the group would demonstrate its collective strength. Around Easter 1976 the Pelham Buildings on Woodseer Street just off Brick Lane, which contained 60 habitable flats, became due for demolition. The squatters soon countered with mass occupation, initially by eight families, though by the end of the year the buildings were home to 300 people. Many of the squatters faced widespread racism in every aspect of their lives; squatted properties were sometimes firebombed and attacked by the far-right National Front. This was compounded by the presence nearby of the local NF branch, which had relocated its office to the Carpenters Arms pub, on the junction between Brick Lane and Bethnal Green Road. NF members would sell their newspaper, *Combat*, under the railway arches at the north end, just a few minutes away from Pelham Buildings. Two other pubs in the area, the Blade Bone and the Salmon and Ball, were notorious for Paki-bashing. Bethnal Green was very much a no-go area.

Yet with the squatted flats containing neither showers nor baths, many of the residents had to travel to the public baths in either Bethnal Green or Poplar, which obliged them to cross through this now racially hostile area. And as in Southall, the police were of little help. BHAG soon stepped in, setting up vigilante patrols, with young supporters taking it upon themselves to patrol the streets at night in defence of the local Bangladeshi community. In this, they were assisted by members of the Race Today Collective. Mala Sen was often the driver on nightly patrols, while Dhondy wrote reports for the paper. As Gedu Miah, a key member of the vigilante groups, recalled:

> Terry [Fitzpatrick] had a Ford Zafire – it's a massive, big car – and we used to go out, eight or nine o'clock in the evening, for night-time patrols. We would stay near the underground

> until it closes ... We were patrolling the whole street until three or four o'clock in the morning – we did this for over a year! Over a year! Can you believe that? And it was seven days – every day we did it! One time me and him was going patrolling – and there was too many of them [racist white youths] and he said, 'You drive the car – I'll go and beat the shit out of them' – and I said, 'I can't even drive', and he said, 'Just put it in gear man and go, go, go!'[8]

Often these vigilante patrols would clash with NF members. One particularly severe incident took place on 13 August 1976, when two young Bengali men leaving their factory shift were attacked by 25 white youths with knives and left seriously injured. In response, the police did very little to catch the perpetrators and instead arrested six Bengali men for being part of a vigilante squad. A new organisation, the Anti-Racist Committee of Asians in East London (ARCAEL), was formed from a coalition of local groups that included BHAG and Race Today, which organised a series of large meetings at Brick Lane's Naz cinema and sit-down protests outside local police stations. That summer ARCAEL organised a 3,000-strong march of mainly Bengali men through the East End, demanding action on racist violence, with individuals such as Khosru Miah and Mala Sen playing a prominent role, quite literally leading from the front. A further demonstration in November saw street battles between ARCAEL and NF supporters, with the police mainly arresting anti-racist protestors.

For Halima Begum, Bangladesh's war of independence was a key event that shaped British Bangladeshi resistance to racism.

> When the war broke out, men like my father who'd been in Britain since the 1950s felt really guilty about not being there to support their families and villages. My father and his friends organised and fundraised for a private carrier to

> get them into Bangladesh so they could fight as part of the liberation movement. They did it so they wouldn't have to go through Pakistani authorities who probably would have massacred them if they found them. So they took great risks to get back to Bangladesh to join the independence movement and they did so not knowing whether they'd actually leave that country alive if the Pakistani military found them.

'I think they were quite radicalised by that', reflected Begum.

> There was something about defending your mother country against the brutal forces of the Pakistani military so that when they came back to face racism in East London, they said enough is enough. It's very similar to the African-American soldiers who fought in the American war in Vietnam. When they came back as part of the civil rights movement, they said enough was enough. They could not unsee the racism any more.

In 1977 the Greater London Council was overwhelmed by the numbers squatting across the city and announced an amnesty for the squatters, giving them the chance to register to secure a tenancy. BHAG drew up a map for the GLC defining a safe living area for the community to minimise the risk of isolated families being on the receiving end of regular racist attacks. It was within this area that families were given tenancies, some in their existing squats.[9]

Finding a home, however, was only half the battle. Racist violence continued in the years that followed, with narratives that Bangladeshis were getting preferential treatment in council housing being pushed by the far right. Again, as we shall underscore in the next chapter, British Bangladeshis refused to be passive victims, organising their resistance in the face of new challenges.

TWICE MIGRANTS: THE AFRICAN ASIAN STORY

Bangladeshis were not the only South Asian diaspora attempting to find home in the 1970s. For East African Asians, the 1970s were a period of great turbulence. As they were to find when many were expelled from Africa, even British citizenship was not truly enough to be accepted in Britain.

> AN IMPORTANT ANNOUNCEMENT ON BEHALF OF THE COUNCIL OF THE CITY OF LEICESTER, ENGLAND. IN YOUR OWN INTERESTS AND THOSE OF YOUR FAMILY YOU SHOULD ACCEPT THE ADVICE OF THE UGANDA RESETTLEMENT BOARD AND NOT COME TO LEICESTER.

So read a full-page advertisement published by Leicester's Labour-run council in the *Uganda Argus* on 15 September 1972. The message was clear and cold: immigrants were not welcome.

Under British colonial rule, tens of thousands of South Asians moved to East Africa. Many arrived as indentured labourers, building the Uganda–Kenya railway under harsh conditions. Over time, a prosperous middle class emerged, largely composed of educated Gujaratis – doctors, lawyers, merchants and civil servants – who had carved out a place between the ruling white elite and the indigenous Black African majority, often confined to the lowest-paid work. As the tide of nationalism rose across East Africa after the Second World War, resentment towards this intermediary community grew. By the 1970s that resentment had hardened into hostility. In January 1971 nationalist leader Idi Amin came to power through a military *coup d'état*. In August 1972 he ordered the expulsion of Uganda's Asian population. They were given just 90 days to leave.

Of the 55,000 Ugandan Asians forced to flee, more than half held British passports, and around 11,000 made their way to Britain. Many came to Leicester, once the second-richest city in Europe, renowned for its hosiery, knitwear, footwear and light engineering industries.[10] But by the early 1970s it was a city struggling with factory closures and rising unemployment. 'Leicester clothes the world', some proudly declared, yet now this Midlands metropolis had begun to unravel: recession hit hard, manufacturing giants collapsed and unemployment soared. Those who came arrived cold, anxious and with little more than the clothes they wore. Though they were technically British citizens, there were no homes waiting for them, no jobs prepared, and certainly no warm reception.

The British press described their arrival as a 'flood' and an 'invasion'. In cities such as Leicester and parts of north-west London, where small Gujarati communities had already taken root, themselves refugees from earlier expulsions in Kenya and Tanzania, families were squeezed into cramped terraces and temporary lodgings, rebuilding their lives from scratch.

Only four years earlier, Enoch Powell had delivered his infamous 'Rivers of Blood' speech, railing against immigration from the Commonwealth. The 1968 Commonwealth Immigrants Act, passed in its aftermath, had already sought to curb the entry of East African Asians. Now, amid economic turmoil and rising inflation, anti-immigrant rhetoric was once again on the rise. The far-right National Front exploited the climate of fear, targeting cities such as Leicester in its campaigns.

Unlike earlier immigration waves, often composed of young men seeking work, many of the African Asians arrived as families. Though often fluent in English and highly qualified, they were routinely denied access to the professional and middle-class roles they had previously held. By contrast, factory owners showed no hesitation in hiring the newcomers. Since their qualifications carried no weight in the British jobs market, class barriers between South Asians would soon break down on the factory floor. As the Race Today Collective noted,

> The ghettoisation of labour meant that the school teacher from Ludhiana, the mechanic from Hoshiarpur, the graduate from Punjab University, the illiterate middle peasant from a village in Azad Kashmir ... [all] found themselves on the same shop floor. Britain recognised no distinctions of class or qualification amongst the Asians whose labour it used.[11]

In particular, factory employers assumed that Asian women would be cheap labour, easy to exploit and too timid to fight back. These assumptions would be proved wrong in dramatic fashion.

DEMANDING THEIR DIGNITY

Many of the new arrivals in Leicester found work at the Mansfield Hosiery Mills in nearby Loughborough, where they were assigned the lowest-paid jobs cutting fabric. The better-paid knitting roles were reserved for white women. Discrimination was rife. Supervisors refused to learn workers' names, shouting 'Oy!' across the factory floor. Asian women faced disproportionate disciplinary action, erratic shift patterns, and were largely paid by piecework, unlike white women, who received a guaranteed weekly wage.

By the autumn of 1972 their patience had run out. In early November 370 Asian workers walked out of the Trinity Street factory. A few days later another 80 workers at the Clarence Street site joined them in solidarity. These workers, most of whom were Asian women, were worn down by years of racist abuse from supervisors and unbearable workloads and were determined to make their voices heard. They marched through the streets of Loughborough demanding justice and staged a protest outside the local Marks & Spencer, accusing the retail giant of profiting from the mill's racist practices. In response, the Leicester branch of the National Front organised a counter-protest, chanting 'Put Britons First!' and attempting to intimidate the strikers.

But the workers were not alone. A solidarity committee comprising sympathetic trade union branches, university students and local anti-racists stepped in to provide support and guidance. Among their advisers was Bennie Bunsee, a South African exile and anti-apartheid activist. His involvement infuriated both the employers and the workers' official union, the National Union of Hosiery and Knitwear Workers (NUHKW), which had initially refused to back the strike, as he was able to assist them in applying serious pressure to make the strike official. Unwilling to be sidelined, the strikers occupied the union's offices, chanting Indian mantras and refusing to leave until the strike was recognised. The union relented: on 4 December it officially backed the strike, agreed to pay strike wages, and took the dispute to arbitration.

The strike would last for eight weeks. Throughout that time, the company attempted to break the workers' resolve by hiring replacement scab labour, but the strikers held strong, manning the picket lines and blocking entry to the factory. Managers even visited workers at home, trying to coax them back. Still, they stood firm.

Eventually, the conditions at the Trinity Street factory drew national attention. A court of inquiry issued a damning report confirming what the women had said all along about their treatment.[12] The *Leicester Mercury* also published an exposé on the Clarence Street site, warning of looming unrest if conditions were not improved.[13] At a public meeting, the union then announced the formation of a new factory committee. Of its 15 members, 11 were to be Asian women, each representing different departments. The committee would meet monthly to discuss working conditions and grievances, ensuring that the women's voices, long ignored, were now firmly part of the conversation. This confirmed it: the strikers had won.

Two years on from this strike, Bennie Bunsee wrote about its impact:

> The relationship between English and Asian girls is different: problems like pricing of articles are discussed together. Swearing has stopped. The Asian workers now have the chance to become cutters and overlockers, which was not the case before. Asian women are given a wages slip – again this was not done before. Some of the Asian women are now trying to learn English and some of the English women know a little Gujerati. The strike finally ended when Asians were granted knitters jobs – but the strike had raised many issues, not least of which was the dignity of the Asians themselves as a people. A familiar slogan of the workers was 'We will not go back like dogs.'[14]

THE IMPERIAL TYPEWRITERS STRIKE

Another notable dispute would occur at the Imperial Typewriters factory in Leicester two years later. Imperial Typewriters, a company taken over by the US multinational Litton Industries in 1966, was at the time one of the largest employers in Leicester. It had already recruited workers from the Indian subcontinent and the Caribbean in the immediate post-war period and took on many of the new arrivals from East Africa too. By 1974 some 1,100 of the 1,600 workers at the factory were South Asian.

With its dated machinery which it used to produce electric typewriters, the factory resembled a Victorian workhouse more than a modern combine, as the mills, factories and foundries that employed Asian workers often did. Instead of capital investment to improve productivity, employers sought to maximise their profit margins by increasing the intensity of work for immigrant labour. The work was gruelling, and the factory floor was often filthy and unpleasant. Hours were long and pay was low. As a female worker told Mala Sen, an activist with the Race Today Collective, 'When I first started work here, I had to make 14 motors per hour. But then they raised the target to 16 and then to 18 and so on. Now it's 22.'[15] Impossible targets such as these often prevented workers from taking breaks, and there was a racial division of labour on the factory floor itself, with Asian workers doing the worst jobs for the poorest pay. Despite making up a majority of the workforce, there was just one Asian shop steward. Workers expressed their grievances to the TGWU factory convenor, Reg Weaver, but they received no union backing.

This was compounded when workers discovered that they had been significantly short-changed on their bonus payments. They were paid a bonus when they reached a target of 200 assembled motors, but according to a 1972 agreement, they were entitled to a bonus once they reached 168 – meaning they were losing out on an additional £52 a week in today's money. It was this discovery that triggered a walkout: on 1 May 1974 39 Asian workers went on strike, which affected four different firms in the city. And while others soon returned to work, the workers at Imperial Typewriters persisted. Guided by unofficial leaders

Hasmukh Kehtani and N. C. Patel, they successfully picketed and leafleted the factory, bringing an additional 500 workers on to the picket lines. Within a few weeks, production had fallen by 50 per cent.

During the strike, workers held grievance meetings where they aired their frustrations about paltry pay and poor working conditions. These testimonies were taped by the strike committee and formed the basis for a list of demands. Many highlighted the racial discrimination they faced: white women pushing past them in the queue to work and getting to choose which jobs they did; Asian workers being denied promotions; racist foremen making their lives hell on the factory floor. More than anything else, this was a strike for respect and dignity in the workplace.

The TGWU continued to refuse to support the strike, with George Bromley, a union negotiator and well-known local Labour Party member, accusing them of failing to follow the proper disputes procedure. His statement, laced with racist undertones, ended with the following remark: 'In a civilised society, the majority view will prevail. Some people must learn how things are done.' He later made a series of wild claims, at one point suggesting that the Chinese Communist Party was funding the strikers. In the union's stead, activists such as Bennie Bunsee took on the role of advisor to the strikers. 'Bennie Bunsee lived in my house', recalled the veteran journalist Amrit Wilson, 'so I was in constant touch with him about the strike.'[16] As with all South Asian workers' strikes during this period, the key support base, she said, were the activists and the community: 'Instead of seeing this community mobilisation as a useful way of organising, unions felt threatened by them.'

Community support was vital, particularly in the absence of strike pay. Four factories with a large Asian workforce donated to the strike fund for the Imperial Typewriters workers and pledged a 24-hour stoppage in solidarity if required. Donations came in from across the country, too, with contributions from the Birmingham Sikh Temple, the Southall Indian Workers' Association and the Edinburgh Women's Conference. On 19 May 2,000 people marched and attended a mass meeting in the inner-city area of Highfield, demonstrating the support the workers had mustered.

Heather Rawling, a student at the University of Leicester at the time, recalled the support of the mainly white workforce at the neighbouring Corah hosiery factory. 'The way they organised themselves was democratic. They elected their own leaders and held mass meetings. They did get their message out to other workers. The hosiery industry was massive at the time, and they were undergoing their own problems with their management, so there was sympathy.'[17]

The pickets themselves were large and lively. Writing in *Race Today* in July 1974, Mala Sen described the picket line as one with a vivacity and style that made it unique:

> Whenever a scab or management representative appears, a fearful yowling and hollering is set up, led invariably by the women who have been stalwarts on the line since the day the strike started. The noise is tremendous as it echoes across the street and between the high buildings … A new element has emerged amongst the strikers … they are fearless and energetic. They have no qualms about attacking the National Front, cheeking the police … and they are powerfully hostile to blacklegs.[18]

'The factory was in a narrow area, so the noise was loud because it was quite enclosed', recalled Rawling. 'There was a lot of support from other workers. I was invited to their strike committees.' The National Front, which had polled 9,000 votes in previous elections, constantly targeted the picketers but, Wilson recalled, 'the scale of the support that the picket had meant they carried on regardless'.[19]

In the end the strike lasted three months. Although the union had never officially supported the strikers, workers sought the support of the TGWU rank and file, writing to branches across the country. The IWA mobilised hundreds to lobby the TGWU's head office in London, which later promised an inquiry into the union's handling of the dispute. On 18 July workers decided to return after the company agreed to review bonuses.

In the aftermath, and despite workers winning a few concessions, many became more assertive in demanding fair treatment at work. One of the workers, Shardha Behn, told *Race Today* that September:

> The first day I got back to work, my foreman asked me what I had gained in the last twelve weeks. He was making fun of me, I know. I told him that I had lost a lot of money but had gained a lot of things. I told him I had learnt how to fight against him for a start. I told him he couldn't push me around any more like a football from one job to another. I told him I now knew many things I didn't know before. In the past, when I used to get less money in my wage packet, I used to start crying at once. I didn't know what else to do. I told the foreman, 'Next time I won't cry, I'll make you cry.'[20]

Following the dispute, the strike committee issued a statement:

> Our struggle has taught us also that black workers must never for a moment entertain the thought of separate black unions. They must join the existing unions and fight through them. Where the unions fail in their duties to black workers, they must be challenged to stand up for their rights. The union is an organisation of all workers, regardless of race,

> colour or sex. Right now, the trade union movement in Britain is functioning as a white man's union, and this must be challenged. In challenging this, we believe in the unity of the working class. This unity must be solidly established in deeds and not in words. It is the main task of the trade union movement to create this unity.[21]

GRUNWICK

The summer of 1976 was brutal. Across Britain, a heatwave scorched streets and strained tempers. In a film-processing factory tucked away in Willesden, north-west London, it was almost unbearable. Inside, there were no windows, no fans – just heat, sweat and the constant hum of machines.

Most of the workers at the plant, the Grunwick processing plant, were women who had recently arrived from East Africa. This was a group that the representatives of the notoriously anti-union firm had explicitly recruited by going door-to-door with leaflets, because they saw them as docile and easy to exploit. Once working for the firm, the women laboured under punishing conditions: if they needed the toilet, they had to raise a hand like a child in school, while a glass-walled office loomed over the shop floor from which a stern manager scrutinised their every movement. Overtime for staff was compulsory and could be imposed at a moment's notice. Pregnant women were denied time off to see a doctor. Workers were ranked on their so-called 'productivity', with no one wanting to be at the bottom of the list; many worked even harder for fear of being sacked. Yet for a full 40-hour week, the women at Grunwick were paid just £28; the national average at the time was £72.

On 20 August 1976 the first spark of anger was struck. Devshi Bhudia, a young Gujarati worker, was ordered by his manager, Malcolm Alden, to sort thirteen crates of outgoing mail before the end of the day. Bhudia found the demand unreasonable. In protest, he slowed his pace. He was immediately dismissed. Three male colleagues walked out in solidarity, standing outside the gates until evening.

That same day, Jayaben Desai, a 43-year-old mother of two, was packing up after a long shift at the Grunwick plant. When a foreman approached her and demanded she stay and work overtime, Desai refused. For this, she was summoned to the manager's office. As she later recalled in an interview with the writer and journalist, Amrit Wilson:

> Before I could say anything, he started to shout at me, saying 'Mrs Desai, you can't talk back to me…' I said, 'I am here to tell you something but if you don't want to listen to me I am not going to listen to you either.' He said 'Mrs Desai don't point at me.' I said 'If you point at me I can point at you.' He said 'I warn you.' I said 'I don't want your warning. I am going to leave this job. I have worked loyally, shown you respect, but I too expect to be treated with respect. You bring me into the office to shout at me and I can't say anything. I just have to listen, I am not going to stand this.'

She then left the office, walked on to the shop floor, and addressed her colleagues.

> 'I am leaving', she declared. 'You all know very well what the management are doing. This has happened to me today. It will happen to you tomorrow. You have to wake up.' Why aren't they employing white people in this factory? Because the white workers would teach them how to treat them. We are not teaching them, that is why they are treating us like this. I told the manager, 'You misjudge people, you think they are daft. But they are not. Some have problems, some because of their circumstances are working here. But I am not like that. You can't treat me like that. I will prove it to you.'[22]

That same day her son, Sunil, had also been humiliated, reprimanded for laughing. 'Stop chattering like monkeys, this is not a zoo', the manager, Malcolm Alden, had said.[23] As Desai was about to leave, she turned to Alden one last time: 'What you are running here is not a factory it is a zoo. But there are many different types of animals in a zoo. Some are monkeys who dance to your tune. Others are lions who can bite your head off. We are the lions, Mr Manager!'[24]

Outside the gates, a small group had already gathered. The young men who had walked out along with Bhudia discussed damaging the manager's car. Desai stopped them. Violence, she said, wouldn't effect change. A union, on the other hand, might. Desai's husband was part of a union, and she saw firsthand the benefits it provided. Her son contacted the Citizens Advice Bureau in Wembley, who suggested they join the Association of Professional, Executive, Clerical and Computer Staff (APEX). By Monday morning Desai and the others were back at the factory gate armed with placards and a petition demanding a union. Their fellow workers were quick to sign. At 3 p.m. that day 50 workers in the mail order department at Grunwick's Chapter Road premises walked out on strike in support of another colleague who had been sacked for allegedly working too slowly.

Along with Desai, Bhudia and the others who were already out, the workers approached the Willesden Law Centre, contacted Jack Dromey of the Brent Trades Council, and began holding mass meetings to build support for their strike. Over the next few days, more workers joined them. Desai and others spent a great deal of time convincing women to join them on the picket line, challenging patriarchal attitudes and engaging with husbands, fathers and fathers-in-law who did not want their relatives taking part. 'Some women had a lot of pressure', Desai reflected. 'They used to be pushed – "Don't go, don't go." Many stopped attending the pickets as well because their families said it was not appropriate that our women should be standing on the picket line. What will people say?'[25] In response, Desai pointed to the proud history of Asian women protesting in the struggle for Indian independence. The efforts of women such as Desai were fruitful – not least because conditions at the sweatshop were so appalling that the women knew that they had to take a stand; their mistreatment could not go on. As Desai declared at the time, 'This is not so much a strike about pay, it is a strike about human dignity.'[26]

To further their action, the striking workers collectively joined APEX, and once in, they demanded union recognition from the firm. They were helped when, on 1 September 1976, APEX declared the strike official, with the workers then receiving strike pay and the backing of the TUC. To this, the response from management was severe: the striking workers were sacked. Undeterred, they remained resolute and continued to assemble on the picket line.

Throughout the end of that summer the strike would build, with 137 out of a total workforce of 490 on the picket line at its height.[27] But in autumn, as the student workers who made up a proportion of the striking workforce returned to their studies, those who remained on strike began to feel increasingly isolated on the picket line. This was heightened by the racist abuse they received from passers-by, with shouts of 'Paki' and 'Go back to Paki-land' frequent.[28]

The strikers turned to the broader trade union movement for support, eventually gaining the backing of prominent trade unionists who framed their strike as part of a broader fight around the principle of the right to organise and the right to join trade unions. Yet in an era in which politicians were seeking to clamp down on the power of trade unions, such action was seen as a grave threat. Just two years earlier, the National Union of Mineworkers had brought down the Heath government after its mass picketing, supported by the wider trade union movement, had successfully shut down the Saltley coking depot, forcing the government to concede to its pay demands.

In the autumn the Grunwick strikers began to picket local chemists, attempting to dissuade them from sending their films to Grunwick for development. They also sought solidarity action from postal workers in an attempt to cut off the main route by which film reached Grunwick's mail-order photo-processing business. On 1 November members of the Cricklewood branch of the Union of Postal Workers formally refused to handle Grunwick mail.[29] Kodak workers, meanwhile, refused to handle Grunwick's photographic supplies. Managers would end up bringing the supplies in themselves, smuggling small quantities through the gates in the boots of their cars.

Such solidarity put serious pressure on the company, and that month Grunwick increased the general wage by 15 per cent, with a further 10 per cent increase planned for April 1977, in a desperate attempt to hold on to its remaining workforce who were tempted to join their colleagues on the picket line.[30] The firm also improved holiday and sickness benefits.[31] They are 'paying everybody higher wages now', Desai told a reporter from *Race Today*. 'The strike has increased the pay to £30 a week and we are told that the management has stopped treating workers like slaves.' 'They speak so politely now.'[32]

But Grunwick had other methods at its disposal. Its manager, George Ward, was backed by an influential right-wing organisation, the National Association for Freedom (NAFF), which funded and handled all of Ward's legal business during the strike. For blacking Grunwick's mail, NAFF threatened legal action against the Union of Postal Workers. Further support for management came on 4 November, when thanks to the efforts of more than a hundred Conservative MPs, they secured an emergency debate in the House of Commons on the solidarity action of Post Office workers. The MPs claimed that their actions had contravened the Post Office Act 1953. With legal and political pressure growing, and in response to the shallow promise made by Grunwick to cooperate with ACAS, the mediation body between unions and employers, the solidarity action was called off.

The strike rolled on into the new year, and in March 1977 ACAS published its report, recommending union recognition by the firm's management, who promptly rejected it. Management also resorted to hiring scab labour, people from all backgrounds, to mitigate the impact of the strike. On the picket lines, meanwhile, striking workers were subject to growing police intimidation and violence, even, as it later emerged, along with their supporters, being spied on by the Metropolitan Police's Special Branch.[33]

In response to these setbacks, the strikers sought to escalate their picketing. Supported by Brent Trades Council, the Grunwick workers toured the country, speaking to trades union branch meetings in an attempt to gather support. When APEX called for a mass picket, supporters from up and down the country came in their thousands. The presence of Arthur Scargill, general secretary of the National Union of Mineworkers (NUM), and miners from Kent, Yorkshire and Scotland frightened the establishment. The NUM was considered the most militant trade union at the time; Prime Minister James Callaghan was so concerned that there could be a repeat of the Battle of Saltley Gate which had brought down his predecessor Heath that he told officials that Scargill 'may have to be warned off'.[34]

In response to the picket line's swelling numbers, the Met's Special Patrol Group, notorious for their violent policing methods in Northern Ireland, were deployed, and Scargill, along with the left-wing Labour MP Audrey Wise and others, were arrested on the picket lines. But the mass pickets – miners, dockers, printers, firefighters and others standing shoulder-to-shoulder with the Asian women workers of Grunwick – remained significant. On 11 July 1977 alone around 20,000 gathered on the narrow streets of Willesden, hundreds of whom were later reported as suffering injuries due to their clashes with the police.

Yet despite all the pressure, Ward refused to budge. His intransigence would pay off; as the dispute continued, APEX and the TUC were gradually pulling back their support, claiming that the strike was unwinnable. Workers felt betrayed. They had been promised solidarity and then hung out to dry. One cold November evening in 1977, more than a year into the strike, four of the strikers, including Desai, began a one-day hunger strike outside the TUC headquarters. The officials inside were unmoved. In July 1978, after 670 days on strike, the dispute was finally called off by the remaining strikers.

Today, Grunwick is celebrated by the labour movement as a tale of triumph. But in the end, without wider trade union backing, the workers lost. This pattern repeated itself in 1992 during the Burnsall strike in Smethwick, when South Asian women protested against inhumane working conditions and racist abuse from managers at their metal-finishing company. It happened again in 2005, when Asian women at Gate Gourmet, a company outsourced from British Airways and based at Heathrow airport, were replaced by agency workers who were willing to do their jobs for less money. The workers protested, and 700 of them were dismissed in just two days. Once again, Asian women felt they had received only lacklustre support from their trade union.

Today, Black and Asian women workers are three times more likely to be on exploitative zero-hour contracts than their white male counterparts.[35] Far too many continue to suffer in precarious, low-paid jobs on bogus self-employment contracts, denied statutory sick pay and protection against unfair dismissal. The dilapidated Imperial Typewriter building in Leicester today houses garment sweatshops where South Asian women continue to work long hours for low pay. Some investigations have revealed workers being paid less than the minimum wage. In the city where a struggle for dignity was waged over fifty years ago, exploitation remains rife.

FINDING A VOICE

Asian women weren't exploited only in the garment factories and on the shop floor, of course; they also experienced this in the home, as the journalist Amrit Wilson found after she came to the UK as a student in the early 1960s. There, despite finding a tight-knit community where, for the most part, everyone looked out for each other, she was struck by the gendered divisions. One particular incident which brought the gendered dynamics home occurred after a Pakistani bus driver invited her for a meal with himself and his wife at his home. Once the meal was finished, he left to go to the pub. 'I said "What about us?" He said "No, no you've got your own dartboard at home." Women were expected to stay at home.'[36]

These and similar attitudes left Asian women in Britain feeling lonely and isolated. Political spaces could be similarly exclusionary. 'A lot of IWA people would go to the pub and come back late in the evening expecting food made', said Wilson. 'The poor woman, she's also working. She's probably doing a job at home sewing.' Wilson felt that the caste discrimination and misogyny of these spaces too often went unaddressed.

Initially, Wilson had planned to go back to India after her studies, but then she got married and decided to stay. 'That's when the scale of racism really hit me', she said.

> Bringing up a child in this country was a very, very tough experience. I remember being attacked on the street, with my baby, and facing a lot of racism within the welfare state. The patronising attitudes and so on. That made me realise that I had to do something.

Wilson knew she could write, and she wanted to put that to good use. In 1978 she published her groundbreaking book *Finding a Voice*, which documented the experiences of South Asian women in Britain.

'The first place I went to was Southall', she recalled.

> I went to a children's project which they were running in some community centre and talked to the kids. I had a little tape recorder. I took it along and I asked the children if they wanted to be recorded. They all loved it. 90% of them were very ashamed of being South Asian. Ashamed of their food, of their language, culture, so many things. It was quite sad, really.

Wilson also spoke to women about the isolation they had felt when they arrived in Britain, the racism they experienced in the NHS and the welfare system, and the prejudice they faced in the workplace. She also detailed the struggles women faced within their ethnic communities, from domestic violence to forced marriage. 'My best interviews just happened by chance', she recalled.

> I remember one day I'd gone to somewhere new and got lost. I was wandering around with my tape recorder, as ever, and I thought I'd ask this woman the way to the tube station. She said, 'Look, I can't tell you, but at home I have a book which can tell you the way', so she took me to her house and then she said, 'You want a cup of tea?' I said OK. Then she sat down and she started telling me about her life. She was a laundry worker, and she had to work so hard. It was terrible. And then she'd come back home and the husband wanted food on the table. He was quite cruel, really.

During the project, Wilson connected with community workers and devoted increasing amounts of her own time and energy to providing a support network for South Asian women.

> [The community workers] told me that there is literally nothing for women. A woman facing violence at home is completely on her own, whereas in India at least, there will be a network of relatives. We toyed with this idea of setting something up. A lot of younger women also got interested, and that's how Awaz was born.

Set up in 1979, Awaz, an Urdu word meaning 'voice', was the first South Asian women's collective in Britain. Drawing most of its support from London, its campaigning and activism played a key role in the struggles of the era. One of its early campaigns revolved around the virginity tests then being carried out on many South Asian women by immigration staff at Heathrow airport. The tests were necessary, officials claimed, because some immigrants were abusing the 1971 Immigration Act, which allowed fast-tracked entry for the fiancées of migrant workers, and it was to determine their marriage status that they subjected women to this degrading inspection. What lay under it was, however, was a series of intensely racist and sexist assumptions about South Asian women; it was, as many considered at the time, essentially a form of sexual harassment. Yet the women subjected to it knew that a refusal to consent meant being sent home. In response, and working alongside the Organisation of Women of African and Asian Descent (OWAAD), which Awaz would later join as a member organisation, the group organised a demonstration and later a sit-in at Heathrow, protesting not just the virginity tests but the treatment of women at the nearby Harmondsworth Detention Centre.

Awaz and OWAAD also campaigned against the over-prescription of Depo-Provera. Wilson described Depo-Provera as 'an injectable contraceptive widely used on Black and Asian women who were seen as the lowest of the working class'. Again, it shone a light on the racist and sexist assumptions of many in the British establishment. The medical establishment, Wilson told me, 'thought these women were stupid and wouldn't be able to take the pill so they gave them this drug'. A 1978 study carried out at the London Hospital in Mile End and Whitechapel found a disproportionately large number of Asian women were being prescribed Depo-Provera, often without fully knowing about its side effects.[37] Similar concerns were raised by the Brent Health Council.

Awaz supported Asian women in their workplace struggles, too. 'There was a factory called Futters in Willesden', recalled Wilson. 'We found there were a lot of miscarriages happening for Asian women [working there]. We asked them [the women] if they would be willing to see a doctor, and so we arranged that. Then we discovered that the miscarriages were connected to the pollutants in the factory.' Both Awaz and OWAAD supported these workers when they went on strike in 1979 over poor working conditions and health and safety concerns.

7
FIGHTING BACK

Suresh Grover froze in shock. There it was: a pool of blood spreading across the pavement. A section of the High Street had been cordoned off and a uniformed police officer gestured for bystanders to move along. It was the long hot summer of 1976, and a racist murder had stunned Southall.

'What has happened here, officers?', the curious 22-year-old asked. 'Go away, it's just Indian blood', was the response. Grover was soon to learn that 18-year-old Gurdip Singh Chaggar, an engineering student, had been stabbed to death by racist thugs the night before. The murder had taken place opposite the IWA-owned Dominion cinema, a symbol of the South Asian community that had begun to plant its roots on British soil. But the blood on the pavement showed that the community was not going to be allowed to exist in peace. Southall was no more a safe haven than anywhere else.

The cruelty of the police response came as no shock to Grover or the wider community. Just a few years earlier, while Grover was living in Nelson, Lancashire, he himself had been stabbed in a racist attack, and despite his pleas, no police action was taken. The broader response was predictable too; after Chaggar's killing, the leading fascist Kingsley Read was quoted as saying, 'One down, a million to go.'[1]

The late 1970s was the era of 'Paki-bashing': homes, shops and places of worship were attacked, while South Asians – young and old – were murdered on the streets. That day, Grover acted instinctively, taking some paint and daubing the pavement near the blood with the words: 'This racist murder WILL be avenged. We'll get you racist scum.'[2]

Grover was not the only one to be enraged. The news of Chaggar's murder reverberated through Southall like a thunderclap. The youth were angry. This was the state of terror in which they lived, day after day, one attack after another. Slurs were hurled out in schools. The sneering mimicry of accents, the ridiculing of their food, the casual contempt for their names. The abuse was relentless. It followed them on the playground, the football pitch and the walk home. Bricks were launched through windows. Assaults took place in broad daylight. All the grinding daily humiliation was underpinned by a quiet understanding: no one would come to their defence.

For Balraj Purewal, who arrived in Southall at the age of eight in 1961, racist abuse was a grim rite of passage from which no Asian child was spared. At his first school, Beaconsfield Primary, white parents would shout outside the school gates, protesting the fact that non-white pupils made up a large majority. Six months later Purewal was separated from his brother and transferred to Tudor Road Primary School, an example of bussing, a policy whereby, to prevent significant numbers of Black and Asian children congregating in one school, the government sought to disperse them. In Southall, this meant children being bussed out of their local areas and transported to schools across the

London borough of Ealing. The aim was to appease those racist parents who resented the presence of Asian children in schools that had traditionally been all-white.

In practice, bussing meant Asian children were isolated even further, and it made them ever more likely to be bullied; alongside the inconvenience of the long journeys, much of the racist violence to which these children were subjected took place on the way to and from school. For Purewal, the abuse got worse at his new school, Dormers Wells High School. For over two years he was unable to stand in the queue for lunch because he was constantly attacked, while during football and rugby bigger white lads would pile on top of him. As for the education system itself, Asian children were often put in separate classes where they were taught demeaning things such as how to use a knife and fork.

Some fought back. Purewal had long admired his older peers who stood up for themselves against the bullies. In his fourth year at high school, he realised that the boys who had until then protected him would soon be leaving. He knew not only that he'd have to stand up for himself, but that he'd have to stand up for the kids in the years below him, too. It was these kids, forced to fend for themselves at school against racist bullies, who would become some of the most fearless fighters against the far right in the years to come.[3]

Suresh Grover had a similar childhood experience to Purewal. Born in Uganda, where his father owned a textile mill, when he was seven years old in 1966 the family moved to Nelson. 'I couldn't speak a word of English', he recalled. 'The first thing I learnt was to keep my head down.' Life for the Grovers in Lancashire was defined by isolation and hostility; Grover's mother, who wore a sari, was frequently abused on the street, and shouts of 'Paki' were commonplace.

At school, the abuse was relentless:

> I was never called Suresh. My woodwork teacher would say, 'Here comes Jimmy, Tarzan's son. He was born on an elephant, swings on a tree', and everyone would laugh. We invited white classmates to our house. Nobody ever turned up. I was never invited to theirs. Not once.

There were numerous confrontations during lunch breaks, with fights often orchestrated by other pupils. 'We just got surrounded and attacked ... We learnt not to open our jaw, because if you did, it would get broken.' Teachers offered no protection, often joining in on the taunts. 'We were spat at, kicked, called "black bastards." It wasn't just words. One of my friends had his jaw broken, another got stabbed. The violence was real.'

Outside the school gates, the danger only grew. 'On Saturday nights, skinheads would come into town looking for us', Grover said. 'We knew which streets to avoid. But even then, sometimes you couldn't escape.' Unlike Southall, Nelson's South Asian community was much smaller, and even more vulnerable to racist violence. 'Ten of us, girls and boys, just stayed together, three Indians and seven Pakistanis, shoulder to shoulder.'

The night he was stabbed, Grover was going to see a Clint Eastwood film with his nephew when a racist gang surrounded them. 'One of them said, "You touched my girlfriend"', Grover said. 'My nephew opened his mouth and the guy just smacked him. You could hear the crack. So I went for him. And the next thing I know is you're on the floor, you get stabbed, there's blood everywhere and they run away.' The police's refusal to act was another reminder that Grover was on his own. 'I saw the guy who beat me go by my house on a daily basis', he recalled. Still, there was a kind of courage that came from being beaten so often. 'The fear goes away. Before, fear of being beaten up would paralyse you. But we survived it. What else could happen?'

Television and the world events he saw through it offered a political language for what Grover was living through. 'When I saw Malcolm X on television', he remembered, 'I thought here is a man who is saying what we feel. The Black Panthers too, the way they walked, the way they carried themselves, it was electrifying. It gave us pride.' Sport was another source of moral strength. Grover recalled the Black Power salute made by two African-American athletes, Tommie Smith and John Carlos, during their medal ceremony at the 1968 Summer Olympics. 'For me, that was everything. That was dignity in the face of hatred.'

By his late teens Grover had grown rebellious and outspoken. 'I worked at Calvert's pies factory in Nelson during my school holidays', he told me.

> Our foreman was the most racist man you could imagine. He wouldn't pay us on time and often docked our wages. We worked nights, and one day we'd just had enough. He called us 'Pakis.' I convinced ten of the other workers to join me, and together we sabotaged the factory. We stuffed Brillo pads and socks into the pies, ruining the entire batch. When the foreman came in the next morning, every pie was destroyed. We were all sacked, of course, but it was worth it.

The pressure of Nelson remained suffocating, though, and Grover felt he would soon end up in trouble. 'There was a fight every day. Either I'd kill someone or someone would kill me. I had to get out. I told my parents I would find work in London.'

It was in London that Grover found what he calls his 'university'. Living in squats, he met people from around the world: Chileans fleeing Pinochet, South Africans fighting apartheid. 'It was my introduction to global politics. Every meal was political. You'd sit down to eat and someone would say, "What do you think about Angola?" It opened my world.' London also gave him space to breathe and new influences. 'Harlem dance theatre turned up and stayed with us. I had never met gay people ... It was such a massive experience for me.'

Politics, meanwhile, seeped into everything. 'I started reading about South Africa, learning about Soweto', he said. Soon, he had thrown himself into political activism. 'I joined a group called the Asian Socialist Forum. That's how I got really into it, having discussions with people from Sri Lanka, Pakistan, Mukti Bahini in Bangladesh.'

By 1974 Grover had moved to Southall. It was, he thought at first, somewhere he didn't need to be constantly looking over his shoulder. But the brutal murder of Gurdip Singh Chaggar served as a harsh reminder that nowhere was entirely safe. In the days following the murder, something shifted. The streets buzzed with tension, and teenagers who had grown up shrinking themselves now walked with clenched fists. Chaggar's death had become a rallying cry for Southall's youth. These young people were done waiting. They were done hiding. The Indian Workers' Association quickly organised a meeting, but local youths, frustrated by their lack of urgency, disrupted it, calling for real action on racism. Frustrated with factionalism and the IWA's failure to give young people a voice, they led a walkout, assembling outside the Dominion and holding their own impromptu meeting to publicise their plan to march on Southall police station in order to demand protection from racist attacks. In a further sign of tensions, while this meeting was taking place a Jaguar pulled up, from which white men yelled racist abuse. One of those in the car then opened a window from which he waved a pickaxe. 'You black bastards', he shouted, 'you fucking Pakis!'

Kalwant Suri, then a young man in Southall, recalled the youths chasing the car. 'They thought they would get away as usual. I and others chased them and some started throwing bottles and other things at their car. They panicked. You could see the fear in their faces.'[4] In the unrest that followed, the police arrested two Asians. In response, hundreds marched to the police station and held a sit-in, demanding their release. There, another arrest was made, further inflaming the situation. Tempers were high and the youths threatened to burn down the police station unless all those arrested were released unconditionally. Their demands were delivered to the police by a delegation of youth representatives and community leaders. In an effort to disperse the growing crowd, the youth delegation was told by the police that those demands would be met. The sit-in was aborted.

Later, however, it emerged that, contrary to what the police had said earlier, those arrested would, in fact, face criminal charges. The youth were furious – at both the police and the community leaders who claimed to speak on their behalf. There was a feeling that these self-appointed community leaders took on the role of mediators, acting in deference to the state, the same state that was racist to its core. From now on, the youth decided, they would take matters into their own hands.

This group of angry young people would soon organise themselves under the banner of the Southall Youth Movement (SYM). They came from various places. Some were members of street gangs such as the Holy Smoke and Tooti Nungs. Others were involved in kabbadi (Indian wrestling), while others came from local colleges. For their insignia, the group chose the Olympic torch, in homage to the actions of the African-American athletes Tommie Smith and John Carlos in 1968, who each raised a black-gloved fist during the playing of the US national anthem.

It was the emergence of the SYM that would come to give shape to the local response to Gurdip Singh Chaggar's killing. In the days after the murder, some local white people had been targeted in revenge attacks, including a Communist Party member and a socialist documentary photographer. The SYM cautioned against this kind of senseless violence, instead urging the youth to organise the strategic self-defence of the community. As many had built up formidable reputations as fighters against racism in schools, their authority was readily accepted, and in the months that followed Southall became a hub of anti-racist resistance. Never again would the youth allow racists to march without challenge. Their rallying cry was 'We shall fight like lions' – and fight they did.

'We realised from the 1970s that the local authorities, the police, the state agencies, had totally excluded us and the only thing that we had was actually just working on the street', reflected Grover, who was closely connected to the group. The experience reframed what he had lived through. 'Racism didn't just attack us; it politicised us. It forced us to ask questions.' But while Suresh Grover already considered himself political, others involved in the SYM were sceptical of broader political campaigns. One of the SYM's earliest slogans was 'no politics', taken up partly in response to the numerous divisions within the Indian Workers' Association and the local gurdwara, with various factions constantly vying for control. For young people like Purewal, far too often those claiming to be community leaders were more concerned with social status and elected office than tangible change.

First and foremost, it was not status that was the priority of the youth movement, it was the defence of their own community. This they achieved by organising regular patrols in the area, and soon they had developed a reputation as formidable street fighters. On one occasion a Pakistani family on a council estate in nearby Hanwell came crying to Balraj Purewal. A white gang had threatened to smash up their home. The SYM mobilised to confront the gang, warning that they would smash up the entire estate if the family suffered any abuse. 'We never had any issues on that estate again', Purewal said.

'We had inherited an idea of fighting injustice from our elders', Purewal continued. While there was something of a generational divide emerging in terms of tactics, such divisions were not always clear-cut, with many elders supporting the youth and adopting self-defence measures too. 'Everybody had a hockey stick at home.'

In late 1977 the SYM squatted a derelict building at 12 Featherstone Road, transforming it into a youth centre. Purewal had become the group's general secretary, and the following year its first full-time worker. The centre had an open-door policy seven days a week, offering legal advice, providing gym facilities, and space for local bands to practise and play. The SYM also ran its own football and kabaddi teams, as well as a youth club at Tudor Road Middle School, which met three evenings a week to provide employment support, mentoring and leadership training. It was these kinds of services to the community that gave the SYM its credentials – and the ability to mobilise.

***

The first major battle for the youth of Southall arose in 1979. In the run-up to that year's general election, the National Front, an openly racist political party that had been holding a series of provocative meetings in other diverse areas, including Islington and Leicester, announced its intention to hold a meeting at Southall Town Hall on 23 April, St George's Day. At this news, the Southall community was in uproar. Ten thousand people signed a petition demanding that Ealing Borough Council cancel the meeting, but to no avail.

In the days leading up to the meeting several large demonstrations were held. Hundreds attended a public meeting and one march was attended by over 5,000 people. Suresh Grover credits Vishnu Sharma, head of the Southall IWA at the time, for building support for the demonstrations. 'His alliances with the anti-Nazi league and the unions were crucial.' The Anti-Nazi League, set up in 1977 by the Socialist Workers Party, was a significant anti-racist organisation during this period. Linked to Rock Against Racism, which ran two giant carnivals in 1978 attended by 80,000 and then 100,000 supporters, it was supported by many trade unions, Labour MPs and the Indian Workers' Associations.

When the day of the meeting arrived, 2,750 police officers were deployed in the area. Some locals had planned a peaceful Gandhi-style sit-in, while that evening the IWA was due to hold a counter-event. The youth were increasingly impatient with both. They believed the National Front would need to be physically opposed.

Then the rumours began. There was talk among those who gathered that the police were planning to get around the sit-in by smuggling NF members into the town hall early. In response, at around noon members of the SYM began to assemble outside the town hall, while Balraj

Purewal led a march along South Road towards the town centre. The police responded by arresting key members of the SYM, provoking further outrage, while scuffles between police and protestors broke out. As the police erected cordons in neighbouring streets, restricting entry even to those residents who were trying to get home from work, bottles and bricks were thrown. Police deployed shields, batons and snatch squads. The arrests increased.

At around 6 o'clock that evening, protestors – by then numbering around 3,000 – tried to break the police cordon that had formed on the High Street near the town hall. To disperse the crowds, mounted police were sent in. They began hitting people with truncheons; one elderly woman was dragged across some broken glass. Meanwhile, a local community centre, the headquarters of People's Unite, where protestors were being treated for injuries, was attacked by the police. Those in the building barricaded themselves inside. In the end around seventy people were arrested, and a number of those who attempted to remain inside were seriously injured, including West Indian community organiser Clarence Baker, who ended up in a coma for five months. Baker later recalled a police officer shouting, 'Get the Black bastard, he's a leader.' They beat him until he was unconscious.[5]

Members of the NF finally began to arrive at the town hall just after 7 p.m. As they arrived, some made insulting gestures from the steps. In response, a group of protestors shouted from the roof of a nearby shop. In the end, only forty individuals, plus a few journalists, actually attended the meeting, which was over by 9:30 p.m.

As the crowds dispersed later that evening, Blair Peach, a 33-year-old schoolteacher from East London, was making his way home down a side street when he was attacked by the police. He was taken into the house of Parminder Atwal, a 24-year-old local. 'I saw a policeman hit [Peach] on the head as he sat on the pavement', he later recalled. 'The man tried to get up, fell back and then reeled across the road to my house.'[6] Later that night, Peach died from a head wound in Ealing hospital. The fatal blow was likely from a lead-filled rubber baton. Suspicion fell on a group of six Special Patrol Group officers. Eleven eyewitnesses said they saw the police attack Peach.

The day after Peach's death, an internal Metropolitan Police inquiry began, headed by Commander John Cass. The results of the inquiry were not made public, and only in April 2010 did the police finally reveal its details, confirming that an officer probably struck the fatal blow. Nobody has ever been charged for Peach's death.[7]

Over the course of the day 700 people were arrested, 342 of whom were eventually charged. In the aftermath a large community effort, the Southall Defence Campaign, was established to support of the detainees, and within a few weeks nearly £10,000 had been raised. Their trials of those charged were to take place at Barnet Magistrates' Court, over 25 miles away, and to help them the community came together to coordinate daily transport, pay legal costs and any fines imposed, and, in cases where defendants were sentenced, to provide financial support to their family members. '78 per cent of those arrested were local people', Grover told me. 'A mixture of middle aged, young and old.' He attended court almost every day for over a year to support the defendants. Yet despite the testimonies of witnesses and a strong legal defence, the conviction rate stood at 60 per cent.

In the years that followed the community would continue to resist racist incursions into Southall and the deaths of Gurdip Singh Chaggar and Blair Peach would be commemorated annually. The SYM, meanwhile, continued both its youth work and its anti-racist monitoring work, confronting racists whenever they reared their ugly heads. As we shall underscore in the next chapter, sometimes such confrontations would prove explosive.

Some on the left viewed movements such as the SYM with suspicion. John Rose of the Trotskyist International Socialists, for instance, while praising its 'ability to mobilise support', saw its 'no politics' attitude as 'an end to a blind alley'. He also queried its attitude to women. 'The passive role of women in Indian society is mirrored in the youth movement', he wrote, 'partly through heavy family pressure but partly also through the chauvinism of the boys.'[8] The SYM in turn remained suspicious of left-wing organisations parachuting in from outside. This, its members considered, was patronising, and they were further compromised by their focus on recruitment for their respective organisations. As Balraj Purewal remarked, 'They saw themselves as the mind and us as the body.'

Yet the criticisms of those such as Rose about the group's sexism were echoed by some local Asian women. Suresh Grover recalled how women would complain to him about predatory behaviour from some men and their deliberate exclusion from political campaigns. For those, a new movement would emerge in the years that followed. Organising under the banner of political blackness, the Southall Black Sisters was set up in 1979, and provided a political home for South Asian women who felt alienated by the macho and male-dominated Asian youth movements. Many of its founding members had been part of the various defence campaigns following the mass arrests in 1979, and they included people such as Surinder Sandha,

Parminder Dhillon, whose father set up a day centre for the elderly on Lancaster Road, and Avtar Brah. Pragna Patel, who revived Southall Black Sisters in 1983, recalled many of its original members being concerned about the lack of interest in issues affecting women from established anti-racist organisations. 'They believed the political struggle had to be waged not just against racism but also against sexism and the discrimination of women, particularly in our own communities.'[9] Alongside challenging institutional racism in housing, employment and immigration, the group prioritised challenging patriarchal oppression and discrimination against women within their own community. They campaigned on various issues affecting South Asian women, including domestic abuse, sexual violence and forced marriage.

Patel alleges that both the SYM and the IWA were patriarchal and misogynist in their own ways. 'I remember, in 1979, contacting the Southall Youth Movement and asking to join it to support the effort to defend the community against the fascists that were marching in the streets and I got no response.' The IWA, she contends, 'was quite a patriarchal institution made-up of largely elderly men who were also quite traditional and socially conservative when it came to issues of family and relationships and so on'.

Southall Black Sisters, although influenced heavily by the wider anti-racist movement, was, Patel said, 'a rebellious child of the anti-racist movement' because it challenged 'the patriarchy, the misogyny and the sexism that these movements, although claiming to be radical, reproduced'. The group united Black, Asian and Arab women under the banner of political blackness and supported various campaigns, including the pickets against virginity testing at Heathrow airport, as well as gaining experience of industrial action during the eight-month-long strike at the Chix bubblegum factory in Slough, which was also led by Asian women.[10]

Yet as Southall stood firm in the face of rising racism, another community in London was about to follow suit.

HERE TO STAY, HERE TO FIGHT

Altab Ali Park is the only park in East London to bear the name of a Bengali. It's a small green space on the former site of a thirteenth-century church. In fact, it was the white chalk rubble walls of this church that gave the wider area in East London the name Whitechapel.

This rare and poignant tribute is a product of tragic circumstances. On 4 May 1978 Altab Ali, a 24-year-old textile worker, was headed home from work along Adler Street when three teenagers cornered him and stabbed him, later confessing at trial that they had targeted Ali because he was a 'Paki'. This wasn't the first racist murder in East London, nor would it be the last. Two weeks before Ali's murder, 10-year-old Kennith Singh was stabbed to death by racists in Plaistow. He suffered eight stab wounds to the back of his head. Two months later, in June 1978, Ishaque Ali died of heart failure after a vicious attack by racists in Hackney.

Yet what made this murder particularly explosive was its context: Altab Ali was murdered on the night of local elections. That year the National Front put up candidates in every ward in Whitechapel, and in the years leading up to the election NF-influenced gangs had terrorised South Asian communities in East London.

Rajon Uddin Jalal, then a young Bengali teen living in Whitechapel, recalled the atmosphere at the time:

> There were racist attacks every day. We knew the streets weren't safe for us. But the murder of Altab Ali was shocking. Groups of us from the Brick Lane area and other neighbourhoods like Commercial Road, where the youth movement was based, we all got in touch and immediately organised an informal meeting. It came about spontaneously. We met in the East London Mosque. We demanded that the premises of the Bangladesh Welfare Association behind the mosque be opened up as a space for us to discuss what actions we should take following the murder of Altab Ali. The community was getting mobilised.[11]

Ten days after the murder, on 14 May, 7,000 people marched from Brick Lane to Hyde Park and then on to Downing Street behind Altab Ali's coffin, calling on the government to take meaningful action against racist murders. The protesters held placards which read 'Here to stay, here to fight', and 'Self-defence is no offence'. 'The protest was led by Bengalis but about a quarter were white demonstrators, mainly from the Anti-Nazi League', recalled Jalal. 'It was the Anti-Nazi League who delivered for our demonstrations. They mobilised a lot of people.'

That same month the Greater London Council released plans to house Bengalis, following the work of the Bengali Squatters Movement; the plan was described by the press as a 'ghetto', language which further emboldened the racists and intensified attacks on Bengalis in Brick Lane. Just a month later, on Sunday 11 June, 150 young racists rampaged through Brick Lane, shouting 'Kill the Black bastards' and smashing up shops and cars.

In the wake of Ali's murder, a number of local youth groups were set up. They included the Bangladesh Youth Movement, the Bangladesh Youth Front, the Progressive Youth Organisation, the Bangladeshi Youth Association and the Bangladesh Youth League. Many provided sports, cultural and social activities for young people, with a focus on community defence, and it was through these youth organisations that a generation of assertive anti-racist activists emerged. When, on the following Sunday, 18 June, a march was organised locally, it was the Bengali Youth Movement alongside the Anti-Nazi League who were responsible.

The pattern was repeated throughout the summer, with further racist attacks sparking renewed anti-racist demonstrations. In these, as in Southall and elsewhere, anti-racist demonstrators proved more likely to be arrested by the police than the racists themselves. 'There was something happening every day', recalled Jalal. 'There would be rallies and demonstrations outside police stations. There were sit down protests in Bethnal Green.'

Another tactic that the local activists used was trailed a month later, on 17 July 1978, when the newly formed Hackney and Tower Hamlets Defence Committee organised a Black Solidarity Day which saw 70 per cent of South Asian shops in the East End close in protest against racist attacks. Eight thousand restaurant and factory workers around Brick Lane also went out on strike for the day. 'We closed down the area', Jalal recalled. 'It was the first ever Black strike against racial attacks. And people from different walks of life came to join us. Workers from the Ford Motor Company came to join us.' Around a thousand workers from the Ford factory in Dagenham came out in solidarity, as did students from several nearby schools. As Jalal said,

> It was an important day because it sent out a signal. We were going to fight for our equal rights as equal citizens of the country, and for dignity and self-respect. We had had enough of scapegoating and Paki-bashing: it was time for the whole community to fight back.

That evening around 2,000 people marched through the East End. When racists in a car provoked the marchers, police arrested three anti-racist demonstrators. In scenes reminiscent of Southall two years earlier, the protestors held a sit-in outside Bethnal Green police station for over an hour until the three were released.[12] That summer would see weekly clashes between anti-racists and the National Front.

There were other lesser-known figures in East London who played pivotal roles in the fight against racism. Many were not members of any formal anti-racist groups that would have received coverage in newspaper reports and therefore have not received the same attention in existing historical literature. There were often informal networks of local residents committed to keeping their communities safe. Halima Begum's family, for instance, were on the frontline in the fight against racism. Living off Brick Lane, they experienced it in its most brutal form when the National Front and other racist thugs would rampage down the street, smashing up homes and restaurants. Begum recalled:

> Whenever there was a racist group of people running down Brick Lane, you'd need to mobilise. Because we physically lived there, we'd be first out on the street. It was happening on our front door. My brothers Kamal and Iqbal were always out organising the physical protection of our neighbours because the police wouldn't defend us.
>
> They didn't organise themselves as an entity. It was more about spontaneous organising, the coming together of a community to protect homes and buildings.

In Brick Lane, the battle lines had been drawn. And in neighbouring Newham, the youth would soon have to fight similar battles.

THE NEWHAM YOUTH MOVEMENT

'I've just gutted a Paki', shouted 17-year-old Paul Mullery triumphantly as he plunged a blade into the heart of Akhtar Ali Baig. It was 17 July 1980, a sunny afternoon, and the attack had taken place in broad daylight. Baig had come out of East Ham station and was walking down the High Street when he was savagely attacked by the skinhead gang – two boys, two girls, aged 15 to 17 – who stopped him, abused him and spat in his face before Mullery stabbed him to death.

The 29-year-old Pakistani student at Queen Mary College had a promising career ahead of him as a chartered accountant. Exams and bookwork were his world. A devout Muslim, he regularly attended the local mosque and was described as a 'respectful, gentle and studious man' by those who knew him in the local press. A new life as a father was just weeks away. His pregnant wife Nasreen was hoping to join him in England. But his dreams of a family life were cut short by a senseless racist murder.

The skinheads, who had been drinking at the Duke of Edinburgh pub that afternoon, had put a £5 bet on who could kill the first 'Paki'. Baig was their chosen victim. As stunned shoppers stopped and gaped, passerby 24-year-old Mick Byrne saw Baig collapse against a wall and attempted to save his life.

> I saw the blood on his jeans and blood coming from his chest ... every now and then he was gasping for breath. He was trying to say something. I tried to calm him down, telling him 'You'll be alright' but then he just went limp and I covered his head with a blanket.[13]

The youth were angry. Over a hundred Asian and Afro-Caribbean young people marched to Forest Gate police station. Outrageously, the police claimed it was not a racist murder but merely a mugging. Angered by such routine disregard, the youth marched back to the spot where Akhtar Ali Baig was murdered and clashed with the police. Sixteen were arrested.[14]

This wasn't the first racist incident in the area. Just a few years earlier, in 1977, Mohinder, Balvinder and Sukhvinder Virk were working on their car outside their family home in East Ham when they were set upon by a group of white men. Racist abuse turned quickly into violence, and in the struggle that followed one of the attackers was stabbed. The brothers' relatives phoned the police, expecting protection. Instead, the officers who arrived promptly arrested the Virks. They were denied bail, treated as criminals rather than victims, and eventually tried at the Old Bailey.

The court proceedings revealed the prejudices of the time. The prosecution relied on testimony from the very men who had instigated the attack, while the presiding judge, Michael Argyle, refused to consider the possibility that racism had played a role. When defence lawyers attempted to raise the issue, he dismissed it as irrelevant. The Virk brothers received sentences ranging from two to seven years in prison. By contrast, those responsible for the killing of Gurdip Singh Chaggar in Southall, a case that bore all the hallmarks of racial violence, received only four years for manslaughter. Community groups noted the imbalance, pointing out that when Asian families sought help, they were criminalised, while their attackers walked free.[15]

The injustice galvanised local organising. In East Ham, Hardev Singh Dhesi, a prominent IWA member, played a key role in establishing the Steering Committee of Asian

Organisations to rally support for the Virks. Dhesi recalled visiting the family at their home to offer his support:

> When they opened the door, there was no male member in the family, as all the males were in prison, just young wives and their young children. In normal circumstances, they wouldn't have invited strangers into their house, but I was amazed to see they just opened the door and said, 'Come in'. After that we went to Barking Gurdwara and organised a public meeting. We invited all the organisations to study the case and formed the Steering Committee of Asian Organisations – there were just over 20 organisations who came together initially. Within two weeks we raised £4,000, a lot of money in those days. We published literature, contacted councillors, the Home Office, and solicitors and asked them to appeal against the sentences. Then we organised pickets for all the days of the appeal.[16]

These campaigns and demonstrations had some success. The following year, the Appeal Court halved the Virk brothers' sentences, with the judge declaring them to be 'law-abiding citizens'.

Yet further racist attacks soon followed the attack on the Virks, including the murder of 10-year-old Kennith Singh in Plaistow in April 1978 and a racist assault on 19-year-old Narinder Singh Marway on Green Street. Marway had been racially abused, spat on and hit on the head with an iron bar. When the police arrived, it was Marway who was arrested, simply for wearing a karaa (a Sikh bangle), which police described as an offensive weapon. A pattern began to emerge: young Asian men who defended themselves against racist attack were punished, while those committing racist violence were shielded by the system.

By the time of Baig's murder in 1980, frustration had reached boiling point. For many, his death confirmed what they already knew – that the police and courts offered little protection. Justice would have to be fought for on the streets.[17] Shortly after Baig's murder, the Newham Youth Movement was set up.

On 19 July 1980, two days after Baig's murder, 2,500 people marched through Newham in protest. A bulletin of the Newham Youth Movement documented the march. 'The tempo and the feelings of the youth was high', they wrote, a mood dampened when, on the way to Forest Gate police station, 'about six Asian youths were arrested', actions which sparked a sit-down protest. Intercession by demonstrators eventually got them released, and the march continued on the planned route. The police, however, tried to divert it towards West Ham Park to force it to disperse. 'The youths forced their way through the cordon of police to continue towards their original destination, chanting slogans such as "Here to stay, here to fight" and "Self-defence is no offence".' In the end, a further 29 people were arrested, leading to the campaign's demands being broadened. Later, a second march was called, after the youth met with the more established group, the Steering Committee of Asian Organisations, which over 5,000 people took part in, and the whole of East Ham was brought to a standstill. Even Black workers from Ford's downed tools and shopkeepers shut their shops for the day.[18]

Years later, Unmesh Desai, a former member of the anti-racist Newham Monitoring Project, recalled the sheer scale of the march: 'What was distinctive ... was that everyone came out, young and old, men and women, Asian and Afro-Caribbean. As friends told me later, it was actually their mothers who got them all up early and said, "Come on, we've all got to go on the march."' It was, he said, 'the most angry and militant march that I'd ever been on. It was truly amazing because, in those days, anywhere east of Liverpool

Street – and this is very difficult to comprehend now – was regarded as a no-go area for black people.'[19]

Further protests were organised during the trial of the four arrested for Baig's murder. Of those on trial, two, Debbie Parker, a pupil at Plashet School, and her brother, James, were known racists. After the murder, the police searched Debbie Parker's bedroom and found material bearing the swastika and letters 'NF' as well as a hat with 'NF' and 'Pakistanis Out' written on it. In a further shocking incident, as Paul Mullery, the killer, was led from the court, he gave the Nazi salute and shouted 'Seig Heil' and 'All for a fucking Paki'.[20]

8
A NATIONAL MOVEMENT

'Forget polar bears – the new Friends of the Earth boss prefers talking about Palestine.' So read a *Daily Telegraph* headline in August 2025, disparaging long-standing anti-racist activist Asad Rehman as he took on another top job, following his tenure as CEO of the anti-poverty charity War on Want. I'd bumped into Asad Rehman on more than one occasion at Palestine solidarity demonstrations, and when I eventually got round to interviewing him at his home in Forest Gate, his decades-long political advocacy was made abundantly clear. His home is very much a mini-museum, adorned with framed posters of anti-racist demonstrations from Newham to Bradford alongside photographs of his political heroes such as Malcolm X, and, much to the *Telegraph*'s disdain, Palestine solidarity banners.

Though Rehman resides in one of the most diverse boroughs of London, he remembered life as a young man growing up in Burnley, Lancashire, where his was one of the few Asian families in a predominantly white working-class town. He can't recall a single day from his childhood that wasn't marked by racist abuse or attacks. 'It was very, very hard', he said. 'The amount of racist violence was off the charts from 1975 onwards.'[1]

His father had come to Britain from Pakistan in 1966, finding work in a knitting factory. Three years later young Asad and the rest of the family joined him. Burnley had once been the largest producer of cotton cloth in the world, but the town that Asad arrived in was suffering severe economic decline. As deindustrialisation took hold, both white and Asian workers lost their jobs as mills and factories began shutting down. In this climate of uncertainty and anger, far-right groups gained ground, capitalising on the despair and fuelling a rising tide of racism throughout the town.

Rehman's first home was in Burnley Wood, where they were the only non-white family at the local school. Conditions were poor – no hot water, a tin bath in the cellar, rats scuttling around in the dark and an outdoor toilet. Worse than the poverty was the violence. Their house sat on a street corner, a spot that became a meeting point for local racists. Rehman remembered countless days when he and his siblings had to stay indoors while people hurled abuse, smashed windows, or worse. At one point, petrol was poured through the letterbox in an attempt to set the house alight.

His mother often found herself trapped inside while men with dogs loitered outside. With no phone in the house, Rehman had to sneak out the back, run through alleyways to a distant phone box, and call the police – who, more often than not, didn't turn up. If they did, it was long after the attackers had gone. In the end, the violence got so bad that Rehman's family were forced to move out, relocating to an area near the local football stadium. But the racism persisted, and even the journeys to school were dangerous. 'We'd be attacked on the way to school, at school, and coming home', he said. Even a simple trip into town meant risking abuse: beer thrown at Asian women, hate-filled graffiti like 'Pakis out' and swastikas daubed across walls. 'Our windows were always broken', he recalled. 'It was relentless.'

Many of the town's Asian children banded together for safety and solidarity. Older kids would escort the younger ones through hostile streets, forming a protective chain to fight off racist gangs along the way. In a school where they were vastly outnumbered, safety came through barricading themselves into classrooms at break time. Teachers, often scared themselves, looked the other way.

Rehman's politicisation was born from this environment. 'The older we got, the more it dawned on us that we'd have to fight back', he said. The pain was psychological as much as it was physical. 'We were being rejected by white society. We were seeing jokes about Black and Brown people on TV. We had nothing positive. No validation. No positive image. It forces you to figure out what is your identity. In school they would say you lot live in mud huts.'

With encouragement from his parents, who valued education above all, Rehman began reading. 'I went to the library and found books. I came back and said, "In the second century in Africa we had civilisation while you were in caves." And they beat me up for it.' That thirst for knowledge led him towards Black political thinkers. 'You inevitably end up with Malcolm X at some point. You start to say, "Wait a minute, look at all these strong Black figures standing up for themselves."' One pivotal moment came when he saw *Roots*, the landmark TV miniseries about slavery. Kunta Kinte's refusal to accept the slave name 'Toby', even under torture, stayed with him.

At 14, Rehman joined the Labour Party Young Socialists. 'As a Pakistani, the language of community appealed to me', he explained. 'The only way our community survived was because of the collective. My father's generation shared a bed and had three different shifts. That was how people saved enough to be able to put down a deposit.' Most Asians at the time supported the Labour Party and instinctively joined trade unions. But even when an Asian councillor was elected, there was disillusionment. 'We were being beaten up and they were having tea with the police', he said. Representation wasn't enough. It was this gap, between symbolic leadership and grassroots struggle, that drove Rehman and others to organise independently. But the community didn't always approve. 'One day I came home and my dad said people were saying I was hanging around with communists and gays', he recalled. 'We had these gatekeeper types, and we were rebelling against them. They thought we'd be kicked out eventually. But we were saying we're here to stay.'

His mother, meanwhile, had joined an English-language learning scheme. One of her tutors was an Indian nurse named Rekha Patel, who had moved to Burnley from Scotland. One day, Rehman struck up a conversation with her about his life – how he and his friends defended isolated families, met at the mosque and fought off racist attacks daily. Rekha told him about the Asian youth movements springing up across the country. Inspired, Rehman established a new local group, the Pendle Asian Youth Movement, in 1982, covering Burnley, Brierfield and Nelson. 'It was very informal', recalled Rehman.

> There was a larger group of people supportive of us in the community but our immediate base was about 25 young people who'd play football together. We had a few meetings. Newham Monitoring Project [an anti-racist group based in East London] came up to do a talk. I'd distribute a lot of leaflets. You'd get information and then disseminate it in a way that makes sense to a bunch of other people, so there was informal political education.

> We'd tell people at the mosque don't buy South African goods, or we're going to do this on Palestine and they'd support us. The mosque was the welfare centre, the advice centre, the religious centre, the community centre – it was everything to everybody in the community. Of course, it played such a huge symbolic role.

And when it came under threat, the community defended it. Religion, too, played a role in shaping collective care. 'My parents were deeply, deeply religious. That influenced their views on the community. They taught me to think that way. Things like, "You know the old lady down the street, go make sure she's all right."'

Asad Rehman's experience mirrors my father's experience growing up in Luton, and indeed that of many other South Asians who felt a similar feeling of isolation in the 1970s. And while there remains comparatively more historical material on the London-based Asian youth movements, owing to the existence of London-based groups such as the Race Today Collective and the Institute of Race Relations, South Asian resistance to racism was not confined to London.

In the late 1970s Asian youth movements were springing up in towns and cities across the UK, playing a vital role in various community campaigns against fascism, racism and deportations. By 1979 there was an Asian Youth Movement (Manchester), and soon branches followed in Birmingham, Pendle, Luton, Newham and Sheffield. There were smaller youth organisations, too, set everywhere from Dewsbury and Batley, in Yorkshire, to Nottingham, Bolton, Haringey and Watford. Though a central organisation did not ultimately emerge, many were informally connected and supported each other's campaigns.

Each of the various Asian youth movements that sprang up during this time took on a particular composition, based on the areas in which they developed. The Asian Youth Movement (Manchester), for instance, was both more diverse and more middle class than many other youth movements, with many of its members being students at the University of Manchester. And while most Asian youth movements were overwhelmingly dominated by young men, AYM Manchester had two key female members, Nilofer Shaikh and Kuldeep Mann, who founded the organisation's women's wing. This wasn't just important for the group's demographics, it also led to a more focused commitment to women's liberation, with the group hosting discussions on the classic text 'The social basis of the women's question', as well as discussions with Amrit Wilson on Asian women in Britain and with a female member of the Tamil Tigers, a militant group fighting for an independent Tamil state in Sri Lanka, to discuss women's involvement in the struggle.

Alongside educational events, the AYM also resisted racist immigration laws and rallied behind many of the Asian women who fought back. One such campaign centred around two Pakistani women, Nasira Begum and Nasreen Akhtar, who were facing deportation – Begum had escaped domestic abuse, while Akhtar's marriage to her British husband was declared invalid by immigration officials. At an event held in November 1979 at Manchester's Longsight library to discuss the women's case, the organisers asked if anyone else in the audience needed help with immigration issues. Up stood Anwar Ditta, a working-class Kashmiri woman who lived in Rochdale. With tears in her eyes she explained that she had been told that her three Pakistan-born children would not be allowed to join her in the UK due to new stricter immigration laws; the Home Office said they didn't believe Ditta's children were hers. The AYM then set up a legal and political campaign in her support, and in less than eighteen months Ditta spoke at over 400 meetings and demonstrations. 'The first time I heard her speak', recalled Mukhtar Dar, a member of the Sheffield AYM, 'there was pin-drop silence. Not an eye was dry in the room. The way she was able to articulate her experiences was just incredible ... She looked and dressed like our mothers and our sisters. She was proud of her background.'[2]

'Every time the Home Office said no, it got me more determined to fight for them', recalled Anwar Ditta in a 2018 interview. 'I had a good response from abroad, nationally, internationally ... A lot of mothers from every culture supported me. I was very lucky.' Ditta recalled a young woman in Liverpool who hugged her and gave her £10 to send to her children in Pakistan. 'In those days 10 pound was a lot of money. Over thirty years now, I still can't forget her.'[3]

'I always loved her broad Rochdale accent', recalled Rehman. 'We held events in support of her in Pendle. Most of the Asian women and the community understood her struggle. We'd go round, getting support for a petition in support.' Support came from overseas too. In August 1980 Irish Republican prisoner Bobby Sands wrote a poem in solidarity with Ditta.

Despite losing her appeal and being left with no further legal avenue, Anwar Ditta persisted in her efforts to be reunited with her family. Her campaign gained momentum and eventually led to a documentary by Granada TV in 1981, which proved that her children were hers through blood tests, forcing the Home Office to make an embarrassing U-turn. Ditta's success inspired others to keep fighting against racist immigration legislation, and she continued to speak at public meetings, exposing the prejudices of the immigration laws of the time. When the cameras were on

Ditta and her children at Manchester airport, following her victory, she deliberately chose to be flanked by Nasira Begum and Jaswinder Kaur, who were still fighting their own immigration cases.

'I was a mother struggling and God knows how many other mothers were struggling ... I didn't want to just be isolated', recalled Ditta in a 2018 interview. 'God knows, with my strength and struggle how many other mothers succeed after that.'[4] Later she would continue her activist work, supporting other causes and going on to speak at an anti-apartheid demonstration alongside Tony Benn and other socialist stalwarts in 1982.

1981 – THE SUMMER OF RIOTS

In the early hours of Sunday 18 January 1981 a fire tore through 439 New Cross Road in south-east London, where Yvonne Ruddock was celebrating her birthday with around sixty guests. Thirteen young Black people lost their lives. Within the local Black community, the tragedy came to be known as the New Cross massacre. At the time it was not uncommon for fascists to carry out firebomb attacks on the homes of Black and Asian families.

Later that year, in July, Parveen Khan and her three children Kamran, 11, Aqsa, 10, and Imran, 2, were killed in an arson attack on their home. Parveen was pregnant, and her unborn child also perished. In both cases, the police failed to investigate the fires properly and no one was charged. Former Metropolitan Police detective sergeant Shaf Mogul later stated that the force was riven by virulent racism. 'It was overtly racist and that came down from high-ranking people', he said. 'The P-word and N-word were used frequently and openly.'[5]

Shirin Housee, who was born in Mauritius and grew up in East London, remembered the New Cross massacre as the moment her political consciousness was truly formed. At the time she was a teenager studying for A levels at Waltham Forest College, taking a politics course that covered racism and the US civil rights movement. On the Monday morning after the fire that killed 13 young people in New Cross, her class was doing what most 17-year-olds do; laughing, chatting and swapping stories about the weekend.

Then their politics teacher walked in.

Housee recalled him as a decent man: deeply political, but usually calm and measured. That morning he was anything but. He was visibly angry and distressed. He snapped at the class, asking whether they had any idea what had happened over the weekend. When Housee asked what he meant, he said nothing. He simply threw that day's newspaper on to the desks.

As they began to read, the mood in the room shifted. The laughter drained away and the class fell silent. 'You could cut the air with a knife', Housee recalled.

She looked up at her teacher and said, 'I'm sorry, I get it now.'

The young people who had died were her age, or close to it. They had been celebrating a 16th birthday. 'This could have been me', she remembered thinking. 'This could have been my friends.' Racism for her was not something abstract or distant. It was neither confined to the past, or to other countries. It was in here and now and it was lethal. 'It's happening on our doorstep', she recalled thinking.[6]

In the months that followed plans were made for a large demonstration. Housee's teacher, who was also a political activist, told the class he expected to see them there at Walthamstow Central station. Housee went. That march, she said, was the beginning of everything. Twenty thousand people marched from New Cross to Hyde Park as part of the Black People's Day of Action. 'I remember seeing cardboard copies of the 13 dead with their names on it. And I just cried. That is what brought it home to me.'

A year later, Housee went to Essex University, which had developed a reputation as one of the more radical universities. Professors such as Paul Gilroy and other black sociologists taught there. Housee was one of several Black and Asian students involved in the Black Students Alliance at Essex University. Asad Rehman also attended, and both immersed themselves in student activism. Beyond organising on campus, they were up bright and early supporting the miners on their picket lines during the 1984–85 strike. And they would later support young people in Bradford who were criminalised for organising the defence of their own community against a fascist threat in 1981. That year was an explosive one when it came to race relations.

***

By 1981 years of unresolved tension between Black communities and the police had reached breaking point. An aggressive expansion of stop-and-search powers, combined with entrenched poverty, poor housing and high youth unemployment, left many inner-city areas primed for unrest. The most serious outbreak came with the Brixton riots in April, followed by further disturbances in Toxteth in Liverpool, Handsworth in Birmingham, Chapeltown in Leeds and Moss Side in Manchester. Each saw confrontations between working-class Black youth and the police. In total, 35 areas of Britain saw disturbances, including Southall.

On 3 July 1981 three coachloads of skinheads from London's East End descended on Southall for a concert at the Hambrough Tavern. They hadn't even reached the venue before they started causing chaos; as they made their way through the town, they terrorised local shopkeepers and passers-by, smashing windows, hurling racist abuse and violently attacking an Asian woman.[7]

Word of the attack spread rapidly through the community. At around 7 p.m., Balraj Purewal was playing football with friends at the Indian Youth Club, but the quiet of the summer evening was broken by the voice of a local woman who leaned out of her window, which overlooked the playground, to shout: 'Boys, white people are attacking and beating our people. What are you doing here?'[8] Minutes later, a supporter of the Southall Youth Movement burst into the club to deliver the same news, and soon hundreds of young people surged out into the streets, determined to confront the intruders.

The police had already refused to arrest those responsible for the attacks on local shopkeepers. Instead, they had escorted the skinheads into the Hambrough Tavern. This imbalance further inflamed the anger among Asian youth.

As dusk settled, SYM members began moving towards the pub's two entrances, catching the police off guard. Fights erupted, and officers scrambled to respond, with riot police soon arriving armed with shields and truncheons. From there the situation escalated swiftly. Police lashed out, striking protestors, and in response a second group of Asian youths attempted to storm the back entrance of the pub. Bricks and petrol bombs were hurled towards the windows. Along Southall Broadway, three long stretches of brick wall were rocked back and forth by crowds of youths until they came crashing down, the bricks gathered and turned into weapons, hurled at lines of advancing officers.

Some older residents joined the resistance, breaking apart their own garden walls and passing bricks to the young people. Others siphoned petrol from their cars to hand over for makeshift bombs.[9]

Wooden pallets were dragged into the street and turned into barricades to prevent police reinforcements from reaching the pub. Inside, the skinheads found themselves under siege. As flames engulfed parts of the building, they fled, seeking cover behind police shields while launching bricks in the opposite direction. Some of them later rampaged down Delaware Road in Hayes. Many young people were injured. Yet few dared go to hospital, fearful that medical treatment would be followed by arrest.

Southall was not alone in its experience of unrest. One of the places that would go up that year was Luton, my hometown. The disturbances were centred around the inner-city area of Bury Park, and came in response to a persistent wave of racist attacks. Like many inner-city districts built around industry, the area had long welcomed waves of migrant workers: its Edwardian terraces once housed Scottish and Irish factory workers, and were later home to Jewish families, then Caribbean ones. But by the late 1960s and 1970s Enoch Powell's infamous 'rivers of blood' speech had fuelled a national surge in racist attacks. One former resident, Amer Abbas, recalled a Jewish butcher saving his father from a 'Paki-bashing' in the late 1960s. 'He grabbed him by the neck and hid him under his till for two hours till the skinheads had left Bury Park.'[10]

By the winter of 1979 racist gangs wearing badges of the 'Anti-Paki League' and the 'British Movement' had been terrorising residents with increasing audacity. Around the same time, Luton West MP John Carlisle made national headlines by calling for immigrants to be 'encouraged to go home'. He demanded a two-year freeze on immigration, his remarks reverberating through Parliament and echoing, more dangerously still, on the streets.

Early one Saturday morning in November 1979, the Shalimar restaurant, one of the only Pakistani eateries in town, was the target of a vicious attack. The Shalimar had long been a sanctuary for exhausted Pakistani taxi drivers – men like my grandfather, who would gather there in the early hours after long night shifts for a hot curry, a cup of tea and some conversation. That night, however, the restaurant was ransacked. Windows were shattered, furniture overturned and the manager stabbed.

The violence continued into the next day, when another sixty skinheads descended on the area, this time targeting Asian youth outside the cinema next door. But this time the community fought back – just as the youth of Southall had done. When the police eventually arrived, rather than tackle the white skinheads, they arrested 15 Asians; none of their attackers were detained. Of those arrested, nine were held without bail for an entire week.[11] The few attackers who were penalised received little more than a £10 fine, while the young men who had defended their community were met with severe penalties, some even being sent to youth detention centres. This heavy-handed and one-sided response spread anger through the community, and the next night a defence committee was formed which sent a telegram of protest to the Conservative home secretary, William Whitelaw.

From there, the violence escalated further. In February 1980 alone, over twenty Asian-run shops were smashed in a single week, while skinheads on motorbikes roamed the streets, intimidating shopkeepers and customers, and West Indian youths were assaulted outside discos.

This, of course, wasn't the first outbreak of racial violence in Bury Park, nor would it be the last. My father, who came of age in the 1970s, remembered streets you simply couldn't walk down as a Black or Asian person unless you wanted your head kicked in. On Boxing Day 1980 he was attending Friday prayers at Luton Central Mosque on Westbourne Road, then just two converted terraced houses a stone's throw from Kenilworth Road Stadium, home to the town's football club. That afternoon, Luton had beaten Chelsea 2–0, and around 1:30 p.m., a crowd of about 200 Chelsea fans gathered outside the mosque, kicking the doors and hurling a brick through a window. Panicked worshippers moved towards the back of the building. Some tried to reason with the mob, only to be met with more missiles. Others ran across the street, broke down a garden wall, and began returning fire.

Muhammad Ikram, whose father arrived in Luton in 1962, remembered that day well. 'It was the only time, aside from the riots that came later, that my dad, a law-abiding citizen, said: "Go outside, son, and protect your community. Go and confront the racists."'[12] Four worshippers were injured and the mosque was severely damaged. Akbar Khan of the Pakistani Welfare Association told the local press: 'The police say they cannot do anything because this was just football hooliganism. But it was nothing to do with football: it was purely a racist attack.'[13]

In the 1970s and 1980s, match days meant shutters down for the few Asian shops nearby. 'It was always a bad day when Luton were playing at home', said Ikram. For Black and Asian kids, those days also meant staying indoors or, if they had to go out, donning oversized parkas to hide their faces. 'The away fans caused the most trouble', my dad recalled. 'They'd break shop windows. Asian people got beaten up and chased.' That isn't to say things were peaceful the rest of the time. 'The school playground was like a prison', he said. 'We Asians stuck together to survive.'[14] His school was mostly white, and older students regularly attacked him while teachers turned a blind eye. His own form tutor called Asian students 'curry face'.

Ikram remembered a time in the early 1970s when there were less than a dozen Asian families in Luton. He and his brothers went to Rotherham High School on the Farley Hill estate. He was the only Asian in his year. 'It wasn't an easy place to be', he told me. 'We were never accepted. We'd be called "smelly Paki". It was everywhere. You'd walk down the street and get called a Paki bastard.' While Ikram's parents' generation thought their time in Britain would be temporary, his was the first generation to say they were here to stay – and they knew that meant they had to be prepared to fight. Their heroes were people such as Bruce Lee, whose films were shown on TV and sparked a wave of enthusiasm for martial arts among Asian kids. 'He was our hero', recalled Ikram. 'He was someone who gave us the confidence to fight back. If it wasn't Bruce Lee, it was Muhammad Ali. There were never any white role models.' This martial arts craze would soon prove its utility to the anti-racist struggle. Ikram recalled one incident in which an Asian lad was being attacked coming out of Rotherham High School: 'His older brothers came up and knocked this fella out with nun chucks.'

Fighting back one way or another was unavoidable. 'That was how you won respect', Ikram said. 'People would always try and press your buttons and me and my brother were taking no shit.' Others in the town fought back in different ways. In February 1977 when the National Front chairman John Tyndall arrived to speak at Luton Town Hall, he was pelted with eggs and met with chants of 'Nazi scum'.[15]

After the Boxing Day attack on the mosque, locals began to organise themselves still further, and on 3 January 1981 an Anti-Nazi League march was held alongside local Muslims outside the mosque, defending it from further attack. The next day over 500 people gathered at Beech Hill School, including the Pakistani Ambassador. The crowd demanded a public inquiry into the police's handling of the mosque attack. But young Asians felt more was needed. 'The ambassador paid lip service. The elders would just talk. We wanted to show our strength', recalled Ikram.

It was this frustration and anger that led to the formation of the Luton Youth Movement (LYM) in 1981. Unlike other youth movements, the organisation was not restricted to Asian youths, but welcomed support from sympathetic Black and white young people too. One of its first actions was to take on a local bus driver who had erected signs in his garden which read: 'No blacks, whites only'. 'He drove his bus through Bury Park and we confronted him', recalled Ikram. 'We wanted him fired.'

Ikram also recalled rumours of a fascist demonstration in nearby Watford. Local youth went to counter-protest. 'Around 30 to 40 of us shot up only to find what looked like a paramilitary brigade of fascists marching down the street. They must have been ex-army the way they were so well-rehearsed. We got chased around that town for hours. We were lucky to make it back.'

Another member of the LYM, Fahim Qureshi, remembered some of their activities. 'We protested against fascist organisations like the National Front when they held meetings in Luton', he said. 'The local council, which owned the library, allowed [those meetings] to happen.'[16] Many found this kind of passive complicity particularly infuriating.

'They never took our views into account as young people and people of colour', Qureshi reflected.

Into spring the actions of the organisation grew in strength, and on 16 May it led a march against racist violence through the town. The march started in Kingsway Park, before pausing at the mosque and then heading to the town hall, where speakers from Brixton and Southall addressed the crowd.[17] Common experiences of police brutality and inaction against racism connected youth from up and down the country. Yet further trouble was arriving, and as the rally concluded, about thirty skinheads stormed the event, shouting 'Sieg Heil' and giving Nazi salutes. Demonstrators fought back and fistfights erupted until the police escorted the attackers away. The same group later attacked an Asian woman and two children, again chanting Nazi slogans.

In the late 1970s and early 1980s attacks on Asian families were a frequent occurrence, particularly on the council estates that dotted the outskirts of Luton, including Houghton Regis and Marsh Farm. 'A lot of families used to get attacked', recalled Qureshi, 'especially in the outlying housing estates. Young people had had enough. They'd seen their parents suffer and they refused to cower down. They flocked to join and took to the streets.' They had had enough, and decided that they too needed to defend themselves. 'We'd sit with families who were targeted. Asian families would have bricks thrown through their windows and racists standing outside harassing them: we'd go out and confront them.'

To protect residents, the LYM's operations ran in shifts: six people inside a house, six more guarding outside. Young people aged 14 to 34 stood on the frontline. 'There was a house repeatedly targeted in Houghton Regis, an area where there was a lot of racism', Ikram said. 'We decided to go camp there for a few nights, and on the last night, we ran out on the attackers.' The LYM also spent a great deal of time painting over racist graffiti in the subways around Luton. Some of its other work involved more direct confrontation, as Ikram recalled:

> There was a National Front house on Midland Road. We smashed their windows. There was another NF pub in town. Their windows got panned in. We knew where to go and what to do. We tried to get out to Southall when they were fighting the skinheads but we were stopped by the police.

On Saturday 4 July, the day after the youth of Southall confronted skinheads at the Hambrough Tavern, there was further trouble. A gang of about thirty skinheads attacked Asian youths in Luton town centre, while two nights later petrol bombs were thrown at the Sikh temple on Portland Road.[18] The violence was building, and by 10 July, in anticipation of further confrontations, shops across Luton were boarded up.

Nor was this confined to Luton; under the government of prime minister Margaret Thatcher, unemployment had risen to levels not seen since the 1930s, and this hit diverse inner-city areas particularly hard, areas which were already grappling with issues such as racist violence and police brutality. In April rioting spread through Brixton, in South London, while just a week later Southall was up in flames.

That Friday night of 10 July, as rioting broke out in dozens of towns and cities across Britain, racist gangs surged through George Street, the main shopping street in Luton town centre, smashing windows and shouting racist slurs. Black and Asian youth fought back, and the violence spread fast. 'Bury Park was like a war zone', said Ikram. 'It was quite horrific really. At one point, we were all pushed into a small residential road. A friend of mine came out to see what the commotion was. He was still wearing his slippers and he got arrested.' Meanwhile, around 200 Asian and West Indian youths stood guard outside the mosque in fear of further attacks, while local taxi drivers ferried defenders across town. When the police arrived bearing riot shields, they made indiscriminate arrests.[19] The youths, bolstered by many more then exiting the local pubs, countered with petrol bombs, bricks and bottles thrown towards police lines. As the *Socialist Worker* newspaper reported that week, 'a few police were injured but many black youngsters carry the marks of police brutality'.[20]

The following year racists speared a pig's head atop the unfinished minaret of what was to be one of Britain's first purpose-built mosques on Westbourne Road. The LYM organised a mass march from Bury Park to the town hall. It was one of the largest demonstrations the town had ever seen. British Movement skinheads attacked the march, while those demonstrating fought back. These clashes continued in towns and cities across the country.

The youth of 1981 had demonstrated that they were willing to fight back by any means necessary – even if it meant burning down everything around them. Years of frustration and anger had reached boiling point and though the flames were eventually put down in the aftermath of the riots, the anger remained.

But such an assertive, and at times violent, approach would be met by fierce backlash from the state, culminating in further clashes on the streets and in the courtroom too.

9
SELF-DEFENCE IS NO OFFENCE

South Asians were forced to defend themselves from a vicious tidal wave of racism from both street gangs and the state. Far too often the police were of little help, and when South Asians resisted racist thugs on the streets, they were criminalised by the state. As more and more organised anti-racist groups developed in the 1980s, on more than one occasion, from Bradford to Newham, they found themselves in the courtroom, making the case for the right to self-defence.

***

Masood Malik was 13 years old when he first saw a fascist. It was in 1975, and the NF – formed only a decade earlier – was putting serious efforts into stirring up racial hatred in towns and cities that had become prominent destinations for recent immigrants from the former British Empire. In Manningham, a heavily South Asian district of Bradford, the city that Malik called home, the NF chose to organise a meeting at a school. 'This', Malik recalled, 'was really stoking the flames.'[1] At the meeting, NF members spat at locals from out of the windows, barraging them with racist abuse. 'That was when it really got to me. I thought – I'm just not going to have this.'

The experience of the youth of Bradford was similar to that of Southall: racist bullying in school, bussing, violence on the streets and inaction from the state. Soon they too would rise up and organise in defence of their communities. In 1977, with the support of the Indian Workers' Association, the Indian Progressive Youth Association was founded, which soon changed its name to the Asian Youth Movement (Bradford) to better reflect the large Pakistani demographic in the area.

To Tariq Mehmood, an AYM member who was born in Pakistan but raised in Bradford, there was no real difference between South Asian, African and Caribbean people: they were all the same to those who wanted to harm them. 'We were called "black bastards" on the streets', he recalled. 'We were commonly united with our African and Afro-Caribbean friends. They didn't know they were black until they came here – I didn't know I was a "Paki" until I came to Bradford. We were united on those common issues of our oppression.'[2] And if they were united on common oppression, they were equally as committed to common liberation, being keenly internationalist and anti-imperialist in their outlook. 'We were not some politically illiterate youth', Mehmood emphasised. 'We were well aware of our anti-colonial resistance and of the horrors of colonialism.' They saw the link between racially targeted people in Britain and the threads of oppression everywhere from Southall to Soweto, and from Gaza to Derry. 'This period was the time of the hunger strikes in Ireland', said Mehmood. 'We were all very much supportive, and part and parcel of the networks to support those movements.'

Political education was a central plank of their agenda, with members frequently meeting in Bradford Central Library and a local left-wing bookshop. The AYM Bradford had about 200 paid-up members and ran a cricket and football club too. The organisation was highly disciplined, forbidding members from being part of any political party (including the Labour Party) in order to prevent infiltration; some of the Bradford AYM's key members had formerly been members of predominantly white Trotskyist organisations, and though these connections influenced their socialist politics, many were also left with a scepticism about organisations they perceived to be lacking any interest in physically defending Black and Asian communities. Members were also not allowed to date women from the families they supported on matters of immigration or racism.

After Margaret Thatcher's election victory in 1979, which she won in part by echoing the NF's rhetoric, claiming that Britain was being 'swamped' by people from a different culture, the role of the AYMs grew more serious. The tensions continued to grow over the next few years, and like many other Black and Asian communities in Britain, by the summer of 1981 many in Bradford were fearful of the potential for increased racist violence. Things ramped up still further when, on 11 July, rumours began to swirl that fascists were planning to march through the area of Manningham. When the police confirmed the news, they told Asian people to avoid going outside that day. Yet given the police's track record of harassing young Asian people and ignoring racist attacks, few were willing to listen. According to Mehmood, young people 'didn't believe that they [the police] would, or that they could', do anything. 'We didn't think they had the willingness, for they themselves were full of racists, in their own ranks – and we had a long history of that struggle against them.'

By this point there had been a split in the Bradford AYM, spurred by a dispute over funding. Mehmood joined the new group, the United Black Youth League (UBYL), which rejected state support, believing it was important to stay independent rather than remain in the youth movement. The new group had a deeply organised, well-developed self-defence operation: 'In Bradford, we were already patrolling the streets for many weeks against gangs of Paki bashers in Manningham', Mehmood said. 'Where I lived, we had embryonic telephone trees. If somebody reported an attack by a gang or somebody else, they would phone the next person and run to get there. We would drop what we were doing and very quickly have fifteen, twenty people over there.'

Having understood the potential scale of violence that their community faced, UBYL members prepared petrol bombs ahead of the Manningham march. Luckily, they were never used, being made with the understanding that they would only be used to defend people from serious injury. For Mehmood, the rationale was simple: 'We were the sons and daughters of that community', he said. The move wasn't about machismo; it was about 'politically organised and conscious action' to defend their friends and families. 'When the police said stay at home, we said, "Come out on the streets." When they said they would look after it, they would patrol the streets, we did.'

On 11 July, with demonstrations organised by South Asians against fascism happening across London, the call went out to the young people of Luton to resist the fascists. 'Our thinking at the time', Malik remembered, was that 'we're going to have to do things for ourselves and not be downtrodden.' Thousands of young people joined, and so strong was the resistance that the fascists didn't dare show their faces, leading to a great cheer from the gathered anti-fascists.

Things, however, would take a darker turn just two weeks later, when 12 young people were arrested and taken in by the police, with extravagant headlines talking of 'bomb factories' being discovered in Bradford and 'Black Gangs' being 'stung', their 'plots to bomb police' uncovered. Two of those arrested were Mehmood and Malik. 'The police made a mountain out of a molehill', Mehmood remembered, 'claiming that we were going to attack police stations. On the contrary, we did not believe in individual acts of terrorism – we still don't – we saw ourselves as victims of terror.'

When the police turned up at Malik's house, they told his father that they just wanted to question him. As soon as they got into the police car, however, they said, 'You better speak. What do you know about petrol bombs?' 'I told them I didn't know what they were talking about', Malik said. 'They said, "You lying bastard, you were there, you made them", telling me when we got to the police station, "You better speak or I'm going kick your arse all around this police station floor." I was 18 years old, thinking *whoa*!'

While those under the age of 21 were held in remand centres, the rest were kept in jail, where Malik remembered being given a tough time, with prison officers making racist comments from behind the cell bars.

It would be months before the accused, who became known as the 'Bradford 12', were taken to trial on 26 April 1982. Walking from the cells to the court, Malik said, was 'daunting'.

> The charges didn't sink in, 'conspiracy to cause explosions'. I didn't really realise the extent of how serious it was until they had a Saturday Court, which is a special court, and there were five stipendiary magistrates sitting there. That's when I thought, *this is very serious*.

Soon the case became a cause célèbre, with a network emerging to campaign for the twelve. Outside court on that first day over 500 local people gathered, chanting songs in their defence, while across the country support groups were established. One of those involved in the support work was Balwinder Rana, who had earlier helped to establish the Kent Asian Youth Federation. That day, as he took a seat in the upstairs gallery of the courtroom, he shouted, 'Self-defence is no offence!' as the defendants were brought into the room, causing the judge to warn that if there were any more interruptions the court would be cleared.

Even the structure of the trial itself was subject to intense political division. Initially, the jury was to have been all-white. 'I was seriously considering not recognising the court and accepting that I was going to go to jail for life', Mehmood remembered. Instead, the defendants called for a jury of their local peers, which wasn't accepted, but as significant local and national pressure grew it led to the appointment of five non-white jurors, with two Asian and three Caribbean people joining the panel. The defendants also insisted that the white people be working-class. To this day, Mehmood believes that these moves saved them, and that had they not gone hard for a balanced jury, the sentences would have been heavy.

One of those representing the Bradford 12 was Michael Mansfield. He recalled a key question at the trial being whether a petrol bomb was truly an explosive substance or merely a pyrotechnic. This led to two moments of light relief, the first 'when co-defending counsel the late Edmund Alexander ... attempted to demonstrate – in court! – how easy it was to assemble a petrol bomb, and how its effect did not constitute an explosion. At the point at which Edmund lit the rag, the judge ducked and made a rapid exit.'

The second was when an explosives expert, Dr Keith Borer, took those present to a nearby courtyard, where he produced 'a crate of milk bottles, half-filled them with petrol, lit the rags and suggested we throw them at a wall to see what happened'. The jurors joined in 'enthusiastically', with 'the meagre result ... a blackened wall' – that is, until 'A window was suddenly flung open and an extremely irate man leaned out, shouting abuse at us: our target had turned out to be the rear wall of the Conservative Party offices in Leeds.'[3]

During the cross-examination by the defence counsel, it soon became clear how much the story had been built up as a media opportunity for the police, making them appear more assertive and authoritative. A sizeable chunk of the police narrative had clearly been fabricated. 'The age-old tactics were used', Mehmood remembered. 'Fit up the verbals, write up your notes afterwards, lie, cheat, deceive.' The defence repeatedly picked holes in the police arguments, as they offered 'lie after lie', Malik said. 'They got ripped to shreds. We found it quite funny, watching the police really getting caught out.' One particularly stark example of fabrication was unearthed during the cross-examination of an officer by Helena Kennedy QC. The officer claimed that he had extensively questioned the defendant Sabir Hussain without taking any notes, apparently asking him some 200 questions to which he received 196 answers, all of which he then recorded. After Kennedy asked if he had compiled Hussain's answers from memory, he replied that he had. 'What was the first question I asked you today?' Kennedy then asked. The officer admitted he couldn't remember.[4]

Throughout the trial the defence highlighted the racist violence against immigrant communities, as well as its deadly consequences. Malik remembered Michael Mansfield's opening gambit, which referred to the New Cross fire.

'It was a really powerful opening, it really got you – even as a young kid of about 18, I thought, *wow*.' As the trial continued, the police were repeatedly shown to be dishonest in their approach to race relations and racist attacks. One Bradford CID deputy head was quoted as having told Pakistani community leaders that there was no such thing as 'racial violence'. Another statement of his, read out at the trial, claimed that:

> Police officers must be prejudiced and discriminatory to do their job. Prejudice is a state of mind drawn from experience. Searching long haired youths in bedraggled clothing produces drug seizures, and searching West Indian youth wearing tea cosy hats and loitering in city centres could detect mugging offences.[5]

How deep this prejudice ran was also demonstrated when a senior policeman stated that being left-wing meant 'anyone against the police and the general running of the country', while being right-wing meant 'anyone who conducts himself within the general running of the country'.[6]

Despite such clarifying moments, the trial was a struggle. 'There were days where we thought we'd done very well', Malik recalled, 'and the odd day when we thought it's not gone well.'

> I feared the worst. We were told – and we were led to believe – the police would hammer us and wanted to make an example out of us. At the time, there were demonstrations up and down the country, in Toxteth, Tottenham, Chapeltown. I thought we were going to get found guilty and would go away for a very long time. We would have got over ten years if we were found guilty.

Fortunately, the multiracial jury was sympathetic to the defendants. Malik remembered jury foreman Wesley Baker, a Caribbean man, after the trial, walking up to the defendants to tell them: 'I would never have been the foreman to find you guilty.' Another juror, one who many defendants were concerned about, was a young white worker who had been arrested as a match-going Leeds United fan. Yet even he would later tell the defendants that 'the police lie out of their teeth'.

While the trial continued, outside court a national campaign to 'Free the 12' grew in strength. Such was its size that those in the courtroom could hear the protests from the stand – Malik found the sound of demonstrators outside to be morale-boosting, while Mehmood believes that without the campaign, 'We would not have won.' Fahim Qureshi, then a leader of LYM, remembered being picked up by his comrade Suresh Grover at Junction 11 of the M1 at 6 a.m. to get to Bradford for the 10:30 a.m. pickets. The band UB40 pledged to do a benefit gig, and the defendants were particularly touched by international support from Sinn Féin, feminist movements in America, and members of the African National Congress in South Africa. All of which was bolstered by the feeling that, as Balwinder Rana recalled, 'any day, we could face a similar situation in Southall, and may need to use the same tactics to defend our community as they did in Bradford'.[7]

Finally, on 16 June 1982, the months of anxiety came to an end when, after a 31-day trial, all twelve of the defendants were acquitted. Qureshi remembered standing on the steps of the court, chanting and singing with a thousand other people, before hearing of the first 'not guilty' verdict. 'Immediately, a massive cheer went up', he said, 'then complete silence, as we were asked to be silent so the other verdicts could be communicated. After the final defendant's verdict was announced, another continuous, massive roar went up.'[8]

Afterwards the twelve defendants were carried out of the Crown Court shoulder-high on a sea of people, and the mood in Bradford was electric. Everywhere there were tears of joy, and the city turned into a gigantic party, with a large contingent of Sikhs from the local gurdwara giving out curry and puris in celebration.

The verdict marked a pivotal moment in British legal history, and a rare victory for anti-racist politics. 'Self-defence is no offence' was the slogan of many of the Asian youth movements, and it was the legal basis of the defendants' victory. As Gareth Peirce wrote in the *Guardian* after the judgment, the court verdict accepted 'the proposition that a society should afford protection to all its citizens and that if it did not, as the evidence they heard showed clearly that it does not, then those unprotected can arm themselves'.[9]

Looking back on the trial four decades later, Masood Malik had no regrets about his actions. 'I'm proud. I've got no shame about what we did to defend ourselves and our communities. If we didn't stand up for ourselves, I think we'd be an even more oppressed community than we already are.' Tariq Mehmood, too, was proud that out of the pain and repression of the period came the proof that 'resistance bears fruit and hope is never lost'. Summarising the beliefs that spurred him, as a young man, to confront fascists and defend a community under siege, he said that all human beings deserve the right to live life in a dignified way. When that dignity is attacked, people must know how to resist.

> If somebody is attacking you by passing racist immigration laws, you can't pick up a gun. If somebody comes to slap you in the face, you can't knock their hand off with a sword. By the same logic, if somebody comes to attack you with a sword, you cannot defend yourself with a feather.[10]

THE SCHOOL STRIKE AGAINST RACISM

It wasn't only Asian radicals in the north of England who began to challenge the ascendant new racism in 1982. That year, Parvaiz 'Goga' Khan, a 15-year-old who lived in the East End of London, moved to Little Ilford School in Manor Park from Trinity Boys' School in Canning Town which he had been attending previously. There, he had been subjected to racist taunts, and attacks were routine – and as for many others, even the journey to school was dangerous. 'We was in East Ham so we'd have to catch two buses to go to this school', he recalled in a 2019 interview.[11] 'What I specifically remember is coming out of that school and getting the crap beaten out of you on the way home just because you was coloured. That was on a regular occurrence. It really toughened me up. It made me into a real tough little kid.' The area, he remembered, was a tough one for the local Asian population. 'You had the local skinheads. You'd walk around East Ham and it'd be Paki scum, get out, NF written on the wall. I was always confused. Get out and go where? I was born in West Ham. Where do you want me to go?'

At his new school things were no better: white youths from nearby schools would wait outside the gates to attack Asian children, and while pupils complained constantly, the authorities ignored them. Things would soon take a turn when, in early autumn, an Asian boy of 12 was badly beaten up by white youths outside the school, so much so that he had to be taken to hospital. Just a few days later a gang of skinheads with iron bars and sticks rampaged through the local streets, kicking and abusing Black people before confronting Asian school children going home from football. Khan remembered one of such attack in particular.

During afternoon break he was chatting with friends when older boys forced their way in.

> Five or six older guys came through the gate and they just started hitting a couple of my friends standing near the gate, punching them and kicking them, shouting racist abuse to them, 'You Paki this, you Paki that', and I'm standing there and thinking what the hell is happening here?

By now he was used to violence, and he no longer ran away.

> As one of them has come running towards me and gone to hit me, I've hit him back. So they wasn't used to this. When the other kids started seeing me starting to fight back they thought, hold on, they all stopped and turned around. So next thing everyone's starting to fight them.

Soon, a teacher emerged and broke up the fight. 'We all went back into school and that was the end of it.' Or so he thought; later that day, police entered Khan's classroom. 'The deputy head and two policemen walked into the class and they said "Right Parvaiz we need to speak to you." They took me down to the headmaster's office and they said there was an incident and there's been a serious assault.' Khan was stunned; he'd never been in trouble with the police before. 'They put me in the back of a police car and they took me to Forest Gate police station and they locked me up in a cell.'

A few hours later, his father arrived. 'I hear the keys jingling and the door opens', Khan remembered,

> and there's my dad standing there with the police sergeant. He says 'Mr Khan, your son has been a very bad boy and he's done a very bad thing and you need to teach him a lesson and he's gonna get into a lot of trouble now.' When I saw my dad, I started crying. I was really scared … I just broke down. He said don't cry. Tell me what happened.

After Khan explained what had happened, he was surprised to find his dad siding with him; he recalled his dad's words to the police officer: 'What did you want my son to do? Did you want my son to be beaten up? Did you want my son to be in hospital?'

Soon word began to spread that the injured attacker was from a notorious racist family from Warrior Square in Little Ilford, and they were planning revenge. Even the teachers quietly suggested that it might be safer for Khan not to return. But he refused: 'I was thinking if I don't come, I've got my two younger brothers in the school, do I leave them to the wolves? Do I leave my friends? Do I leave all the other kids?' Khan had been training at a gym above the local gurdwara, and he was able to get the support of the older Asian boys should trouble ensue again.

One afternoon a group of Asian kids had gathered outside the school. 'The younger kids who lived around Warrior Square on the other side of Manor Park were petrified', recalled Khan. 'They said, "We're scared to go home. We're scared because we know them guys live around there and they're gonna beat us up. They're gonna be waiting for us." So we said let's walk around in a group.' After they had escorted the younger Asian children, Khan and the others were walking along Dersingham Avenue when a car screeched up in front of them. Out came three white men, scruffily dressed in jeans, bomber jackets and trousers, swearing and yelling racial abuse at the children. 'It was a cream colour Vauxhall Cavalier', he said, 'and three guys jumped out with truncheons.' Two of Khan's friends were attacked, with the men throwing them into a nearby front garden. 'Our first reaction was that these are the guys that said they're coming to attack us to kill me. So, natural reaction, half of the kids that were with us run off. A few of us that stayed started fighting back.' Within minutes, uniformed police officers, dog handlers and a police helicopter were on the scene.

> The next thing I specifically remember a small van, a police dog van that screeched up at the front, policeman's jumped out opened the doors of the little van, the dog's come out of the van and that's when everyone's run. I've run and the police dog come running up to me and I've just stopped. The policeman said hands behind your head and sit down. Another police car come and they've arrested eight of us. Put us in the sherpa vans and took us to Forest Gate police station. And two of my friends were quite seriously injured from what I recall and they were put in the cells.

One of the eight, Kalbir Singh Khala, was hit on the head several times by a police truncheon, and was so badly injured that he had to be taken to hospital. A 19-year-old, Inder Johal, lost his front teeth in the attack. 'I remember they kept coming in and looking at us', Khan remembered, 'and said that you guys just beat up police officers you're in big trouble you're really going to go to prison and that's when we realised bloody hell these guys that just jumped up and attacked us are police officers. They attacked us. We didn't go out looking for them.' The men were plainclothes police officers, members of the locally based District Support Unit.

Much like the Bradford 12, the eight Asian youths who were attacked that day by the police officers sparked a national movement. The Newham 8, as they came to be known, were charged with affray, actual bodily harm and grievous bodily harm. They were Parvaiz Khan (age 15), Curjit Hunjan (17), Bhupinder Singh Sangha (16), Kulwinder Matwala (21), Vipun Pathak (18), Uttuyaka (16),[12] Dalbir Johal (19) and Kalbir Singh Khela (19).

The Newham 8 belonged to a local youth centre, Stardust, which got behind them, with two of the youth workers, Satnam Singh and Caroline Sikorski, playing a key role in the Newham 8 Defence Campaign. They were also able to rely on the support of the Newham Monitoring Project (NMP), at the time one of the best-resourced anti-racist groups in the country. The NMP was set up in early 1980, following the racist murder of Akhtar Ali Baig. It was made up of concerned Black and Asian people who wanted to monitor the level and extent of racist attacks in the borough and the response of the police and the local authority. In its 1983 annual general report, Gulshun Rehman from the NMP management committee said that the focus of the NMP had widened to 'dealing with cases of police racism, harassment, for example, stop and search, detention without charge for an unreasonable length of time, etc., and in many cases physical abuse and violence'.

In June 1982 the project was granted funding by the left-wing Greater London Council, led by Ken Livingstone. It meant that the group was able to employ a full-time worker, Unmesh Desai, and establish an advice centre in Forest Gate; in 1983 it set up a 24-hour emergency service to provide support to victims of racist violence and police brutality. The NMP played a key role in assisting the community-led campaign in support of the Newham 8. Such was the swell of support that within just 24 hours of their arrest, around 500 people had gathered for a public meeting.

'We had a meeting in the local gurdwara which was in Roseberry Avenue', recalled Khan. 'The local elders actually understood what had happened. And they said "No, we're not gonna allow our children to go to prison and take this. They haven't done anything wrong."' What helped was the recent attacks at the school. 'What happened the week before?

These guys came into the school to attack them. These guys went there to defend the little kids. Where was the police?'

While there was a great deal of anger and unity among young Asian people in the Newham area, and many who wanted to form and take charge of their own defence campaign, there were deep divisions too. These tensions emerged when several local community and religious leaders began to vie for the campaign's leadership. As Unmesh Desai recalled: 'On the night the eight were arrested, the temple leadership got a good local Asian solicitor whom the youths felt could be trusted with conveyancing but not with a political case like this.'[13] So, through a local teacher, they got in touch with the NMP, and through it with the solicitor Gareth Peirce. 'The Bradford 12 case had recently finished', Desai said. 'We didn't know who this solicitor Gareth Peirce was, but we knew that she'd done the case ... Without knowing us, without our guaranteeing that she was going to get the case, she took a taxi and just came rushing down to the project.'[14]

With Peirce and others, Desai went to a meeting then taking place in the gurdwara. 'The gurdwara leadership', he said, 'were making big speeches, one after another, with all sorts of blood-curdling threats.' When they requested that the local youths be allowed to talk, the leadership gave them the floor: 'We said, "Look, can we hear this woman, Gareth Peirce, who defended the Bradford 12, and the Bradford 12 are an inspiration to us all?" Gareth made this amazing speech, basically winning the whole audience over – it was proposed that Gareth be appointed the solicitor to the campaign.'[15] The self-appointed community leaders were, he said, 'furious'. 'They felt we'd hijacked the campaign from them – which, of course, we had. But it was not deliberate, we were no great master strategists with a master plan; it was basically something that happened spontaneously.'[16]

On 5 November 1982, the day of the first court appearance of the Newham 8, there was a historic school strike. Around 500 schoolchildren crowded outside the front of the Old Bailey in a mass picket. Iram Syed, who was 12 years old at the time, recalled being involved at a sit-in at Plashet School alongside other pupils. Her older brothers were studying at Little Ilford School alongside Goga Khan, and she understood firsthand why they felt the need to take matters into their own hands. Two years earlier Akhtar Ali Baig had been murdered in Newham in broad daylight. The level of fear in the Asian community was overwhelming at times. 'We had to be very very careful when we were out', said Syed.[17]

> I remember my brother being beaten up at a bus stop by some white youths and his watch being taken away from him. They used racial slurs and things like that and I remember him saying he needs to start doing weightlifting and things like that so he can fight back.

Support for the school strike came from several neighbouring schools such as Langdon School and Trinity School. Syed was not surprised by the scale of support. For her, this campaign was broader than just an individual case.

> I just remember feeling at the time that everything was so unfair. There was just this overwhelming fear all the time. We knew we were being protected by our own. The police were not there to protect us.

The pickets continued throughout the trial, supported by local and national organisations, and were successful in drawing press and public attention to the case, as well as emphasising to the judge and jury that they were dealing with an issue of national concern. The NMP and other antiracist organisations, meanwhile, launched a fifteen-month long campaign, with meetings held up and down the country about police racism. Further action saw 2,000 people marching through the streets of Newham, while the group also counted on the support of Arthur Scargill and the National Union of Mineworkers, as well as anti-apartheid campaigners and Irish Republicans.

The trial lasted for six weeks, and the lies and racism of the police officers were demonstrated clearly throughout. Just as during the trial of the Bradford 12, it was Michael Mansfield's cross-examination that exposed the fabrications of the police. On this occasion it was Sergeant Aylott, one of the three plainclothes police officers, who was publicly embarrassed:

> Mansfield: 'Why did you say it was 100 Asians, when your notes say 30?'
> Aylott: 'I was dazed when I wrote my notes.'
> Mansfield: 'The statement is dated 2 months later. Were you dazed when you wrote that?'[18]

When the trial concluded, four of the defendants were acquitted of all charges. Four others, however, were found guilty on the main charge of affray, while individual charges were dismissed except for one conviction for a minor charge of common assault. Not a single perpetrator of the series of attacks on schoolchildren at Little Ilford School in 1982 was prosecuted. As the Newham 8 Defence Campaign pointed out at the time:

> There must be something wrong with our society when 8 young men aged 15–21 without any previous record face conspiracy charges and undergo a 6-week long trial for the 'mere' crime of responding to a situation where they saw no other alternative but to organise their own defence![19]

The NMP continued to compile dossiers of cases of racist violence. In 1983 a total of 156 cases were reported. A simple breakdown showed them to be: police harassment 76 (49%), racial harassment and attacks 68 (43%), other 12 (8%). One Asian woman in a council house in Manor Park reported:

> When the white family who live next door had a party, they threw milk bottles and emptied ours and their dustbins in our front garden. The noise was so loud, we didn't sleep till 5 a.m. Every time we come out of the house, they shout 'Pakis' even when we come out to say goodbye to friends and relatives. We live as silently as possible so as not to attract attention – anything that would start the harassment again.[20]

According to the NMP, in the overwhelming majority of cases the police took no action against the racists. So when the racists went on the rampage in summer 1984, the local community would again be forced to take matters into their own hands – and to confront the state too.

NEWHAM 7

On 7 August 1984 a series of racist attacks took place in the area, with white youths driving around in a car targeting Black and Asian people at random. In one particularly horrific incident, a partially disabled Asian youth was taken by force to Wanstead Flats, a large park nearby, and hit with a hammer.

In response, a group of Asian youths went to the Duke of Edinburgh pub in nearby Upton Park, a well-known meeting place for the National Front, to confront some white youths who they believed were behind the attacks. A fight broke out, and the police arrived quickly on the scene, arresting one of the Asian youths and charging him with 'conspiracy to assault persons unknown, possession of an offensive weapon and causing actual bodily harm'.[21] Over the next few weeks six more Asian youths were arrested in connection with the incident. While three of the white youths involved in the fight were released without charge the next day, five of the seven Asian youths were kept in remand for seven weeks, with no information given to their parents and requests for bail refused. Solicitors had to issue a writ for habeas corpus before the Asians were released.

It wasn't only the Asian youths who comprised the Newham 7 who felt as though they had been discriminated against. A few months later, on 29 November, a 16-year-old Black boy Eustace Pryce died after being stabbed in the head outside the Greengate pub on Barking Road in nearby Plaistow. As the NMP recalled:

> Eustace, his brother Gerald and some other friends were driving down the Barking Road when an Asian friend pulled up alongside and told them that, minutes before, he had been racially abused by a gang of youths. Eustace and his friends went to confront the gang. A fight broke out when the Canning Town gang armed themselves with baseball bats and one of the white youths drew a knife on Eustace, stabbing him in the head. Some plainclothes police officers had witnessed the tail-end of the incident from a passing bus. When they arrived on the scene, it was Gerald Pryce, and not the killer of Eustace Pryce, who was taken to the police station and questioned for several hours. An aunt tried to see him but was refused.[22]

Three weeks later, Gerald Pryce, the brother of Eustace, was charged with affray.

As in the Newham 7 case, the treatment of a Black youth contrasted sharply with that of a white. Martin Newhouse, who was arrested and charged with Eustace Pryce's murder, was granted bail on the grounds that it would be wrong to keep him in jail over Christmas; Gerald Pryce, on the other hand, was denied bail and kept in jail. When he was finally released, bail conditions restricted his movements and prevented him from returning to Newham to visit his pregnant girlfriend.

In the aftermath, Asian and Afro-Caribbean youth would unite in a joint campaign for justice, and on 27 April 1985 a National Demonstration against Racism was held in Newham. Three thousand people turned out in support of both the Newham 7 and the Justice for the Pryces campaign. The march was due to go past Forest Gate police station before finishing with a rally in Plashet Park, but in the end the marchers barely passed the station. As soon as they reached it, police snatch squads charged into the crowd, pulling out young Asian and Afro-Caribbean people and violently assaulting them. Ten protestors were then taken into the police station and arrested.

The demonstrators refused to march any further; they said they would remain outside Forest Gate police station until the ten were released. This they did for two hours, with protesters gathering outside the station while police officers made various promises about when the ten would be released. By 6 o'clock, as dusk was falling and the number of demonstrators had dwindled, police reinforcements from all over London had arrived and began to mass in the side streets round the police station. When, a few minutes later, an Afro-Caribbean girl was pulled off a wall by her hair by a police officer, the crowd surged forward to protect her. Hundreds of officers charged out from the side streets, forming a military-style wedge that cut through the crowd, sending demonstrators flying. Scores of people were injured and some were chased into side streets and attacked by the police. Thirty-four arrests were made.

A second march soon followed, on 11 May. This time the march was allowed to complete its route, but when the demonstrators reached their rallying point in Plashet

Park, all but one small gate had been locked by the police. As 2,000 people were funnelled through this one gate, it became obvious that one small spark would cause a conflagration. When a Black youth was manhandled by the police, the crowd surged forwards; police on horseback emerged from the side streets, as did riot officers, who marched into the park, linked up in a military formation and charged, forcing everyone to run. Many people were seized, thrown into police vans, assaulted and later dumped on to the street. Later, in a show of strength, police officers in riot gear marched up and down Green Street and High Street North. Solicitor Gareth Peirce compared that day to Orgreave, when striking miners were met by vicious police violence on a picket line just outside Sheffield.[23]

Finally, on 13 May 1985, the trial of the Newham 7 began at the Old Bailey. But the trial would offer little reprieve from the litany of racist assaults; during the lunchbreak of the second day, one of the defendants, Parvaiz Khan (who had also been prosecuted as a member of the Newham 8), was racially abused and violently assaulted by ten prison wardens in the court cells, provoked by his refusal, as a Muslim, to eat a pork pie. When he came back to the courtroom his face was covered with bruises, his eye swollen. The trial had to be delayed for two days. Fortunately, the presence of TV reporters ensured that images of Khan's badly bruised and swollen face were flashed on television screens and printed in newspapers – not only in the UK, but in India and Pakistan too.

When the case was resumed there were to be further embarrassments for the authorities. Two police officers awaiting cross-examination were discovered in court rifling through the defence files – with the ludicrous claim that they were checking the layout of the court. Other officers, meanwhile, were exposed in their lack of ethical and professional standards when defence lawyers demonstrated how they had compiled notes together, breaking police rules. Furthermore, their response to the horrific wave of racist attacks that had culminated in the fight at the Duke of Edinburgh pub, the court heard, was to keep a meeting place for Asian youth – the local Wimpy bar opposite the pub – under constant surveillance. The police's chief prosecution witness, a waitress at the Wimpy, admitted under cross-examination that she had previously been asked by the police to act as an informer on Asian youths using the premises, especially what they were saying about racist attacks. No such police surveillance, it barely needs saying, was deployed to keep checks on white racist organisations.

For those standing trial, the defence rested on the idea of community self-defence – that reasonable force was permissible in the prevention of a crime. In the end four of the youths were found guilty of affray. But one of the results of the trial was that the police's actions were held up for public ridicule. Concerted community pressure also ensured that Gerald Pryce was not convicted, though the murder charge against Martin Newhouse was dropped in favour of a charge of affray, for which he was sentenced later that year.

Above all, the unity of the Asian and Afro-Caribbean youths on the marches had shown that it was possible for determined young Black people to make a stand against racism and to influence the way their communities were policed. The forces of 'law and order' had been severely humiliated. The pretence, at least, of police accountability would in future be adhered to. The Black community, as even the courts acknowledged, had a right to defend itself.

10
SOLIDARITY

In June 1982, one month after the acquittal of the Bradford 12, the Shizan restaurant in Darnall, Sheffield, was attacked by 15 racist youths. The police, based at a station just one mile away, took twenty minutes to arrive, leaving the manager and four restaurant workers to defend themselves in the meantime.[1] When the police did arrive, they arrested one of the victims of the attack, Ahmed Khan, and charged him with 'malicious wounding'.[2]

This was not an isolated incident; the area around Sheffield had seen many such racist attacks, including assaults on taxi drivers, restaurant workers and people leaving a local mosque.[3] These events would trigger the founding of another of the era's youth movements, the Sheffield Asian Youth Movement.

Its founding members had come to know each other during the Bradford 12 campaign. During that campaign the Sheffield Support group had brought together local youths as well as several students from the university, including members of the Black consciousness group formed a few years earlier. One of those who helped found the movement, Matloub Husayn-Ali-Khan, the son of a local steelworker, worked as an engineer in a foundry in the city, a job few Asians at the time had access to. While at work he had experienced significant racism, which had prompted him to become involved in the Sheffield Campaign Against Racism (SCAR) in the late 1970s, an organisation then chaired by the district secretary of his union, the Amalgamated Engineering Union. SCAR brought together trade union branches, Labour Party branches and church groups, but many local youths felt it was incapable of mounting a sufficient defence of their communities. Their experience in the Bradford 12 campaign had taught them about the importance of autonomous organisation.

Later, after hearing a member of the Bradford Asian Youth Movement, Anwar Qadir, speak at a meeting in late 1980, urging them set up 'a self-defence group of ethnic youth', Husayn-Ali-Khan would help found the Sheffield AYM which, though organised as South Asians, also maintained links with other organisations like the Campaign Against the Immigration Laws. Crucially, aside from a small grant for a printer, the organisation was financially independent.

Following the attack on the Shizan restaurant, the Sheffield AYM picketed outside it as well as outside the local magistrates' court. The organisation also began to draw attention to other racist attacks in the city as well as the failures of South Yorkshire police in dealing with them. In August that year 350 people, led by the AYM, marched towards the city centre to 'highlight grievances over alleged police attitudes to racist attacks in the city', chanting slogans like 'Self-defence is no offence' and 'Stop police harassment'. As one member told the local press, 'We have shown … that Asian youth have a voice of their own which has been ignored over the years by some people in prominent positions.'[4] Much like their counterparts in Luton and elsewhere during the early 1980s, the Sheffield

AYM organised the defence of families who had repeatedly been attacked and carried out regular street patrols. 'The city centre coach station was one of the many areas where the fascists put up their racist graffiti and we went out there to challenge them', recalled Mukhtar Dar, another founding member of the group.[5]

To avoid repercussions from their parents, some of the AYM left home and moved into an AYM house, owned by Matloub Husayn-Ali-Khan, code-named 'The Bus Shelter'. 'In the basement, we had weight training facilities and upstairs we had our offices', recalled Dar. 'We kept newspaper cuttings of attacks and minutes from Community Police Liaison Meetings, including a big thick folder called the "fascist file". This listed all the names, addresses, and workplaces of local fascists.'

The Sheffield AYM operated as a cadre-based organisation, with a core group of committed members who could mobilise a wider base when necessary. 'We started to flypost the Darnall area', recalled Dar.

> There were probably about twenty-five or thirty people on the streets. We had scouts at the front, and there were police vans in front of them. We were prepared to flypost while the police were on the streets and even the police station while the police were inside; we had a code through whistles, whereby once the police started looking back, we'd whistle, slow down, and disappear into the side streets before regrouping.

With their backs against the wall, the AYM also began organising self-defence classes. 'Our existence was reduced to what we called "combat breathing"', said Dar.

> Twenty-four seven, we didn't know when the attack would take place. We would sit in cafés, waiting for the pubs to empty, and inevitably the racists would come drunk and

> shout abuse at the waiters, and it would kick off. But we'd be there, and we'd be tooled up. We weren't particularly big, but we were organised and we turned victims into fighters.

Dar also recalled a restaurant owner, a man named Raja, whose business was petrol-bombed. 'We started organising meetings there, and from being a victim, he became a fighter and a key member of the Asian Youth Movement.' Another member, Zaffar, was followed and arrested by the police on fabricated charges. 'We would picket the police station until he was released', Dar said.

Another of the group's members, Badsha, a British Bangladeshi, joined the Sheffield AYM when he was 16. 'My older brother was a military man', he said. 'He'd come out of war. We were brought up to defend ourselves.' 'My nickname was bash because I'd get into loads of fights.'[6] Badsha attended several meetings and found camaraderie among those with similar experiences. 'Everyone felt equal and valued. There was no leader as such.' One incident he remembered vividly:

> A car of skinheads called us Paki bastards while we were in the park. A few days later, I saw one of them and told my brother 'That's the twat' and he said, 'Well either you smash him or I smash him.' I beat the crap out of that guy. It gave me confidence. Him and his mates were shocked. They kept themselves to themselves after that.

Alongside their support for specific campaigns, the Sheffield AYM had a broader programme of political education for its members. Mukhtar Dar said that the programme included the history of racism and colonialism as well as the looting of the Indian subcontinent. 'We'd take our members away for residentials, show films and study pamphlets.' Putting the historical jigsaw together, members of the Asian youth movements developed strong anti-imperialist principles and saw themselves as internationalists. Young Asians from Birmingham, Sheffield and Newham even took delegations to Northern Ireland. 'Ireland was an important struggle for us', Dar reflected.

> I remember when I was arrested for graffitiing 'free the Bradford 12' in Sheffield – I was taken to the police station and verbally and physically abused by the Special Branch, and as they were chucking me out, there was an Irish man being dragged in with his face almost on the floor and his hands behind his back. He shouted 'Tiocfaidh ár lá', which means 'Our day will come'. Ireland was England's first colony; and, for us, providing unconditional support to the Irish people in their national liberation struggle was a litmus test of our anti-imperialism. What we were going through in terms of our struggle against racist violence – we could see the Irish people were coming through a similar struggle.

Matloub Husayn-Ali-Khan went to Northern Ireland twice, once with the Troops Out movement, an organisation focused on securing the withdrawal of British troops from Northern Ireland, and once with a delegation of Asians. 'I remember us Asians marching down Falls Road [in Belfast] one April. It coincided with the anniversary of the Easter Rising. We met Sinn Féin who were really good welcoming people.'[7] It wasn't simply in terms of solidarity campaigns where the connections between Ireland and Sheffield emerged. 'Everything they practised in Northern Ireland', said Husayn-Ali-Khan, the police and the state 'brought here in terms of surveillance and state violence. The soldiers would point a gun to your head and intimidate you when you marched. They'd come in army Land Rovers. You'd think this is like a bloody military occupation.'

The Sheffield AYM supported other national liberation struggles too. The three key ones, in addition to the Irish struggle, said Dar, were 'the struggle in South Africa against apartheid, the gaping wound of human consciousness; the suffering, the fortitude, and the resilience of the Palestinian people, a massive source of inspiration for us; and, of course, the Kashmiri struggle, [which] was really key.'

The Sheffield AYM was building alliances closer to home too. 'While we organised autonomously, we were not separatists or cultural nationalists', Dar said.

> We were involved in many broad fronts and supported other struggles against injustice. This was a period of intense political upheaval and class struggle. You had the Yorkshire Ripper on the rampage killing women. When women were beginning to organise, to reclaim the night, it echoed our experience; so there was a natural empathy, and natural alliances formed. The fear that they felt was a fear that we felt with racism on the streets. We visited every inner-city Black area. We went to Toxteth, St Paul's, Manningham, Chapeltown, Southall, and Handsworth to build connections and widen our networks.

Perhaps one of the most important stories of solidarity, involving not just the Sheffield AYM but other South Asian activists too, was the support given to the National Union of Mineworkers during its strike of 1984 and 1985.

SCARGILL'S SOUTH ASIAN ARMY

One summer morning in Sheffield, Mukhtar Dar stood beneath his friend's bedroom window clutching a handful of pebbles. When he sent the pebbles sailing through the air, the thud against the windowpane woke up his friend, Sadiq.

It was 18 June 1984, and the National Union of Mineworkers (NUM) had called for a mass picket outside the Orgreave coking plant just outside Rotherham, a nearby town, aiming to disrupt the supply of coke that travelled from there to a power station in Scunthorpe. The months prior had seen several skirmishes between miners and the police, with the miners' leader, Arthur Scargill, being himself arrested at the plant just a month earlier.

When Sadiq emerged from his house, rubbing his eyes, he walked towards a minibus where half a dozen of his comrades from the Sheffield AYM waited. It was 5 a.m., and most were yawning and stretching. Loss of sleep was a worthy sacrifice.

When Sadiq and his comrades arrived on the picket line later that day, hoping to build solidarity with people facing an assault by the state that they recognised, they received far from a warm welcome. 'What the fuck are the Pakis doing here?' shouted one miner. Furious, Sadiq turned to Dar. 'Shit man', he said. 'You get me up at five in the morning and I come here and get this racism from the miners?' Dar, then 24 years old, was quick to respond: 'Well bro, we can see the bars and some of them can't.'

These bars, the bars of racial antagonism, were identified by Karl Marx in 1870. They were, Marx wrote, the 'secret of the impotence of the English working class' – a secret 'by which the capitalist class maintains its power. And the latter is quite aware of this.'[8]

For Dar, the struggle against racism had to be based on class. When his comrades in Bradford were on trial for preparing to defend their communities from fascists in 1981, Dar and members of the Sheffield AYM submitted resolutions to working men's clubs and trade union branches across Sheffield. 'We spoke at those meetings', recalled Dar. 'We had no choice. The only allies we saw were in the labour movement and trade unions.'[9]

Three years later, Dar recognised the commonality of the struggle taking place in nearby pit villages and encouraged his comrades to join the picket lines.

> There were individuals within those communities who had racist views. But when we went into those mining communities, we recognised that just as we were a tight-knit community, they were too – a community constituted by its relations to the means of production; and, as a community, they saw their future being eradicated.
>
> They had the same hatred for the police as we did, for the scabs, for the people who were selling out within their ranks. So, there were a lot of synergies and there was a commonality. And not just with the miners – with the Irish communities, with the African Caribbean communities, we had common experiences and a common fight. Even though we organised autonomously, we saw our struggle as one.

Dar described the solidarity shown by miners during the Grunwick strike as a pivotal movement. 'We watched films of the strike at Asian Youth Movement Day schools. As soon as the miners arrived by the coachloads the atmosphere changed. The police took a step back and the miners swelled the ranks.'

A year after Grunwick, Birmingham Trades Council elected Maurice Ludmer as its new president. Ludmer was a Jewish anti-fascist who worked closely with Jagmohan Joshi and the IWA in fighting the colour bar and racist discrimination in the Midlands more generally. Ludmer died in 1980, but he was succeeded by Paul Mackney, who continued to uphold his anti-racist values. 'The Indian Workers' Association had a regular presence at the trades council meetings', recalled Mackney of that time. 'In those days, we used to get meetings of up to and even over 200 people.'[10] Mackney's partner served as secretary of the Birmingham Campaign Against Racism and Fascism – a broad coalition that included the Birmingham Trades Union Congress (TUC), the IWA, the Bangladeshi Workers' Association, and several African and Caribbean organisations across

Birmingham. The group organised numerous counter-demonstrations against the far-right National Front and forged closer ties between trade unions and ethnic minority communities. These ties were to prove crucial over the next few years.

The IWA had backed the miners when they went on strike in the 1970s. When they went out again in 1984, support remained steadfast, as the money and food raised in collections made evident. 'I can remember Avtar Singh Jouhl, president of the Indian Workers' Association', Mackney recalled, 'and some mates walking into the Sparkhill Labour Club every Wednesday night. They'd collect food donations from all over the city and a significant sum of money – £2,000 or so every week – would come into the Labour Club.' The funds and food would then be divvied up and sent to miners across the Midlands and South Wales.

For his 1987 book *Birmingham and the Miners' Strike*, Mackney interviewed several miners and local trade unionists. Eric Lippitt of Lea Hall colliery in Staffordshire recalled support from South Asian communities in Wolverhampton and Walsall. 'We went to this shop run by an Indian bloke', he said. 'He'd been robbed the night before and yet he gave us food. That was what we call support. I thought it was fantastic.'[11] Nigel Ashfield, from the same pit, spoke at an IWA meeting in Leamington, which raised over £400, while on Friday and Saturday nights, miners' wives from Littleton and Lea Hall would go round the Wolverhampton pubs with Kamaljit Singh and other IWA members. 'That's fairly extraordinary if you think about it', said Mackney. 'Miners from mid-Staffordshire going to Wolverhampton to collect money at Desi pubs.'[12]

Mackney explained that Black and Asian communities were often the most generous when it came to collecting for the miners facing poverty in their year on strike. Street collections on Soho Road in Handsworth, a deprived area with a significant number of Black and Asian residents, were known to be among the best supporters, and miners often squabbled over who got that 'patch'. Miners who conducted fundraising at Petticoat Lane market in East London made similar observations about Indian stall holders. Meanwhile, it was estimated that well over £5,000 was collected at Birmingham's Sikh temples, most of it going to the Birch Coppice Hardship Fund. In May Baba Bakhtaura Singh, a well-known and much-loved Punjabi folk singer then fighting the state's efforts to deport him, performed at one of Birmingham's first miners' support benefits.[13]

Nigel Flanagan, who grew up in the Harehills area of Leeds, had similar recollections. Many of his friends worked at the nearby Allerton Bywater pit and in the Selby 'super mines' just outside Leeds. He recalled going door to door in the Harehills area alongside others in the East Leeds Miners' Support Group, giving out bin bags and telling residents that they would return the next day to collect the bags hopefully loaded with food to be distributed to strikers' families living in Harehills or Gipton. If any was left over, it would be taken to the Allerton Bywater pit. 'It became very clear that the households that contributed the most and on a regular basis were in the South Asian communities', said Flanagan.

> They also encouraged us to ask the numerous corner shops for donations, which we did. By the end of the strike a lot of the food collectors like myself had 'regulars' who would chat and ask about the strike. A few times we took some strikers with us to talk to people just as a thank-you exercise.[14]

As well as giving donations, people travelled the distance between the cities and the pit towns. Ex-miner Denis Doody, who grew up in Fitzwilliam in West Yorkshire, recalled the IWA visiting his village in 1984. 'Most of them were members of the Communist Party', he said. 'Mick McGahey came with them. They brought two or three van loads of food and toys and everything over, and they came into one of the clubs in the village.'[15] Doody recounted IWA visits to neighbouring villages, too. 'It was quite a culture shock for some people in overwhelmingly white areas, but the people were overwhelmed by the generosity.'

Doody also recalled the solidarity of Indian construction workers, Kashmiri taxi drivers, and local mosques across West Yorkshire which raised money. In particular, he recalled the solidarity of a Pakistani friend, Abdul, who opened up his social club and helped facilitate local NUM meetings. 'He did a hell of a lot of solidarity work for the community', Doody said. 'The Kashmiri community [was] very good to us. Ordinary people. The Pakistani Workers' Association [that was] mainly based around Yorkshire [was] also very supportive and did a lot of fundraising.'

At other times, miners came to visit South Asian communities. Hardev Dhillon – who had arrived in the UK from India in 1963 and set up a branch of the IWA in Greenwich in 1965, where in 1968 he forced the hand of the Transport and General Workers Union to allow 300 of his South Asian colleagues working at a factory in Woolwich to join (which the union had initially refused) – reached out with his IWA branch to NUM branches in Kent. 'We promised to fund them and provide food', he recalled. 'When they travelled to London for demonstrations, we housed them in local houses in the area. Miners came from across the country. Some of them stayed in my home.'[16]

Then, of course, there was the vital element of picket line solidarity. Nishaharan Vaithilingam was a founding member of Black People Support the Miners, a group set up in 1984 that organised Black and Asian solidarity under the banner of political blackness. He had been politicised through the anti-apartheid movement at university after offering to help design posters, and the frequent racist taunts he endured were enough to turn him into a full-fledged anti-fascist fighter, one also involved in the campaign to free the Bradford 12 in 1981. 'Black People Support the Miners would usually meet up at the Chinese Information Centre on Shaftesbury Avenue, near Leicester Square', recalled Vaithilingam. 'That was a free advice service for Chinese workers. The two people who worked there, Bobby Chan and Wabi Zeng, were involved in the campaign. We used to have people like Cecil Gutzmore and others from the African Caribbean community organising under this umbrella too.'[17]

The group would pool their money to hire coaches and visit picket lines in Nottingham and Wales, as well as undertaking political education. Using his love of design, Vaithilingam produced a 'Black People Support the Miners' badge as well as informational leaflets. The group had stalls at Notting Hill Carnival, where they discussed the dispute and raised much-needed funds.

In one particularly striking case, Vaithilingam recalled fundraising outside a Tesco alongside the anti-racist groups, Southall Monitoring Group and Southall Black Sisters. 'I remember an older Asian couple in their sixties coming out with a trolley full of their shopping. When we talked to them about the strike and explained what the miners were going through, they left the whole trolley and went inside to do the shopping all over again.'

***

Despite the racism that Sadiq witnessed at Orgreave, Mukhtar Dar and his comrades from the Sheffield AYM stayed to see the battle that ensued. Six thousand police officers from eighteen different police forces, tooled up with batons, riot shields and helmets, attacked the miners and their supporters, leaving many with serious, lifelong injuries. Dar recalled running for his life, jumping through gardens and over hedges. The state had unleashed a brutal wave of violence, the likes of which many had never seen before.

South Asians were only too familiar with such violence from the state. And it was these joint struggles that they shared with mining communities and others that acted as a crucible for the creation of empathy, solidarity and resistance. Dar commented: 'You had the miners, you had the Irish, you had the African and Caribbean youth. Years and years of police brutality, death in custody and sus laws: it was just a tinderbox waiting to erupt.'[18]

Nigel Flanagan and others in the East Leeds Miners' Support Group learned a lot from their interactions with Black and Asian communities during the strike. 'Harehills and neighbouring Chapeltown had suffered from riots and police aggression from the early 1980s. The swapping of experiences of police behaviour was brought up many times.' Friendships were formed in other ways, too, Flanagan notes. Focusing on a common cause broke down barriers in Harehills and forged a greater sense of togetherness within the community. 'The atmosphere changed. You saw people out shopping who donated food, or in the park, or out and about and you'd stop and talk. You'd joke and banter about the food donated. We rarely mixed in pubs and clubs for all sorts of cultural reasons', he said. 'But I do remember, though, after the strike going out in Leeds city centre with a group of Asian lads I had met through the food donation work.'

Vaithilingam also recalled a great deal of socialising that took place during this period. On one occasion, after providing support on a picket line in Wales, Black and Asian people joined miners in a pub. A Welsh miner's wife who had once expressed racist views found herself dancing with Black and Asian people. 'She was very emotional', he said. 'She told us that she only read from *The Sun* newspaper and had a completely different image of black people. She had never come across black people socially in that way. She expressed deep regret about her views and was very happy to meet us.'

The strike and the solidarities that it forged helped to change the attitudes of many others too. In 1985, when riots spread across Handsworth against police repression, the miners Mackney interviewed told him they understood the root cause of the unrest. 'The miners who got involved with the Handsworth people could see it all', said Allen Stevenson. 'It was obvious it had been brewing for a while. Everything led to the police.'[19] As Eric Lippitt said of the Lea Hall strikers: 'They recognise the problems blacks face because they met them through the strike. They said, "Well this is what unemployment, bad conditions, bad housing causes. What do they expect?"'[20]

Nor was solidarity a one-way street. In 1984 striking Asian women workers at Kewal Brothers, a sweatshop in Birmingham where some were paid just £1 an hour, received support from the wider trade union movement. Upon hearing that Bhagwant Singh was involved in supporting the women, Cannock miners, with barely enough money to feed their own families, hired coaches to take 150 Lea Hall and Littleton miners to the Kewal picket line. A strike spokesperson would later go up to Lea Hall, and the two groups of workers would organise joint fundraising events.

Denis Doody suggests that support of 'all of the workers' was one of the defining features of the NUM under Arthur Scargill's leadership. 'The colours, the nationalities, were irrelevant to us. And that was the ethos within the union.' In practice, this policy had the potential not only to turn trade unionists into stronger and more effective organisers, but also to promote an internationalist outlook. Doody explained that it was through his interactions with local Kashmiris in Yorkshire that he became aware of the struggles of Kashmiris under occupation and their struggle for self-determination – one struggle among many that he continues to support. 'I certainly looked at things as an internationalist and I still do today', he said. 'We're knocking on now, but quite a few of us miners have been attending the Palestine solidarity rallies in London and here in Yorkshire.'

For Mukhtar Dar, the key lesson from the dispute is that alliances are forged in struggle. 'Unity is not something that happens in the abstract', he said. 'It's something that you have to fight for. It's something that is built in struggle. It's in struggle that we test each other, that we break down barriers, that we hold each other to account, and that we challenge each other on our prejudice and our shortcomings.'[21] It was the young Asian activists as much as anyone who were challenged, he added, specifically in their assumption that every white person was racist until proved otherwise.

> We went to the mining communities, we stayed in the halls at night with them, and when they spoke to us and we saw the anger in their eyes and the hatred that they had for the police, they just echoed what we were going through. From that came incredible, profound friendships that endured and have lasted. I will never forget sitting with the miners'

> wives as they sang 'We are women, we are strong.' It really moved us.[22]

These experiences profoundly shaped the Asian youth who saw the value in coalition-building and uniting communities.

The Sheffield AYM continued to campaign against racism in the city in the late 1980s, attracting the attention of the authorities. 'We knew they were tapping our phones and monitoring us', said Raj.[23] 'I caught them outside my house monitoring me', recalled Matloub Husayn-Ali-Khan. 'I chased them away. They would take photos of us.' Husayn-Ali-Khan recounted one incident when he was arrested:

> I asked one of our members Shabaz to do a poster for our Kashmir march. The police came and arrested us for flyposting and took us inside for the first time. It was revenge. They knew we were from the Asian Youth Movement. They had a vengeance because we had exposed the names and badge numbers of racist police officers. We had good links with solicitors. The worst they could do was to use the sus laws and fine us.

'South Yorkshire police were bad news back then – what they did at Orgreave, what they did at Hillsborough. Complete lies', said Husayn-Ali-Khan. 'I was at Hillsborough in 1988. We used to monitor the far right there. It was the same team and the same match. I remember how dangerous and scary the tunnel was and I didn't return the following year when the disaster happened.'

Towards the late 1980s some of the Sheffield AYM had moved out to other cities. Remaining members continued to organise under the Campaign Against Racial and Police Harassment banner and the Sheffield Defence Campaign. Many of their activities took place at the Commonground Resources Centre. It was a space used by the Sheffield Black

Women's Group, Socialist Feminist Group, Troops Out and other left-wing campaign groups, giving young Asians the opportunity to build links with other groups.

ASIAN WOMEN'S ORGANISATIONS

While the case of the solidarity movements that sprang up around the miners' strike shows the power of solidarity within and between groups, there were still divisions. One of the deepest involved the question of gender. Much as in the earlier generation of activist groups, in the Asian youth movements of the late 1970s and early 1980s Asian women found little space. If the earlier generation could blame this male dominance in part on the then overwhelmingly male pattern of migration, for later organisation what separated men and women were cultural barriers and the nature of the activities they were involved in.

'Particularly in Lancashire and Yorkshire, the communities came from overwhelmingly rural settings in Pakistan', said Asad Rehman.

> They bring with them that cultural snapshot of Pakistan as they remember it and they try to reintroduce that. There was still a whole thing about 'Girls shouldn't do this. Girls shouldn't do that.' There were young Asian women sneaking out to go to public meetings and marches. That was much harder in Burnley where if you walk down the street, everybody knows you and your parents. It was very traditional policing over the community. Women were not afforded the same political spaces. We were a working-class community. Most men worked in the factories. Most women stayed at home. Some did piecemeal work from home.[24]

Some campaigns, such as the Anwar Ditta Defence Campaign and family reunification campaigns, did, however, involve many women. Even then, said Rehman, there was a reticence from parents about young girls being involved in organised political campaigns. 'It wasn't completely reactionary but it was very noticeable that there were not many young Asian women because they faced barriers at home. We shouldn't underestimate the level of misogyny within our community.' Self-defence campaigns, in particular, were male-dominated. 'We took a very masculine approach, physical defence of our communities. There was a macho element to that. It would have been hard for Asian women to find a place in some parts of that movement.'

In many instances, Asian women set up their own organisations, tackling issues that disproportionately impacted them and creating inclusive spaces that they could turn to for support. In 1983, for example, Southall Black Sisters, the group originally founded in 1979, was revived by Pragna Patel, who procured a Greater London Council grant to set up a campaigning centre to support Black and Asian women. The group advocated on behalf of victims of domestic and other forms of gender-related violence as well as providing advice on housing and immigration. 'I was very much inspired by the law centre movement which was at its height at the time', recalled Patel.

> This was an important community-based grassroots movement that had sprung up across the UK which was trying to both meet the material needs of people in their everyday lives, providing advice and advocacy on a range of issues from employment to immigration to housing to social care, and at the same time, bridging law and activism.
>
> Very quickly, women started coming in for support. Our reputation for supporting women spread through word of mouth and the issue that they presented with, first and foremost, was violence against women and girls in the home And so, that is what determined the agenda. We didn't have a predetermined agenda. It was set by what the women's needs

> were and what their needs were in relation to support and protection from violence and rape and sexual harassment and so on.
>
> Certainly, these women's needs were being unmet by anti-racist organisations and statutory agencies. The state wasn't interested in protecting women in those days. There were very few refuges for women.[25]

But setting up such an organisation was far from easy, and Patel recalled a very hostile reception from many influential community members. 'Religious institutions and elders didn't like us because we challenged them. Members of the Indian Workers' Association lobbied to close us down in the early 90s.'

> The reason we faced such hostility is nobody wanted to be truthful about the fact that yes, as a minority, we need to challenge state oppression, but we also need to challenge internal forms of oppression that are equally life-threatening and equally soul-destroying for other sections of society, including women and children.

One of the first big campaigns the group organised was a women's march through Southall in support of Krishna Sharma, a woman who hanged herself after suffering years of domestic violence and abuse. SBS publicly shamed her family, gathering outside their house with placards that stated: 'They say it's suicide: We say it's murder.'[26] The group also supported campaigns to free Asian women who fought back against their abusers, supporting high-profile cases such as that of Kiranjit Ahluwalia and Zoora Shah. Victims of such abuse would often become some of the fiercest advocates for others, and SBS often relied on the support of women they'd already supported when it came to mobilising for demonstrations and campaigns. 'They understood immediately what it meant', said Patel.

The group also built connections with women's groups across the UK and often had the support of the wider feminist movement in their campaigns. Birmingham Black Sisters, set up in 1982, and for similar reasons, supported many similar campaigns. They campaigned on behalf of Iqbal Begum, a Mirpuri woman convicted of murdering her abusive husband. One morning, after suffering domestic abuse for years, Begum had had enough. She pushed her husband, who fell backwards and hit his head. He was rushed to hospital and later died. Begum didn't speak English, and was afforded inadequate legal representation and no interpreters. At one point, when entering a plea she had said 'galti', the Urdu word for mistake, but the judge and jury mistook this for 'guilty'.[27] Birmingham Black Sisters advocated on Begum's behalf while she was in prison. They exposed the racism of the courts, which had failed to offer an interpreter. The Birmingham-based campaign was successful and Begum's sentence was reduced.

Politicised by the New Cross massacre, Shirin Housee, who had cut her teeth on student activism at Essex, would come to play a key role in Birmingham Black Sisters. In September 1984 she began studying for a masters at Birmingham University, but quickly became disillusioned with academia, preferring to focus her energy on street politics.

> I met this woman. Maljinder, who was in the year above me, and she felt the same. We were alienated by this very elitist institution and so we left university, gave up that degree and joined the Birmingham Black Sisters, attending our first meeting and that was our introduction to street politics.[28]

Birmingham Black Sisters were also active in the West Midlands anti-deportation campaign, supporting individuals such as the folk singer Baba Bakhtaura and social worker Mohammed Idrish. 'We supported the Palestinians, the miners and their wives during their strike and the women whose husbands, partners, brothers or fathers had been arrested during the 1985 Handsworth riots', recalled Housee. 'The support was childcare, food support and sometimes just meeting the women and talking to them.'

Birmingham Black Sisters was a relatively small group, with a core membership of around fifteen at its peak. They met every week on a Friday night at a trade union office in Birmingham city centre. And while Southall Black Sisters took funding from the state, Birmingham Black Sisters refused all external funding, believing, like many anti-racists at the time, that their political activism would be co-opted, and relying instead on fundraising and support from the broader labour movement.

While Birmingham Black Sisters often criticised the Birmingham AYM (who they referred to as Asian Young Men, for their lack of women members), and the AYM in turn accused Birmingham Black Sisters of being too middle class, the two groups often campaigned together on key issues. 'The sexism was definitely there', recalled Housee. 'I remember swearing at some of them when we saw them in the street because of their sexism.' But, emphasised Housee, some members were better than others. 'It would be wrong to tar the whole group with one brush. I had decent political conversations with some of the men on all things from the riots to international issues.'

Perhaps the campaign that would gain the greatest prominence for Asian women in the early 1980s came in 1982. The winter that year was an unusually cold one, with temperatures in January dropping below –25°C in some parts of the country. Hamid Ali, a young immigrant from Bangladesh, was at the time residing in a Brick Lane tenement flat without central heating. On one particularly bitterly cold afternoon in March Ali turned on his paraffin wax heater, and a spark caught on the curtain, sending flames racing up the wall. The fire quickly engulfed Ali's home. Ali burned to death.

In January that year Ali's wife, Afia Begum, and her 18-month-old daughter Asma had been granted an entry certificate to join her husband in the UK, where her father and other family members already lived. After taking her flight from Bangladesh, she arrived at Heathrow airport in June, where she was told that her entry permit was no longer valid. The death of her husband, she was told, meant she was no longer eligible. She was granted temporary leave to remain in order to settle her husband's affairs, but after that she would be scheduled for deportation.

In January 1983, after less than a year in the country and with her deportation imminent, Begum went into hiding. Soon this caught the attention of the Sari Squad, a group composed of four young Asian activists, Palavi Parekh, then aged 21, Nita Datta (20), Parajati Teare (29) and Ghazala Faizi (26). They launched a public campaign in Begum's defence, galvanising a large number of South Asian women behind them. Their activism continued through late 1983 and into the next year, with one striking action, in August 1983, seeing them tie themselves to the railings outside the home of the then home secretary, Leon Brittain. On being arrested, the women were taken to Rochester police station, where they were subjected to humiliating strip searches while male police officers jeered. They faced further racist abuse once the case was brought to trial, this time from the jury, and it eventually saw them hit with a fine of £1,000.[29]

Despite the work of the activists, on 3 May 1984 the police bundled Afia Begum and her baby into a van, and sent them off to Harmondsworth detention centre near Heathrow airport. Two days later, on Saturday 5 May, Begum was deported. On the day of the deportation, the Sari Squad, alongside East London Workers against Racism and 200 supporters, protested outside Heathrow, but to little avail. Even so, the Sari Squad continued to fight for Afia Begum: later that month, thirty Sari Squad members and their supporters hired a bus so they could take Begum's case to the European Court of Human Rights, where the court ruled that the deportation was unconstitutional. The European Parliament passed a motion, carried by 70 votes to 67, that condemned 'this act as callous and showing the racist and sexist nature of the United Kingdom immigration laws'. Labour MPs, including Jeremy Corbyn and Harry Cohen, reiterated this argument in the House of Commons.[30]

Despite not being able to prevent Begum's deportation, the Sari Squad had taken on the Home Office and exposed its racism on the international stage. Far from being passive victims of racist immigration laws, Asian women had once again fought back.

HOW SOLIDARITY DIED

By the late 1980s most of the Asian youth movements were more or less defunct. Some former members went on to be involved in groups such as the Kashmiri Workers' Association and the Pakistani Workers' Association. The PWA was particularly important for many activists. 'The Pakistani Workers' Association was initially set up by Pakistanis who came here as students', Mukhtar Dar, formerly of the Sheffield AYM, told me.

> They were involved in supporting the struggle against American imperialism in Vietnam. They were active in the big demonstrations in London; Tariq Ali was involved with

> them. After, some of them went back to Pakistan and played a pivotal role against dictatorship, and in supporting the Balochi national liberation struggle.[31]

Later, a second phase of the movement emerged, to which Dar and others would belong. This began in 1984 and remained active until 1992, with AYM members in Bradford, Manchester, Birmingham and Sheffield involved. In Manchester, the group were involved in the Ahmed Iqbal Ullah Memorial Committee after the murder of 13-year-old Ahmed Iqbal Ullah, who was stabbed to death in a school playground after defending a younger Asian boy from racist bullying. They were also involved in justice campaigns for Mohammad Siddique, who was killed by racists; Tahir Akram, killed by racists in Oldham; and Tasleem Akhtar, a young girl who was murdered in Birmingham.

Dar would join the PWA in 1985, after travelling to Pakistan with several other members of the youth movement. This visit was deeply moving. 'When I went to Pakistan and saw the number of people dying due to natural causes – except they weren't natural, they were to do with the colonial looting that had taken place – I knew we had to connect the struggle against racism here with solidarity with and support for struggles back in Pakistan', he told me. 'I ended up joining PWA because we were getting older and we were no longer youth', he said. 'The PWA also had a strong women's wing, and we organised International Women's Day rallies every year.'[32]

Dar recalled a PWA International Women's Day rally with speakers from the Nicaragua solidarity campaigns, the South West Africa People's Organisation, the African People's Revolutionary Party and the Black Panthers. 'The men were looking after the creche and picking up the kids;

the women were the ones speaking on the platform. Back in those days, we were really challenging those attitudes.' 'There were two phases of the PWA', explained Dar.

Badsha, another former Sheffield AYM member, believes some members of the Asian Youth Movement had started by then to become more nationalistic. 'I was from Bangladesh and the discussions on Kashmir didn't resonate as much', he said. 'Some groups felt like they were all just Pakistani. I felt my culture was left out so I felt the need to create a Bangladeshi youth organisation.'

In other towns and cities, the issue of state funding proved to be the most contentious one. Members of the Bradford 12, for instance, split from the Bradford AYM to set up the United Black Youth League because the AYM had accepted state funding. Over time, many groups became more orientated towards youth work instead of radical political activity. Some, such as Marsha Singh in Bradford, would even go on to become prominent Labour politicians, while others found roles on community relations councils and race relations bodies.

As the twentieth century wore on, anti-racist activism in Britain was increasingly institutionalised. For Dar, this was one of the key developments that led to the movements' demise. 'They smash your kneecaps with racism and then they give you crutches in the form of grants to stand up on', said Dar. 'The youth of 1981 and 1985 were an almighty lion that could roar and could bite. The system got scared, and looked to how the struggle in America was contained. The system created the race relations industry.'[33]

'Unfortunately, many people were co-opted. The struggle moved from the streets and into council chambers. Suddenly, jobs came into being where people would be paid to tackle discrimination.' 'As working-class youth', Dar added, 'we could see this phenomenon playing out in front of us. We had communities of Asian and African-Caribbean people, who were united against a commonality of racism, suddenly becoming divided because crumbs were thrown into the ghettos.'

Such decline and division would have consequences for decades to come.

11
RUSHDIE, RIOTING AND RELIGIOUS DIVIDES

In December 1988 the quiet market town of Bolton exploded. Thousands of Muslims marched in protest, not against a racist attack, nor a National Front rally, nor the brutality of the police. Their fury was aimed instead at a book: *The Satanic Verses* by Salman Rushdie.

The novel's satirical treatment of Islam had already sparked outrage across the Muslim world. In Bolton, copies of the book were set alight outside the town hall, flames rising into the winter air as demonstrators denounced what they saw as blasphemy. In Bradford, too, book burnings drew global attention, scenes that would become emblematic of Britain's fraught debates over faith, identity and free speech.

A few months later, in February 1989, Ayatollah Khomeini of Iran issued a *fatwa*, calling for Rushdie's death. The edict transformed an already bitter controversy into a global crisis. Around the world, television screens showed images of angry British Muslims chanting slogans, a sight that provoked a wave of commentary about 'free speech', 'fanaticism' and, increasingly, the supposed 'clash of civilisations'.

While protests in Sheffield and Dewsbury over *The Satanic Verses* largely passed without incident, tensions in Bradford flared on 17 June 1989 when a group of 300 Muslim youths were taunted by a group of white men, including members of Bradford City FC's notorious hooligan firm, The Ointment, with cries of 'Rushdie!' Bottles and stones soon filled the air, and police in riot gear descended on the scene.[1] The violence of that night and the retaliatory attacks by white gangs in the weeks that followed marked a grim foreshadowing of the racial conflicts to come.

The far right saw an opportunity. Having lost momentum after the 1980s, groups such as the British National Party (BNP) and the remnants of the National Front began to rebrand their hate. Muslims were now their preferred enemy.

Despite the absence of formal organisation, Asian youth remained angry, assertive and ready to mobilise. Their frustration found new expression a week after the protests of 17 June when the BNP attempted to march through Savile Town in the heart of Dewsbury's South Asian community. The BNP, a far-right political party that was formed several years earlier by former leading members of the National Front, claimed to be supporting white parents who had withdrawn their children from local schools in protest at the growing number of Muslim pupils. In response, the Kirklees Black Workers' Association organised a small counter-demonstration. But rumours spread that the BNP intended to burn the Qur'an in public, prompting around 800 Muslims to gather in Dewsbury's city centre.

Heavy-handed policing, which sought to push demonstrators back into Savile Town, quickly turned confrontational. Mark, a former member of Leeds Anti-Fascist Action, recalled how some police officers joined in with racial slurs, further angering young Asians. He said the police protected the BNP while targeting the Asian youth.[2]

Clashes broke out, and the Scarborough pub was set alight. Meanwhile, Asian market traders reported racial abuse from

BNP activists as police diverted their attention elsewhere. The riot exposed how racial tensions, inflamed by deindustrialisation and poverty, were simmering just below the surface.

RELIGIOUS DIVIDES

More trouble was to come on 6 December 1992, after Hindu nationalist extremists from the Vishva Hindu Parishad destroyed the Babri Masjid, a sixteenth-century mosque in Ayodhya, India. The demolition triggered months of intercommunal rioting across India, leaving 2,000 dead. Soon, the events in India would have an impact in Britain. They would also expose some of the new fault lines then emerging in Britain's Asian communities. The unity that once bound Hindus, Sikhs and Muslims under the banner of political blackness was fracturing. Racism persisted, but communities were now increasingly organising along religious lines rather than through shared working-class or anti-racist struggles. In a moment with great symbolic weight, when anti-racist activist Amrit Wilson raised the issue of the demolition of the mosque with Jayaben Desai, Desai shocked her by celebrating it. She was, she revealed, now a member of the VHP in the UK.[3]

Across Britain, Hindu temples in Derby, Bradford, Birmingham, Bolton, Oldham and elsewhere were firebombed in apparent retaliatory attacks.[4] Symbolically, even the Indian Workers' Association community centre in Huddersfield, an organisation devoted to secularism and South Asian unity, was attacked, the word Indian alone enough to invite violence. Iqbal Sacranie, a Muslim community leader, claimed that these reprisals were provoked by Hindus distributing sweets in celebration outside a Bradford temple.[5]

This newly fractious atmosphere was aided by a policy of state multiculturalism, one that had already taken the wind out of the sails of the once ascendant Asian youth movements. Groups such as the Council of Mosques and the Hindu Council would now speak on behalf of entire communities; circumventing mass community engagement, which would, no doubt, pose challenges for the state, authorities settled for a far easier and mutually beneficial vision of community engagement, through the prism of self-proclaimed community leaders. The plurality of voices, particularly those of women and young people, would go unheard.

In such an atmosphere, Asian youth, though assertive and militant in opposing racist gangs, did not gravitate towards the left. Nor did they feel any connection with the self-proclaimed community leaders, who had assumed the role of mediators on the race relations committees. Instead, Wahabi-salafist Muslims, subscribing to a more puritanical version of Islam, began to grow in number. Backed by Saudi petrodollars and buoyed by victories (with the help of US forces) against the Soviet Union in Afghanistan, some established a presence in Britain and started recruiting young Muslims alienated by both white racism and an elderly leadership in the mosques that too often (literally and metaphorically) did not speak their language.

Asad Rehman saw the shift play out in real time.

> You've got this idea of multiculturalism, using these gatekeepers. And at the same time, you've got the rise of religious identity. You've got half these young people finding salvation by becoming deeply religious. Deeply, deeply religious. I'm going to grow my beard, dress in Islamic clothes, do all of these things etc.[6]

A distinctly Muslim identity was beginning to crystallise. For many young people, this identity offered a sense of dignity and solidarity in a country that continued to marginalise them. In this, it was helped by international events: the genocide in Bosnia and the Chechnyan war of independence in Russia further alienated many young British Muslims. Some of this new energy was captured by the Salafist group Hizb ut-Tahrir, which began recruiting Muslim students on university campuses in the 1990s.

For other communities, there were different factors at play. In 1984 Indian forces stormed the Golden Temple, Sikhism's holiest site in Amritsar, as they sought out separatists who had taken refuge there. The operation led to the deaths of thousands, according to Sikh groups. Shortly afterwards the then Indian prime minister, Indira Gandhi, who had ordered the raid on the temple, was assassinated by two of her Sikh bodyguards. Her death triggered anti-Sikh riots, which only furthered a strong sense of Sikh identity. These events would send ripples across continents; the Khalistan movement, a separatist movement that sought to create a homeland for Sikhs in the Punjab region, soon began picking up support among the Sikh diaspora in Britain now that the Indian Workers' Association, already a declining force, was losing its once strong influence in the gurdwaras.

GROWING TENSIONS

The late 1980s had seen successful efforts to challenge housing discrimination, making it increasingly difficult for local authorities to allocate housing on the basis of race. As a result, a growing number of Black and Asian families began moving into majority white working-class estates. But vicious street level racism had not subsided. In south-east London, this was demonstrated by a wave of racist murders in the early 1990s. In February 1991 15-year-old Rolan Adams was murdered in a racist attack in Thamesmead, a large estate in south-east London. The following year 16-year-old Rohit Duggal was stabbed to death outside a kebab shop in Eltham, while in April 1993 Stephen Lawrence was murdered in a racist attack in the same area. A number of racist street gangs operated across south-east England during this period, regularly terrorising families. The British National Party, in many ways a successor to the National Front, also maintained its headquarters in nearby Welling.

Meanwhile, Asian youth across Britain continued to battle, out of necessity, against racist gangs and, very often, a racist police force too. On 8 September 1993 17-year-old Quddus Ali was attacked by a gang of eight while returning a video to a rental shop near his home in Tower Hamlets. The assault left him with brain damage and a crippled leg after he was kicked repeatedly in the head. He lay in a coma for four months.[7] When his friend attempted to report the attack, police told him to go home. They were 'too busy' to take his statement.[8]

The local community responded with a peaceful vigil of 600 people outside Whitechapel Hospital, which was met with lines of riot police. The vigil ended in violence, with nine youths charged with riot. Meanwhile, a white man charged with the attempted murder of Quddus Ali was immediately released on bail, deepening the anger of many.[9] As locals demanded justice for Ali, they also rallied in support of the arrested youths, the Tower Hamlets Nine as they soon became known.

One of the Tower Hamlets Nine was Halima Begum's brother Abdul Samad (known to friends as Kamal), an amateur kickboxer who trained at Repton boxing club in Bethnal Green. 'My late brother would show up in Brick Lane when the skinheads were there', recalled Begum.

> They'd have fist fights to stop them from hurting older Bengali men and women. My brother wasn't involved in organised politics but he was part of a group called the Brick Lane Massive. They were not a criminal gang. They protected elderly men and women while they were doing the shopping.[10]

In a sign of the new times, just over a week after the murder Derek Beackon won a by-election in Millwall, on the Isle of Dogs, becoming the BNP's first councillor in the process. Running on the slogan 'Rights for Whites', he exploited white anxieties over jobs and housing in a borough ravaged by deindustrialisation. The Liberal Democrats had helped stoke this resentment by claiming that Bangladeshi tenants were being given preferential treatment, a narrative the BNP capitalised on. Racist attacks surged in the aftermath. On 25 September Kamiljit Kaur, an Asian mother living on the nearby Teviot estate in Poplar, required forty stitches after a wooden stake was hurled from a seventy-foot balcony. She reported that racist incidents had increased since the BNP victory.[11]

In response to the electoral success of the BNP, a new group, Women Unite Against Racism, was set up in 1993. Youth workers such as Georgie Wemeyss worked alongside Bangladeshi women such as Julie Begum and Halima Begum to confront rising racism on housing estates. Halima Begum remembered the important role they played in tackling the BNP at the ballot box. She recalled the BNP deliberately trying to intimidate local women before the 1993 election. 'Given the low electoral registration for women, we decided that the most effective activities for women would be to get women into the voting registers so they would be eligible to vote in the May local elections of 1994.' Alongside this, WUAR tried to stop the BNP from selling its newspapers in Brick Lane.

There were other groups that opposed the BNP. Anti-Fascist Action (AFA) had revived the tradition of militant anti-fascism and fought many physical battles against racist groups across Britain. In October 1993, alongside groups such as the Indian Workers' Association, AFA was involved in the infamous Battle of Welling, when 40,000 anti-racists clashed with the police outside the BNP's headquarters. The HQ, a source of constant protest and controversy, was eventually forced to close.

Despite this resistance, for many young Asians life in Britain remained a daily struggle. They faced unemployment, racist attacks and limited opportunities, while the collapse of the Asian youth movements meant that the radical, grassroots spaces where anger once found expression no longer existed. In their place stood self-proclaimed community leaders, whose primary role was to mediate rather than challenge. They became the state's interlocutors, courted by police, politicians and race relations bodies and treated as gatekeepers of communal peace. But who elected them? What authority did they wield? And why were such diverse religious groups treated as monoliths? Increasingly, religious authority, property wealth and biradri (kinship) networks mattered more than political ideology.

The northern mill towns, meanwhile, suffering deindustrialisation and decline and increasingly segregated along racial lines, became the backdrop for recurring episodes of racial tension. Some young Asians, struggling with poverty and unemployment, turned to gang culture and street crime. 'They were largely driven into that because of inequality, poverty, poor housing, and making those life choices', said Asad Rehman. 'That's what then left all of these young people without a political understanding and answer to what was coming, both in terms of racist violence from the far right and state repression, when they then began to resist.'

The next major flashpoint came in June 1995, in Manningham, Bradford, when two police officers claimed that they had been insulted by local Asian youths playing football on a residential street. The youths, however, alleged that an officer had driven over one boy's foot and harassed them. When one of the youths fled into his home, his sister tried to prevent his arrest, later stating that both she and her baby were assaulted in the process.

The confrontation quickly escalated. Crowds gathered outside the house, police reinforcements were called, and by nightfall Manningham was in open revolt. Cars were set alight, businesses attacked, and violence spilled into the city centre. At 10 p.m. a group of young men marched to the local police station, demanding the release of those arrested and protesting against years of mistreatment at the hands of a racist police force. The scene echoed a familiar pattern: over-policing, economic neglect and political exclusion had combined to create a tinderbox.

Local MP Max Madden, deeply alarmed, secured a parliamentary debate on the unrest. He described a generation of young Asians who were 'angry, alienated and frustrated' – young men and women who felt that 'no one listens to us', 'no one cares about us' and 'no one helps us'.[12] Madden insisted that Bradford's problems were not unique: 'Like so many other inner cities and urban areas, we endure high unemployment, extremely poor housing, little open space and few community facilities.' Quoting the journalist Lucy Ward, who had interviewed local young Asian women, he said: 'A lot of Asian youths feel like second-class citizens, missing out on good jobs and good education.'[13] Another of those interviewed by Ward, Nageena Altaf, said 'It's horrible and sad to see them go to such extremes. It just shows how resentful they felt', while Razia Saman pointed out: 'Asian boys have a lot of hatred for the police, who were warned beforehand it could get as extreme as it did.'[14]

Madden also cited journalist Alam Khan's interviews with young men. One, Arif Khan, had told him that 'For some people the rioting was the only way they could be heard. They were frustrated at being pushed back all the time', while Aziz Rehman pleaded, 'We have got many ideas on how to make Manningham a better place, but nobody listens to us.'[15]

Although the immediate trigger for the 1995 Manningham riots was a confrontation with the police, the underlying causes – unemployment, racial tension and poverty – had been festering for years. Manningham in 1995 should have been a wake-up call. Yet few lessons were learned. In 2001 the cycle would repeat itself with even greater consequences, as northern towns and cities erupted once more into violence.

THE 2001 RIOTS

Oldham, in Greater Manchester, was once the cotton-spinning capital of the world, employing over 50,000 people in its mills at the beginning of the twentieth century in a town then known for its wealth. But the decline of the textile industry had taken its toll, and by the mid-twentieth century there was widespread unemployment and poverty. It was in this Oldham that Pakistani migrants and Bangladeshi migrants worked the nightshifts in declining mills in a last-ditch effort to revitalise an industry on its last legs. Still the decline continued, and now these new arrivals were impacted too. Between 1971 and 1991, 15,000 jobs in the Oldham textile industry disappeared; in 1980 alone 11 mills closed, cutting the size of the town's industry by 30 per cent.[16]

Like other Lancashire towns, Oldham was not immune to racist violence. Deej Malik Johnson, of mixed West Indian and English ancestry, recalled his first day at school. 'I learned racism straight there. Being called the P-word. The other kids would hit me and my mate Samuel who was the other mixed-race lad with sticks', he recalled. 'We would get this crap all the time. There was National Front graffiti. Oldham was never a safe place to be in as a person of colour.'[17]

On 26 July 1989 14-year-old Tahir Akram was brutally murdered in the predominantly Pakistani area of Glodwick by a group of armed white youths. Akram had gone to post a letter for his father when the attack took place: from a passing vehicle, he was cold-bloodedly shot in the neck and died before reaching hospital. Despite the fact that his attackers had previously shot and injured Vincent Grady, an African man, and Abdul Gafor Rajpoot, an Asian youth, both the local police and the press denied that the murder was racially motivated. When the Asian community planned a protest in the murder's aftermath it had to be called off in the face of massive hostility from the town's authorities and the local press.[18]

This wasn't the only incident in the town to hit the news: five years earlier, in nearby Burnage, 13-year-old Ahmed Iqbal Ullah was murdered in a school playground after defending younger Asian boys from racist bullying, while a year later, in Glodwick, 15-year-old Nusser Rafiq suffered a broken bone and extensive bruising after he was hit by a car as he made his way home from school. The driver, described as a 16-year-old white male, yelled 'Black bastard' at Nusser before running him down and dragging him ten feet.[19] There was also the case of Gulfraz Nazir and his family, who had been subjected to years of racial harassment by gangs of racist youths armed with crowbars and hammers, who regularly tried to attack their shop in the predominantly white area of Limeside in Oldham. When the police were called, they failed to turn up in time to make a difference. Finally, in 1999, Nazir organised with friends to defend his family from the gangs. The result was a running battle on the streets between armed white youths and Asians.

With the continuing failure of the police and the authorities to tackle the racists, violent confrontations between groups of whites and Asians became more common. Inevitably when the police did arrive to break up a mêlée, it was the Asians who bore the brunt of police heavy-handedness. Soon the police and the local newspapers began to portray Asians as the perpetrators, rather than the victims.[20]

Institutional racism was baked into housing allocation too. In the 1960s and 1970s Pakistani and Bangladeshi workers settled in and around the town centre in areas such as Glodwick and Westwood, conveniently close to the textile mills that employed them. White residents were able to move to the suburbs and access council housing, while Asians, with larger families, faced longer waiting times – and discrimination too.

A formal investigation by the Commission for Racial Equality into the local authority's housing allocations in 1991 found that the council was discriminating against Asian applicants by segregating them from white households into the centre of town and placing them in lower-quality housing on the Clarkwell and Waterloo Street estates. The council had also failed to review its allocation policy and its ethnic data on households.[21]

As in London, the Asians who did get council housing on predominantly white estates faced racist violence, with many instead opting for the safety of their own areas. And this segregation in housing inevitably led to segregation in education, with some school catchment areas containing near 100 per cent populations of just one ethnic group. Even in mixed areas, white parents could opt for separate schools.

It was this segregation, rooted in racism, that would lead to an escalation in racial tension in the years that followed. For young Asians, youth unemployment remained high and educational attainment low. There were few opportunities outside of poorly paid work and growing resentment at perceived neglect from people in positions of power. The Alexandra, Coldhurst and Werneth wards of Oldham, where South Asians disproportionately resided, ranked among the most deprived 1 per cent nationally on the UK government's Indices of Deprivation 2000.

Unlike the 1970s and 1980s, the South Asian community was much larger and much more assertive. When racist gangs attacked, Asian gangs fought back with even greater ferocity. The segregation of communities led to mutual distrust, while sensationalist media narratives about no-go areas and police narratives minimising racist attacks on Asians while sensationalising Asian-on-white attacks exacerbated tensions. In 1999 Oldham's police chief superintendent, Eric Hewit, released figures which stated that out of 250 racially motivated incidents in one year, the majority involved violence against whites by Asians.[22] He then used these figures to argue that the real problem was not racial attacks against Asians, but crimes committed by Asian gangs. The local press lapped it up; the *Lancashire Evening Chronicle* ran a front page story with the headline 'Violent racial crime rockets: three out of four victims are white', while the *Oldham*

Evening Chronicle had 'Fears growing over plague of racist attacks by Asian gangs'.[23] Yet the truth behind the sensationalism was that Asian victims of racism had long since given up reporting incidents to the police; when they did report incidents, they were not always recorded as racist attacks. The mugging of a white victim by an Asian gang would, however, be recorded as a racially motivated assault. It would also be reported that way in the local press, while racist attacks on Asian taxi drivers barely got a mention.

As the writer Arun Kundnani observed at the time, there were also tensions within South Asian communities:

> This new generation had also been sold short by its own self-appointed community leaders. The state's response to earlier unrest had been to nurture a black elite which could manage and contain anger from within the ranks of black communities. Where a middle class existed it was co-opted; where one did not, it was created. A new class of 'ethnic representatives' entered the town halls from the mid-1980s onwards, who would be the surrogate voice for their own ethnically-defined fiefdoms. They entered into a pact with the authorities; they were to cover up and gloss over black community resistance in return for free rein in preserving their own patriarchy. It was a colonial arrangement which prevented community leaders from making radical criticisms, for fear that funding for their pet projects would be jeopardised. The authorities hoped that if they threw some money at the bigwig blacks, they would stop complaining. And the community leaders proved them right.[24]

Authority within and outside the Asian community had little credibility or respect from an increasingly rebellious youth and they were left with few resources too. 'The result', Kundnani wrote,

> was that black communities became fragmented, horizontally by ethnicity, vertically by class. Different ethnic groups were pressed into competing for grants for their areas.

> The poor and the still poorer fought over the scraps of the paltry regeneration monies that the government made available to keep them quiet. Money that did come in was spent, after empty 'community consultation exercises', on projects that brought little benefit, particularly to the increasingly restive youths. Worst of all, the problem of racism came to be redefined in terms of ethnic recognition so that to tackle racism was to fund an ethnic project, any ethnic project, no matter how dubious.[25]

In Oldham, the British National Party began to argue that it only had a problem with Muslims, not African-Caribbeans or Hindus and Sikhs. Islam, it claimed, was an inherently separatist and dangerous religion, while focusing on 'Muslims' rather than Pakistanis and Bangladeshis helped them to avoid anti-racism legislation.

Baseless myths soon began to circulate in white areas that Pakistanis disproportionately received funding, especially for the construction of mosques. Despite this, the evidence suggested the opposite: 52 per cent of Pakistanis and 61 per cent of Bangladeshis lived in the worst 10 per cent of deprived areas, compared to 7 per cent of white residents, according to the deprivation index used by Oldham Council.[26] Yet in the six years prior to the riots of 2001, the majority of regeneration grants went into predominantly white areas. Westwood and Glodwick received £16 million in 1995/96, whereas Hathershaw and Fitton Hill – predominantly white areas – received £53 million.[27]

The result of this could be seen on Saturday 28 April 2001, when, both before and after the Oldham Athletic v. Stoke City football match, there were a number of racist incidents, including racist abuse by Stoke fans walking towards the ground. Bangladeshi youths fought back, throwing petrol bombs and attacking a pub. Later, in another precursor of what was to come, the National Front attempted to hold a series of marches in defiance of a three-month ban on political marches by the home secretary. They were opposed by the Anti-Nazi League and groups of young Asian men.

Things reached a head on Saturday 26 May, after a group of twenty football supporters were observed during the day drinking in local pubs, and one was arrested for racist chanting. Later that same day a fight broke out between an Asian youth and a white youth. Family and friends joined in, some summoned by mobile phone, including some of the football supporters, who attacked Asian houses in the street. Bricks were put through windows, doors kicked and cars damaged, before the attackers were challenged by a group of Asian men.

Soon news spread that Farida Azan, who was seven months pregnant, had been showered with glass when a group chanting racist abuse smashed her front window. Another Asian woman sat in her car clutching her baby while yobs jumped on the bonnet and glass smashed around her.[28] The police responded by donning riot gear, arresting Asians who fought back and attempting to disperse the increasingly angered crowds of local residents. Soon there were violent clashes between local Asian youths and the police too.

As the night went on the disorder escalated. Some of the Asian men attacked the Live and Let Live pub as they returned to Glodwick, where a large group assembled in Waterloo Street to march towards the town centre. Cars were overturned and destroyed. In the days that followed further incidents broke out, including the firebombing of the *Oldham Evening Chronicle* offices as well as the house of the deputy mayor, Councillor Riaz Ahmad.

Soon these scenes would spread, first to Burnley and Leeds in June, and then Bradford in July. Though they all had their own specific local triggers, there were many similarities. In each place, disillusioned young Asians, tired of racist gangs, police heavy-handedness and lack of opportunity, took to the streets tooled up and ready to push back against anyone who got in their way.

Asad Rehman was in Burnley during the riots. He recalled racist thugs targeting Asians in the predominantly white working-class Burnley Wood area. 'They were systematically trying to burn people out of their homes. People's cars were being burnt out. Windows were being put in. Families were basically jumping out of the back. They knew where the Asian families were and were targeting them.' By this point he was working for the Newham Monitoring Project, which often found itself assisting communities across Britain, particularly when it came to legal advocacy work. 'For me, the saddest thing about that period is actually the fact that so many young people ended up with criminal offences and spent and did time', he told me. 'If there had been the equivalent of what we had in the 80s, they would have run a community self-defence campaign. They would have got really good lawyers, and half those kids would never have spent prison time.'

Seeking to make an example out of the youths, the sentences that many of those involved received were harsh. One individual was given four years for throwing three stones, another was sentenced to eleven months in jail for picking up, but not throwing, two stones. 'In Oldham and in Bradford, there was no organised political defence', Rehman said. 'It ended up with everybody fighting individual criminal charges. So lots of people went down.'

> In Burnley, we ran a political defence campaign and most of the young people got off the charges. The difference was when these things had happened in the past, we had organised

communities and groups like the Asian Youth Movements so the resistance was much more structured and understood. There was more of a concept of community self-defence.

***

A few months after the 2001 riots in the north of England, the 9/11 attacks took place in New York. Overnight, Muslims became public enemy number one. Fear, distrust and suspicion greeted the ever-growing Muslim community and racist attacks intensified.

In the years leading up to this, the BNP had increasingly turned its attention to electoral politics, seeking to capitalise on white working-class disillusionment with the Labour Party. Influenced by Le Pen's National Front in France, the party launched a campaign against Islam, and in the 2002 local elections the party gained three councillors in Burnley. A year later it would do better again, gaining an additional 13 councillors in the town. It would even spread its influence to London and Brussels: in 2009 the BNP gained a seat on the London Assembly as well as two members of the European Parliament. It would go on to win half a million votes in the 2010 general election.

Despite these alarming electoral gains, the prevalent narrative was that overt street racism was on the decline. The days of the National Front marching into Black and Asian communities appeared to be over. But it didn't take long for a new far-right movement to take to the streets yet again.

I was 12 years old when the English Defence League marched through Luton. I still remember my science teacher pleading with us on a Friday afternoon not to venture into the town centre the following day. I'd never seen so many police officers in my life. That same day, as EDL members roamed the streets chanting anti-Muslim slogans,

Prime Minister David Cameron declared that state multiculturalism had failed. Future London mayor Sadiq Khan publicly criticised the speech, accusing Cameron of writing propaganda material for the EDL.[29]

There was, indeed, plenty of propaganda in the British press bolstering the EDL's rise. In the years leading up to that day, tabloid papers such as the *Sun* and the *Daily Mail* routinely demonised Muslims. Local loudmouth Tommy Robinson, who set up the EDL in an abandoned Luton warehouse in 2009, claimed to be taking on the political establishment, which he claimed had silenced criticism of Islam. In reality, politicians and pundits had routinely demonised Muslims and legitimised bigotry. The EDL built an online presence on Facebook and began recruiting from football hooligan firms to establish a serious street presence. There were fears that Luton could explode into violence.

In the end, however, there were no scenes reminiscent of 2001. Anti-fascist activists occupied the railway station to prevent EDL members from entering the town. Two large counter-protests, one in Bury Park (the heart of the Asian community) and another in the town centre, outnumbered the 3,000 EDL supporters who had descended on Luton. Balwinder Rana, founder of the Kent Asian Youth Federation in 1969, helped organise the counter-demonstration and led a Sikhs Against the English Defence League contingent, opposing Tommy Robinson's attempts to recruit Sikhs into his anti-Muslim campaign. Fahim Qureshi of the Luton Youth Movement recalled the defiance of local youths: 'There were 3,000 Asian youths who stood in Bury Park, the very heart of the Asian community, and blocked the whole of Dunstable Road to prevent the EDL coming into the area.'[30]

The episode got me and my peers asking questions. Who were the EDL? What exactly were they defending? Why did they hate us? In the years that followed, there were more EDL marches. Then, as the EDL began to splinter, other groups such as Britain First and the Football Lads Alliance filled the void.

Questions of identity surfaced early. I attended an all-boys state comprehensive in Luton. Almost every student was Muslim, either Pakistani or Bangladeshi. Naturally, we gravitated towards a sense of Muslim identity. Groups such as the Muslim Defence League emerged in Birmingham, Bolton and Stoke, composed mainly of Asian youths who wanted to resist the EDL. The logic was simple: if we are attacked as Muslims, we will defend ourselves as Muslims.

Then there were events overseas. On Eid, we would hear our uncles rail against Western imperialism in our living rooms. Many of us couldn't point to Iraq or Afghanistan on a map but we knew they symbolised the West's oppression of Muslims. A small minority were drawn to extremist groups advocating jihad; others, like me, found common cause with the British left, which emphasised anti-imperialism and showed concern for working-class communities struggling with deindustrialisation and poverty.

In 2014 Israel launched Operation Protective Edge, killing over 2,000 Palestinians in Gaza. I vividly remember seeing a news report of four children killed while playing football on a beach. I felt helpless and desperate to act. A group of us handed out Palestine badges and leaflets at school, drawing the attention of senior staff. The recent Trojan Horse scandal in Birmingham had heightened fears of Muslim political activity, and the media had grown obsessed with ISIS, particularly stories of young Muslims joining their ranks. State surveillance became tangible. Police visited classmates' homes for wearing Palestine badges, and our school even had a special constable stationed on site.

We resented the state. Labour and Conservative alike sounded the same, making party politics largely irrelevant. Foreign policy, however, mobilised young Muslims in ways domestic politics rarely could. A generation before us had marched against the Iraq War; some had even organised school strikes. Many of us did take an interest in current affairs even if the organisations such as the Asian youth movements that had once offered a space to channel that interest into something meaningful no longer existed.

For a lot of people in towns like mine, the notion of a unified Asian identity didn't really exist. Though there were many shared cultural interests and tastes, there were widening class divides too. We heard stories of Pakistani landlords exploiting Pakistani tenants, Indian managers exploiting Indian workers, takeaways paying illegal migrants £2 an hour.

The 2016 EU referendum told another story. Far from a story of white working-class anger, many Asians, of varying religious and class backgrounds, also voted Leave. Towns such as Luton, Bradford and Birmingham voted for Brexit. Still, it was frequently said that the era of 'Paki-bashing' was a distant memory. That racism was 'not in your face' any more. There were early warning signs that this was not the reality. Alongside the racist murders of people such as Mohammed Saleem in 2013 and Muhsin Ahmed in 2015, there was an increase in racist hate crime both after the EU referendum result and during the height of the pandemic.

In August 2024 violent, racially motivated attacks returned with shocking ferocity.

EPILOGUE

'People here are tired, scared and feel forgotten.' I'm in Basildon, Essex, speaking to a Muslim woman, Nabila,[1] about rising racist violence. It's November 2025 and she's reeling off a number of racist incidents that have occurred in the past few months. A man throwing glass projectiles from a residential building at Muslim children, a 7-year-old girl developing an anxiety disorder and sleeping problems after her mum was followed in a Tesco car park, drivers speeding up when hijab-wearing Muslim women cross the road and refusing to stop at zebra crossings.

Nabila is exhausted. She's been called the P-word, feels increasingly unsafe and tells me the real impact of such abuse. Almost all of it is directed at Muslim women, often in front of their own children. It affects their everyday lives. One woman has stopped going to her favourite park after several racist incidents; another stopped doing the school run for two weeks after vile racist abuse. Kids are bullied at school, and women constantly watch over their shoulders. The local mosque, meanwhile, has been targeted with racist graffiti.

'My wife and baby are growing up here', one Muslim man told me in the aftermath of the incident in late August. 'I want to move out of the area. I just cannot stay here.'

Nabila is not just a victim. She's a hero. She invites me to attend a listening circle where other Muslim women are sharing their experiences of racist abuse and calling on the council and the police to act on such incidents. She offers to drive Muslim women to the meeting, takes minutes, and she has shared a detailed report with me outlining several racist incidents and testimonies from victims. She does this work unpaid, on top of raising two children as a single mum.

She wanted to hold the meeting at the local mosque but they refused to give her the space. It's not the first time she's had run-ins with the mosque committee. At Friday prayers, the chair reiterates what he told me a few months earlier when I reported on the attack on the mosque. 'There's no Islamophobia here. Get your facts right. We have a good relationship with the council. We don't want any issues.'

People like him are often positioned as spokesmen for the Muslim community. I say men because they are almost always men. They are positioned as the community leaders while women barely get a hearing. Nearly twenty-five years on from Arun Kundnani's analysis of the damage that self-proclaimed community leaders and gatekeepers have caused to British South Asian communities, I'm seeing it play out in front of me.

A quick Google search tells you that there have indeed been several racist incidents in Basildon in recent years. This dynamic is not unique to Basildon. Far too often, when the racists have marched through British towns and cities, there have been voices who have cautioned against taking action. Some have come from a place of concern. They fear for their child's safety. They don't want their kids facing jail time as we saw in the aftermath of the 2001 riots. But too often, the failure of leadership has emboldened racists and made communities more vulnerable to racist violence.

Today, even with the shocking racist riots of 2024 and the increasingly brazen and unapologetic racist narratives from politicians and pundits alike, ignorance remains about the experiences of smaller, more geographically isolated Black and Asian communities in Britain. Strength in numbers in large multicultural towns and cities has bred complacency. From Brick Lane to Bradford, a generation of young South Asian people are growing up without truly understanding the gravity of the word Paki. Occasionally, they may get a glimpse from their elders of what life was like in the 1970s and 1980s, but that is totally different from having to live through the era.

There are lessons here for those actively involved in anti-racist activism today. Many South Asians will come out to defend their own communities when required, but few consider themselves part of a national anti-racist movement. Political blackness, the banner under which Black and Asian people organised collectively, no longer holds currency. It's a concept that few Black and Asian people relate to in Britain today. The catch-all term 'BAME' can also mask both inequalities and tensions that exist within ethnic minority communities. Those tensions have, at times, resulted in violence between these communities, as demonstrated by the 2005 Handsworth riots between Birmingham's long-established Pakistani and West Indian communities, and the 2022 Leicester disturbances between Muslims and Hindus.

And then, of course, there's the growing class divide within the South Asian community. British South Asians increasingly have competing interests and contrasting fortunes. What does Rishi Sunak becoming Britain's first Asian prime minister mean for an exploited Asian woman working in the garment industry for £2 an hour? What is the point of four Asian home secretaries since 2018 who have all made life harder for migrants and the children of migrants who come after them? Why would working-class South Asians celebrate the growing number of Asian billionaires in Britain when the majority of South Asians remain low-wage earners? According to the Child Poverty Action Group, 67 per cent of Bangladeshi children and 58 per cent of Pakistani children live in poverty.[2] A recent study by the Fawcett Society also found that women of Bangladeshi and Pakistani heritage in the UK earn almost one-third less per hour than white British men.[3]

***

The anti-racist movement in Britain today remains dominated by the white left. Too often it lacks credibility and clout in Black and Asian working-class communities. There are many anti-racist marches but not so many monitoring groups and community-organising initiatives.

Many questions are raised by recent developments. Do we need a form of political organising that transcends the confines of identity given that so many who share our skin colour are aiding and abetting the racist atmosphere in Britain? And what does that look like?

Perhaps what we require is a strategic approach to anti-racist organising, one that allows for constructive criticism and a plurality of tactics and approaches to defeat racism. One lesson we can draw from the histories discussed in these pages is that we cannot allow disagreement in terms of tactics and methods to develop into a much nastier sectarian divide. Another lesson is to prioritise time, energy and resources based on where the real threat is. It's easier to mobilise in diverse urban areas, but what about the smaller, more isolated Black and Asian communities, which, in the words of Nabila, feel hopeless? Who will inspire them? Who will support them? Who will protect them when they're on the receiving end of racist violence?

The Asian youth movements often supported families on outlying housing estates who were vulnerable to racist violence. In an era without social media, they were able to connect with activists and victims of racist violence up and down the country. Their resourcefulness at a time when Asians had few resources is inspiring. Today, when there are much greater resources among British South Asians both in terms of wealth and technology, what might our resistance look like? Who is doing the work of connecting communities up and down the country? And how do we navigate new challenges in the form of religious divides and the growing number of South Asians being influenced by far-right narratives about newcomers?

People such as Suresh Grover of the Southall Monitoring Project are figuring out some of the answers to these questions. Others, with a radical past, have retreated from the battlefield, preferring to settle for cosy community relations and council jobs. People are complex, and while I've highlighted many inspiring examples of individuals who contributed to the anti-racist struggle, some betrayed their earlier principles in their later lives. Lala Har Dayal, for instance, the publisher of the radical *Ghadar* newspaper in the early twentieth century, later renounced his youthful radicalism. Avtar Singh Jouhl, from 1960s Birmingham, accepted an OBE despite the IWA's rich history of anti-imperialism. Unmesh Desai, when he became a councillor, cut funding to the Newham Monitoring Project despite once being a leading figure in it.

In telling the inspiring stories of the past, we cannot also shy away from the contradictions. Misogyny, casteism and corruption weakened the movements. Many let their egos get ahead of building unity in the service of the anti-racist struggle. Some hold grudges to the present day. In some ways, these historical contradictions and conflicts, which still plague movements today, offer a degree of hope. That the challenges we face are not unprecedented and that generations before us were navigating similar struggles and had to figure out ways to overcome them.

A generation before me learned from both the successes and failures of the generation that came before them. And they, in turn, learned from those that came before them. As Mukhtar Dar reflected:

> We in our generation stood on the shoulders of giants; we learned from them and organised to take the struggle forward. My message to young people today is that we have a legacy, a glorious history of struggle. Take that forward. Use it as a bulwark to inform you, to inspire you, and to organise. The struggle in itself was a creative process. In our most inspired moments, we imagined a world free of exploitation and oppression. Study the great strides forward by human beings around the world where people tried to change the course of history to create a more egalitarian society, and learn from their shortcomings as well as their achievements. Don't just be aware of what you are fighting against. The most important task is to know what you are fighting for.[4]

Fahim Qureshi of the Luton Youth Movement offers a similarly urgent call to the youth of today: 'Come out and organise, Take up the baton. We're sleepwalking into disaster if we don't organise ourselves and confront racism. It's only because we confronted racism in the streets and politically that there were changes made at that time; we need to do the same thing now.'[5]

This book is my attempt to shine a light on the lives and experience of those who came before us, not as passive subjects of racism and colonialism, but as active agents of change. History did not simply happen to them. They shaped it through courage, creativity and collective action. And in the same way, history is being shaped now.

As racism rears its ugly head with increasing ferocity, will we learn the lessons of the past or repeat the same mistakes? The next chapter of this story will be shaped by us and the lesson from history is clear: Racism will not be defeated from above. It will only be defeated by us – ordinary citizens who refuse to look away.

LIST OF INTERVIEWEES

Mohammed Ashraf (2025)
Halima Begum (2025)
Mukhtar Dar (2020, 2023, 2024)
Unmesh Desai (2025)
Hardev Dhillon (2023)
Suresh Grover (2025)
Shirin Housee (2025)
Matloub Husayn-Ali-Khan (2024)
Muhammad Ikram (2025)
Rajon Uddin Jalal (2024)
Deej Malik Johnson (2024)
Badsha Khandaker (2024)
Paul Mackney (2024)
Masood Malik (2022)
Tariq Mehmood (2022)
Raj Mistry (2024)
Pragna Patel (2025)
Balraj Purewal (2025)
Fahim Qureshi (2019, 2022)
Balwinder Rana (2020, 2022)
Heather Rawling (2024)
Asad Rehman (2024, 2025)
Iram Syed (2025)
Nishaharan Vaithilingam (2024)
Amrit Wilson (2024, 2025)

NOTES

PREFACE

1 Jane Howard, 'Doom and glory of knowing who you are', *Life Magazine*, 24 May 1963.

PROLOGUE

1 A. Sivanandan, 'On lived theory – an interview', Institute of Race Relations archive.
2 Edward Vibart, *The Sepoy Mutiny as Seen by a Subaltern: From Delhi to Lucknow* (London: Smith, Elder & Co., 1898), pp. 149–50.
3 Utsa Panik, 'Revisiting the "drain", or transfer from India to Britain in the context of global diffusion of capitalism', in Shubhra Chakrabarti and Utsa Patnaik (eds), *Agrarian and Other Histories: Essays for Binay Bhushan Chaudhuri* (New Delhi: Tulika Books, 2017).
4 C. Bates, 'The history of South Asian global migration', in M. J. Borges and M. Y. Hsu (eds), *The Cambridge History of Global Migrations Volume 2: Migrations, 1800–Present* (Cambridge: Cambridge University Press, 2023), p. 74.
5 Naresh Chandra Sourabh and Timo Myllyntaus, 'Famines in Late Nineteenth-Century India: Politics, Culture, and Environmental Justice', virtual exhibition, 28 July 2015, Rachel Carson Center for Environment and Society, https://www.environmentandsociety.org/exhibitions/famines-india (accessed 24 March 2026).

1 THE HIGHGATE REVOLUTIONARIES

1 *The Indian Sociologist: An Organ of Freedom, and Political, Social and Religious Reform*, 1, no. 1, January 1905.

2 Indulal Yajnik, *Shayamji Krishnavarma: Life and Times of an Indian Revolutionary* (Bombay: Lakshmi Publications, 1950), p. 130.

3 Lokmanya Tilak, letter to Shyamji Krishnavarma, 10 July 1905, in Bal Gangadhar Tilak and M. D. Vidwans (eds), *Letters of Lokmanya Tilak* (Poona: Kesari Prakashan, c. 1966), pp. 255–6; British Library (BL), Oriental and India Office Collections (OIOC), India (Pondicherry), 5 November 1908, NNR Madras, 12 December 1908, L/R/5/113.

4 *The Indian Sociologist*, August 1905.

5 *The Indian Sociologist*, August 1906.

6 James D. Hunt, *Gandhi in London* (London: Promilla, 1993), p. 94.

7 *The Indian Sociologist*, October 1906.

8 O. B. Laursen, 'Spaces of Indian anti-colonialism in early twentieth-century London and Paris', *South Asia: Journal of South Asian Studies*, 44, no. 4 (2021), p. 628, https://doi.org/10.1080/00856401.2021.1943773.

9 Harindra Srivastava, *Five Stormy Years: Savarkar in London (June 1906–June 1911)* (New Delhi: Allied Publishers, 1983).

10 Rozina Visram, *Asians in Britain: 400 Years of History* (London: Pluto, 2002), p. 92.

11 *The Indian Sociologist*, August 1907.

12 Richard J. Popplewell, *Intelligence and Imperial Defence: British Intelligence and the Defence of the Indian Empire 1904–1924* (Abingdon: Routledge, 1995), p. 128.

13 Vinayak Damodar Savarkar, *Newsletters from London*, 5 June 1908, BJP eLibrary, https://library.bjp.org/jspui/handle/123456789/291 (accessed 24 March 2026).

14 Savarkar, *Newsletters from London*, 5 June 1908.

15 David Garnett, *The Golden Echo* (London: Chatto & Windus, 1953), vol. I, p. 145.

16 Visram, *Asians in Britain*, p. 155.

17 BL, War Department, Records of the Commander in India (WDRCI), 12 December 1908, Neg. 3094–3096, India Office Records (IOR); WRDCI, 26 December 1908, Neg. 3094–3096, IOR; 'Establishment of a Miniature Rifle Range at India House, Highgate', IOR/L/PJ/6/920, file 384.

18 Detective Chief Inspector's report, 4 September 1909, HPB, October 1909, 110; 'Information about the Revolutionary Party in London given by H.K. Koregaonkar of the India House', 1910, BL, IOR/R/1/1/1076, file Con B I A 4; Peter Heehs, *The Bomb in Bengal: The Rise of Revolutionary Terrorism in India, 1900–1910* (New York: Oxford University Press, 1993).

19 'Information about the Revolutionary Party'.
20 'Information about the Revolutionary Party'.
21 V. D. Savarkar, *The Indian War of Independence, 1857* (London: n.p., 1909), p. 50.
22 Garnett, *The Golden Echo*, vol. I, p. 145.
23 R. A. Padmanabhan, *V. V. S. Aiyar* (New Delhi: National Book Trust India, 1980), p. 34.
24 Padmanabhan, *V. V. S. Aiyar*, p. 36.
25 Padmanabhan, *V. V. S. Aiyar*, p. 41.
26 Popplewell, *Intelligence and Imperial Defence*, p. 129.
27 Nicholas Owen, *The British Left and India: Metropolitan Anti-Imperialism, 1885–1947* (Oxford: Oxford University Press, 2007), p. 73.
28 BL, WDRCI, 12 June 1909, Neg. 3094–3096, IOR.
29 Popplewell, *Intelligence and Imperial Defence*, p. 129.
30 Popplewell, *Intelligence and Imperial Defence*, p. 129.
31 Savarkar, *The Indian War of Independence*, p. 443.
32 Alex Tickell, *Terrorism, Insurgency and Indian-English Literature, 1830–1947* (Abingdon: Routledge, 2011), p. 135.
33 'Dhingra, Madar Lal', Proceedings of the Central Criminal Court, 23 July 1909, *Old Bailey Proceedings Online*, sessions paper t19090719, https://www.oldbaileyonline.org/record/t19090719 (accessed 3 March 2026).
34 'Trial of Dhingra', *Manchester Guardian*, 24 July 1909, pp. 8–9; 'Dhingra, Madar Lal', Proceedings of the Central Criminal Court, 23 July 1909.
35 Garnett, *The Golden Echo*, vol. I, p. 153.
36 *The Times*, 7 July 1909.
37 Owen, *The British Left and India*, p. 75; Mohandas K. Gandhi, 'Curzon Wyllie's Assassination', after 16 July 1909, in *The Collected Works of Mahatma Gandhi* (*CWMG*), E9/245; 'Dhingra Case', 23 July 1909, *CWMG*, E9/252; Gandhi to Kallenbach, 7 August 1909, *CWMG*, P96/15.
38 Mohandas K. Gandhi, letter to Lord Ampthill, 30 October 1909, *CWMG*, vol. 9, p. 508.

2 PUNJABI PIONEERS

1 Maia Ramnath, *Haj to Utopia: How the Ghadar Movement Charted Global Radicalism and Attempted to Overthrow the British Empire* (Berkeley: University of California Press, 2011), p. 24.
2 Harish K. Puri, 'Revolutionary organization: a study of the Ghadar movement', *Social Scientist*, 9, no. 2/3 (1980), p. 56.

3 Savitri Sawhney, *I Shall Never Ask for Pardon* (New Delhi: Penguin, 2008), p. 82.
4 Puri, 'Revolutionary organization', p. 59.
5 Anita Anand, *The Patient Assassin* (London: Simon & Schuster, 2019), p. 197.
6 *R.* v. *Udham Singh*, Central Criminal Court (Old Bailey), 4–5 June 1940, The National Archives, Kew, London (TNA), DPP 2/728.
7 N. V. Rajkumar, *Indians Outside India: A General Survey* (Foreign Department, Indian National Congress, 1951).
8 BL, African and Asian Studies Reading Room, IOR/L/PJ/12/645.
9 Silas Webb, '"The typical Ghadar outlook": Udham Singh, diaspora radicalism, and Punjabi anticolonialism in Britain (1938–1947)', *Socialist Studies*, 13, no. 2 (2018), pp. 41–4.
10 'Indian Workers' Union or Association: Reports on Members and Activities', 1942–1947, BL, IOR/L/PJ/12/645.
11 Rozina Visram, *Asians in Britain: 400 Years of History* (London: Pluto, 2002), p. 271.
12 Visram, *Asians in Britain*, p. 267.
13 The ILP was a socialist political party which sought to increase working-class representation in Parliament. It helped set up and heavily influenced the contemporary Labour Party before disaffiliating due to ideological differences in 1932.
14 'Indian Workers' Union or Association: Reports on Members and Activities', 1942–1947, BL, IOR/L/PJ/12/645.
15 'Indian Workers' Union or Association: Reports on Members and Activities', 1942–1947, BL, IOR/L/PJ/12/645.
16 Amartya Sen, *Poverty and Famines: An Essay on Entitlement and Deprivation* (Oxford: Oxford University Press, 1982), p. 52.
17 'Indian Workers' Union or Association: Reports on Members and Activities', 1942–1947, BL, IOR/L/PJ/12/645.
18 'Indian Activities', 1 June 1945, BL, IOR/L/PJ/12/646.
19 David Petrie, letter to Alexander Maxwell, 15 January 1946, TNA, HO 45/25460.
20 IPI to Mr Silver, 20 March 1942, BL, IOR/L/PJ/12/645.
21 'Indian Workers' Union or Association: Reports on Members and Activities', 1942–1947, BL, IOR/L/PJ/12/645
22 'Indian Notes', 14 November 1942, BL, IOR/L/PJ/12/646.

3 SEAFARER STRUGGLES

1 Joseph Salter and R. Marsh Hughes, *The Asiatic in England: sketches of sixteen years' work among Orientals* (London: Seeley, Jackson and Halliday, 1873), pp. 150–1; see also Rozina Visram,

Ayahs, Lascars and Princes: Indians in Britain, 1700–1947 (London: Pluto, 1987), p. 35.

2 Visram, *Ayahs, Lascars and Princes*, p. 36.

3 Joseph Salter, *The East in the West; or, Work Among the Asiatics and Africans in London* (London: S. W. Partridge, 1895/1896), p. 16.

4 'Lascars' grievances', *Dundee Courier*, 6 May 1901.

5 TNA, ASSI 52/212/17.

6 TNA, HO 144/1106/200455.

7 Sophia Duleep Singh, message written on her 1911 Census return, Faraday House, Hampton Court, TNA, RG 14/3561.

8 Anita Anand, *Sophia: Princess, Suffragette, Revolutionary* (London: Bloomsbury, 2015).

9 Visram, *Ayahs, Lascars and Princes*, p. 253.

10 Tanroop Sandhu, 'The Indian and British Workers' candidate', *Tribune*, 15 May 2024, www.tribunemag.co.uk/2024/05/the-indian-and-british-workers-candidate (accessed 4 March 2026).

11 Shapurji Saklatvala, 'India in the Labour world', *The Labour Monthly*, 1, no. 5 (1921), pp. 440–51.

12 'Colored population elated over Labor victory', *The Savannah Tribune*, 30 November 1922.

13 Jacob Zumoff, *The Communist International and US Communism, 1919–1929* (Leiden: Brill, 2014), p. 325.

14 TNA, KV2/614, 275–277, 'From J Potter Wilson to Saklatvala', 24 September 1921.

15 Anthony Cox, *Empire, Industry and Class: The Imperial Nexus of Jute, 1840–1940* (Abingdon: Routledge, 2013), pp. 139–41.

16 Daniel Edmonds, 'Shapurji Saklatvala, the Workers' Welfare League of India, and transnational anti-colonial labour organising in the inter-war period', *Twentieth Century Communism*, 2020, no. 18 (2020), p. 21.

17 Edmonds, 'Shapurji Saklatvala', p. 22.

18 BL, IOR/L/P&J/12/143.

19 Caroline Adams, *Across Seven Seas and Thirteen Rivers: Life Stories of Pioneer Sylheti Settlers in Britain* (London: Eastside Books, 1994), p. 42.

20 Visram, *Ayahs, Lascars and Princes*, p. 231.

21 BL, IOR/L/P&J/12/234.

22 Visram, *Ayahs, Lascars and Princes*, p. 232.

23 Sir Frederick Hall, question concerning N. J. Upadhyaya and agitation among Indian seamen, HC Deb, 17 June 1927, Hansard, vol. 208.

24 Adams, *Across Seven Seas*, p. 41.

25 Adams, *Across Seven Seas*, p. 42.

26 Shapurji Saklatvala, 'A few thoughts on Party work', *Daily Worker*, 20 July 1934, RGASPI 495/100/938.
27 D. Featherstone, 'Maritime labour, circulations of struggle, and constructions of transnational subaltern agency: the spatial politics of the 1939 Indian seafarers' strikes', *Antipode: A Radical Journal of Geography*, 55, no. 5 (2023), pp. 1411–32.
28 Glasgow Trades and Labour Council Minutes, 23 August 1939, Glasgow Trades Council Minute Book (Glasgow Trades Council archives).
29 Adams, *Across Seven Seas*, p. 43.

4 EARLY STRUGGLES IN POST-WAR BRITAIN

1 Campaign Against Racism and Fascism & Southall Rights, *Southall: The Birth of a Black Community* (London: Institute of Race Relations, 1981), p. 1.
2 Peter Fryer, *Staying Power: The History of Black People in Britain* (London: Pluto, 2018), p. 379.
3 Kevin Searle, '"Mixing of the unmixables": the 1949 Causeway Green "riots" in Birmingham', *Race & Class*, 54, no. 3 (2013), pp. 44–64.
4 Zig Layton-Henry, *The Politics of Immigration: Race and Race Relations in Postwar Britain* (London: Wiley-Blackwell, 1992), p. 37.
5 Dilip Hiro, *Black British, White British: A History of Race Relations in Britain* (London: Grafton, 1992), p. 36.
6 Fryer, *Staying Power*, p. 383.
7 Fryer, *Staying Power*, p. 379.
8 Race Today Collective, *The Struggles of Asian Workers in Britain* (London: Creation for Liberation, 1986), p. 8.
9 Race Today Collective, *The Struggles of Asian Workers*, p. 9.
10 Dominic Sandbrook, *White Heat: A History of Britain in the Swinging Sixties* (London: Abacus, 2009), p. 666.
11 Race Today Collective, *The Struggles of Asian Workers*, p. 10.
12 Race Today Collective, *The Struggles of Asian Workers*, p. 10.
13 Harsh Punja, 'The need for unity: an interview with Vishnu Sharma', *Race & Class*, 58, no. 1 (2016), p. 103, https://doi.org/10.1177/0306396816643048.
14 Race Today Collective, *The Struggles of Asian Workers*, p. 10.
15 Roger Cox, interview 2016, quoted in Yuri Prasad, 'Here to stay, here to fight: how Asians transformed the British working class', *International Socialism*, 153, 19 December 2016, http://isj.org.uk/here-to-stay-here-to-fight/ (accessed 4 March 2026).

16 Roger Cox, quoted in Yuri Prasad, 'Here to stay, here to fight'.
17 Roger Cox, quoted in Yuri Prasad, 'Here to stay, here to fight'.
18 Campaign Against Racism and Fascism & Southall Rights, *Southall: The Birth of a Black Community*, p. 15.
19 '"Sit-in" strike at giant mill', *Lancashire Evening Post*, 25 May 1965.
20 *The Guardian*, 9 June 1965.
21 DeWitt John, *Indian Workers' Association in Britain* (Bombay: Oxford University Press, 1969), p. 48.
22 Cyril Dunn, 'How Little India went to the polls', *The Observer*, 28 April 1968.
23 Sasha Josephides, 'Towards a History of the Indian Workers' Association', Research Paper in Ethnic Relations No. 18, Centre for Research in Ethnic Relations, University of Warwick, December 1991, p. 16.
24 Josephides, 'Towards a History of the Indian Workers' Association', p. 16.
25 Benjamin W. Heineman, *The Politics of the Powerless: A Study of the Campaign Against Racial Discrimination* (Oxford: Oxford University Press, 1972), p. 110.
26 Heineman, *The Politics of the Powerless*, p. 110.
27 'The Sikhs of Smethwick', BBC documentary, 2016.
28 Husna Anjum, 'How immigrant workers singing their sorrows in Black Country pubs gave birth to British Bhangra', *Birmingham Live*, 22 September 2024, www.birminghammail.co.uk/black-country/how-immigrant-workers-singing-sorrows-29945522 (accessed 4 March 2026).
29 Avtar Singh Jouhl, quoted in 'Life-long class fighter against racism', interview with Sheila McGregor and Esme Choonara, *International Socialism*, 164, 17 October 2019, http://isj.org.uk/life-long-class-fighter/ (accessed 24 March 2026).
30 Graham Stevenson, *Migrants & the TGWU*, 10 April 2020, https://grahamstevenson.me.uk/2020/04/10/migrants-the-tgwu/ (accessed 24 March 2026).
31 Mark R. Duffield, *Black Radicalism and the Politics of Deindustrialization: The Hidden History of Indian Foundry Workers in the West Midlands* (London: Avebury, 1988), p. 88.
32 Robert Leeson, *Strike: A Live History, 1887–1971* (London: Allen & Unwin, 1973), p. 217. The dispute itself is unnamed in Mathers's recollections.
33 Leeson, *Strike: A Live History*, p. 217.
34 Leeson, *Strike: A Live History*, p. 217.
35 Leeson, *Strike: A Live History*, p. 218.

5 BLACK POWER

1 'Immigrants main election issue at Smethwick', *The Times*, 9 March 1964, p. 5.
2 'The day I called Malcolm X to fight racism in Birmingham's white only pubs', *The Mirror*, 13 June 2015.
3 Tariq Ali, *Street-Fighting Years: An Autobiography of the Sixties* (London: Verso, 1987), p. 104.
4 Martin Luther King, Jr, 'Letter from Birmingham Jail', 16 April 1963.
5 'The day I called Malcolm X to fight racism in Birmingham's white only pubs'.
6 A. Hambler and R. Seifert, 'Wearing the turban: the 1967–1969 Sikh bus drivers dispute in Wolverhampton', *Historical Studies in Industrial Relations*, 37, no. 1 (2016), p. 59; Gurharpal Singh, 'British multiculturalism and Sikhs', *Sikh Formations*, 1, no. 2 (2006), pp. 159–60.
7 *Express and Star*, 25 February 1969.
8 *Express and Star*, 10 March 1969.
9 *Express and Star*, 10 March 1969.
10 *Express and Star*, 8 April 1969.
11 Enoch Powell, speech given to the general meeting of the West Midlands Area Conservative Political Centre, 20 April 1968, Birmingham.
12 National Opinion Poll (NOP) Reports, April 1968: 'Poll on Enoch Powell's immigration views'.
13 Author interview with Balwinder Rana, 2020. Unless otherwise indicated, all subsequent quotes from Balwinder Rana in this chapter are taken from this interview.
14 *Coventry Evening Telegraph*, 29 April 1968, p. 43.
15 *The Sun*, 11 January 1969, pp. 1–2.
16 A. Sivanandan, *A Different Hunger: Writings on Black Resistance* (London: Pluto, 1982), p. 25.
17 'Report of the General Secretary', presented by J. Joshi at the National Conference of the Indian Workers' Association, Nottingham, 7–8 November 1970 (produced by the Central Executive Committee of the Indian Workers' Association, Great Britain), pp. 14–15, Birmingham Library Archives and Heritage Service, Avtar Jouhl and the Indian Workers' Association Collection, File MS 2141-A-1-4.
18 'Man Alive: What's the Truth about Hells Angels and Skinheads?', BBC TV documentary, directed by David Filkin, 1969.
19 Bernard Weinraub, 'Tensions in London's East End', *The New York Times*, 5 April 1970.

20 Weinraub, 'Tensions in London's East End'.
21 Weinraub, 'Tensions in London's East End'.
22 Ishaque (chairman Pakistani Workers' Union) and Alex Hart (chairman Working People's England), 'Bourgeois justice for Pakistani workers', *Red Mole*, vol. 1, 1 May 1970.
23 Stephen Ashe, Satnam Virdee and Laurence Brown, 'Striking back against racist violence in the East End of London, 1968–1970', *Race and Class*, 58, no. 1 (2016), pp. 34–54, https://doi.org/10.1177/0306396816642997.
24 Pakistani Progressive Party leaflet, Institute of Race Relations, File 01/04/04/01/04/01/17.
25 Pakistani Progressive Party leaflet, Institute of Race Relations, File 01/04/04/01/04/01/17.
26 Ishaque and Hart, 'Bourgeois justice for Pakistani workers'.
27 Ishaque and Hart, 'Bourgeois justice for Pakistani workers'.
28 'Protection groups to be formed by Pakistanis', *The Times*, 20 April 1970; 'Pakistanis vote for vigilante force', *The Guardian*, 20 April 1970.
29 Kenneth Leech, *Brick Lane, 1978: The Events and Their Significance* (London: Stepney Books, 1994).
30 'Irish left-wingers to join Pakistani "Bovver" squads', *Daily Telegraph*, cited in Ashe, Virdee and Brown, 'Striking back against racist violence', p. 47.
31 Ashe, Virdee and Brown, 'Striking back against racist violence'.
32 'Rise of race-hate thugs', *Sunday Telegraph*, 12 April 1970, London School of Economics, File SHORE/8/16.
33 'Growing problem of racial violence in London's East End', *Morning Star*, 13 April 1970, London School of Economics, File SHORE/8/16.
34 Quoted in Ashe, Virdee and Brown, 'Striking back against racist violence'.
35 Ishaque and Hart, 'Bourgeois justice for Pakistani workers'.

6 FINDING HOME

1 Adam Almeida, *Pushed to the Margins: A Quantitative Analysis of Gentrification in London in the 2010s* (London: Runnymede Trust and Centre for Labour and Social Studies, 2021).
2 Author interview with Rajon Uddin Jalal, 2024. Unless otherwise indicated, all subsequent quotes from Rajon Uddin Jalal in this chapter are taken from this interview.
3 Shabna Begum, *From Sylhet to Spitalfields: Bengali Squatters in 1970s East London* (London: Lawrence & Wishart, 2023), p. 10.

4 Begum, *From Sylhet to Spitalfields*, p. 66.
5 Author interview with Halima Begum, 2025. Unless otherwise indicated, all subsequent quotes from Halima Begum in this chapter are taken from this interview.
6 Author interview with Mukhtar Dar, 2023. Unless otherwise indicated, all subsequent quotes from Mukhtar Dar in this chapter are taken from this interview.
7 Farrukh Dhondy, *Fragments against my Ruin: A Life* (London: Verso, 2024), p. 182.
8 Begum, *From Sylhet to Spitalfields*, p. 139.
9 For a more detailed history of the Bengali Squatters Movement, see Begum, *From Sylhet to Spitalfields*.
10 League of Nations' Bureau of Statistics, 1936.
11 Race Today Collective, *The Struggles of Asian Workers in Britain* (London: Creation for Liberation, 1986), p. 10.
12 Commission of Industrial Relations, *Report of a Committee of Inquiry into a Dispute between Employees of the Mansfield Hosiery Mills Ltd., Loughborough, and their Employer* (London: HMSO, 1972).
13 *Leicester Mercury*, 24 November 1972.
14 Bennie Bunsee, 'Women in struggle: the strike at Mansfield Hosiery', *Spare Rib*, 21 (1974), p. 19.
15 Mala Sen, 'The strike at Imperial Typewriters', *Race Today*, 6, no. 7 (July 1974).
16 Author interview with Amrit Wilson, 2024.
17 Author interview with Heather Rawling, 2024. Unless otherwise indicated, all subsequent quotes from Heather Rawling in this chapter are taken from this interview.
18 Sen, 'The strike at Imperial Typewriters'.
19 Author interview with Amrit Wilson, 2024.
20 *Race Today*, September 1974.
21 *Race Today*, September 1974.
22 Amrit Wilson, *Finding a Voice: Asian Women in Britain* (Wakefield: Jaraja Press, 2023), p. 74.
23 Anitha Sundari and Ruth Pearson, *Striking Women: Struggles and Strategies of South Asian Women Workers from Grunwick to Gate Gourmet* (London: Lawrence & Wishart, 2018), p. 112.
24 Sundari and Pearson, *Striking Women*, p. 113.
25 Sundari and Pearson, *Striking Women*, p. 120.
26 A. Rossiter, 'Risking gossip and disgrace', *Spare Rib*, 54 (1977), p. 18.
27 Sundari and Pearson, *Striking Women*, p. 114; Scarman Report, 1977, p. 7, https://www.margaretthatcher.org/document%2F11 1943 (accessed 4 March 2026).

28 Sundari and Pearson, *Striking Women*, p. 122.
29 Sundari and Pearson, *Striking Women*, p. 122.
30 'Grunwick gates: the entry to unionisation', *Race Today*, June 1977.
31 Sundari and Pearson, *Striking Women*, p. 123; Scarman Report, 1977, p. 16.
32 *Race Today*, October 1976.
33 Rob Evans, 'Covert police spied on strikers and their supporters in iconic dispute', *The Guardian*, 13 April 2016.
34 Alan Travis and Home Affairs Editor, 'Callaghan had Scargill watched as Grunwick dispute escalated', *The Guardian*, 27 December 2007.
35 A. Klair, 'BME women far more likely to be on zero-hours contracts' (London: Trades Union Congress, 2023).
36 Author interview with Amrit Wilson, 2025. Unless otherwise indicated, all subsequent quotes from Amrit Wilson in this chapter are taken from this interview.
37 W. Savage, 'The use of Depo-Provera in East London', *Fertility and Contraception*, 12, no. 3 (1978), pp. 41–7.

7 FIGHTING BACK

1 *The Observer*, 13 June 1976.
2 Author interview with Suresh Grover, 2025. Unless otherwise indicated, all subsequent quotes from Suresh Grover in this chapter are taken from this interview.
3 Author interview with Balraj Purewal, 2025. Unless otherwise indicated, all subsequent quotes from Balraj Purewal in this chapter are taken from this interview.
4 Balraj Purewal, *Southall Youth Movement 1976–1984* (self-published, n.d.), p. 104.
5 Jay Rayner, 'Blair's Britain', *The Guardian*, 14 March 1999.
6 *London Evening News*, 24 April 1979.
7 John Cass, *Investigation into the Death of Blair Peach*, internal report for the Metropolitan Police Service, completed July 1979; released publicly April 2010.
8 John Rose, 'The Southall Asian Youth Movement', *International Socialism*, 91 (September 1976), pp. 5–6.
9 Author interview with Pragna Patel, 2025. Unless otherwise indicated, all subsequent quotes from Pragna Patel in this chapter are taken from this interview.
10 'Chix workers gain more support', *Socialist Challenge*, 144, 24 April 1980.
11 Author interview with Rajon Uddin Jalal, 2024. Unless otherwise

indicated, all subsequent quotes from Rajon Uddin Jalal in this chapter are taken from this interview.

12 *Brick Lane 1978: The Turning Point*, Four Corners exhibition catalogue (2022), p. 29.

13 'Eyewitness tells of dying student after East Ham stabbing', *London Evening News*, 18 July 1980.

14 Newham Monitoring Project and Campaign Against Racism and Fascism, *Forging a Black Community: Asian and Afro-Caribbean Struggles in Newham* (London: Newham Monitoring Project/ Campaign Against Racism and Fascism, 1991), p. 40.

15 Newham Monitoring Project and Campaign Against Racism and Fascism, *Forging a Black Community*, p. 36.

16 Newham Monitoring Project and Campaign Against Racism and Fascism, *Forging a Black Community*, p. 37.

17 Newham Monitoring Project and Campaign Against Racism and Fascism, *Forging a Black Community*, p. 41.

18 Newham Monitoring Project and Campaign against Racism and Fascism, *Forging a Black Community*, p. 41.

19 Newham Monitoring Project and Campaign against Racism and Fascism, *Forging a Black Community*, p. 42.

20 Newham Monitoring Project and Campaign against Racism and Fascism, *Forging a Black Community*, p. 43.

8 A NATIONAL MOVEMENT

1 Author interview with Asad Rehman, 2024. Unless otherwise indicated, all subsequent quotes from Asad Rehman in this chapter are taken from this interview.

2 Author interview with Mukhtar Dar, 2023. Unless otherwise indicated, all subsequent quotes from Mukhtar Dar in this chapter are taken from this interview.

3 Interview with Anwar Ditta, conducted by Jennifer Vickers for Ahmed Iqbal Ullah RACE Centre & Education Trust, 2018.

4 Interview with Anwar Ditta, conducted by Jennifer Vickers for Ahmed Iqbal Ullah RACE Centre & Education Trust, 2018.

5 Vikram Dodd, 'Met police accused of giving up search for 1981 Walthamstow arson attacker', *The Guardian*, 9 April 2024.

6 Author interview with Shirin Housee, 2025. Unless otherwise indicated, all subsequent quotes from Shirin Housee in this chapter are taken from this interview.

7 Campaign Against Racism and Fascism & Southall Rights, *Southall: The Birth of a Black Community* (London: Institute of Race Relations, 1981), p. 63.

8 Balraj Purewal, *Southall Youth Movement 1976–1984* (self-published, n.d.), p. 217.
9 Purewal, *Southall Youth Movement*, p. 223.
10 Author interview with Amer Abbas, 2021. Unless otherwise indicated, all subsequent quotes from Amer Abbas in this chapter are taken from this interview.
11 'Luton racist attacks', *Fight Racism! Fight Imperialism!*, July/August 1980.
12 Author interview with Muhammad Ikram, 2025. Unless otherwise indicated, all subsequent quotes from Muhammad Ikram in this chapter are taken from this interview.
13 *Luton News*, 31 December 1980.
14 Author interview with Mohammed Ashraf, 2025. Unless otherwise indicated, all subsequent quotes from Mohammed Ashraf in this chapter are taken from this interview.
15 *Luton News*, 10 February 1977.
16 Author interview with Fahim Qureshi, 2020. Unless otherwise indicated, all subsequent quotes from Fahim Qureshi in this chapter are taken from this interview.
17 *Herald and Post*, May 1981.
18 *Herald*, 9 July 1981.
19 *Socialist Worker*, 18 July 1981.
20 *Socialist Worker*, 18 July 1981.

9 SELF-DEFENCE IS NO OFFENCE

1 Author interview with Masood Malik, 2022. Unless otherwise indicated, all subsequent quotes from Masood Malik in this chapter are taken from this interview.
2 Author interview with Tariq Mehmood, 2022. Unless otherwise indicated, all subsequent quotes from Tariq Mehmood in this chapter are taken from this interview.
3 Michael Mansfield, *Memoirs of a Radical Lawyer* (London: Bloomsbury, 2010), p. 273.
4 'Reflecting on the Trial of the Decade: the Bradford 12', *Race Today*, August 1982.
5 *Telegraph & Argus*, 13 September 1981.
6 Anandi Ramamurthy, *Black Star: Britain's Asian Youth Movements* (London: Pluto, 2013), p. 141.
7 Author interview with Balwinder Rana, 2022. Unless otherwise indicated, all subsequent quotes from Balwinder Rana in this chapter are taken from this interview.
8 Author interview with Fahim Qureshi, 2022. Unless otherwise

indicated, all subsequent quotes from Balwinder Rana in this chapter are taken from this interview.

9 Ramamurthy, *Black Star*, p. 145.

10 Taj Ali, '"Self defence is no offence": remembering the Bradford 12', *Tribune*, 20 October 2022, https://tribunemag.co.uk/2022/10/self-defence-is-no-offence-remembering-the-bradford-12 (accessed 4 March 2026).

11 Journey to Justice, 'The Newham 8, police racism and community action', https://jtojhumanrights.org.uk/local-stories/local-stories-posts/the-newham-8-police-racism-and-community-action (accessed 4 March 2026).

12 This is the defendant's name as recorded in the sources.

13 Newham Monitoring Project and Campaign Against Racism and Fascism, *Forging a Black Community: Asian and Afro-Caribbean Struggles in Newham* (London: Newham Monitoring Project/Campaign Against Racism and Fascism, 1991), p. 51.

14 Newham Monitoring Project and Campaign Against Racism and Fascism, *Forging a Black Community*, p. 51.

15 Newham Monitoring Project and Campaign Against Racism and Fascism, *Forging a Black Community*, p. 52.

16 Newham Monitoring Project and Campaign Against Racism and Fascism, *Forging a Black Community*, p. 52.

17 Author interview with Iram Syed, 2025. Unless otherwise indicated, all subsequent quotes from Iram Syed in this chapter are taken from this interview.

18 Newham Monitoring Project, *Annual General Report* (1983), p. 34.

19 Newham Monitoring Project, *Annual General Report* (1983), p. 44.

20 Newham Monitoring Project, *Annual General Report* (1983), p. 8.

21 Newham Monitoring Project and Campaign Against Racism and Fascism, *Forging a Black Community*, p. 54.

22 Newham Monitoring Project and Campaign Against Racism and Fascism, *Forging a Black Community*, p. 54.

23 Newham Monitoring Project and Campaign Against Racism and Fascism, *Forging a Black Community*, p. 57.

10 SOLIDARITY

1 Anandi Ramamurthy, *Black Star: Britain's Asian Youth Movements* (London: Pluto, 2013), p. 155.

2 Ramamurthy, *Black Star*, p. 155.

3 'Attack on cabbie brings police talks with Asians', *The Sheffield Star*, 2 June 1982.
4 'Asian in protest march', *The Sheffield Star*, 16 August 1982.
5 Author interview with Mukhtar Dar, 2023. Unless otherwise indicated, all subsequent quotes from Mukhtar Dar in this chapter are taken from this interview.
6 Author interview with Badsha, 2024. Unless otherwise indicated, all subsequent quotes from Badsha in this chapter are taken from this interview.
7 Author interview with Matloub Husayn-Ali-Khan, 2024. Unless otherwise indicated, all subsequent quotes from Matloub Husayn-Ali-Khan in this chapter are taken from this interview.
8 Karl Marx, letter to Sigfrid Meyer and August Vogt, 9 April 1870.
9 Author interview with Mukhtar Dar, 2024.
10 Author interview with Paul Mackney, 2024. Unless otherwise indicated, all subsequent quotes from Paul Mackney in this chapter are taken from this interview.
11 Paul Mackney, quoted in Taj Ali, 'How South Asians Sustained the Miners' Strike', *Tribune*, 29 April 2024, https://www.tribunemag.co.uk/2024/04/how-south-asians-sustained-the-miners-strike (accessed 9 June 2026).
12 A Desi pub is one owned or managed by a landlord of Indian heritage.
13 Taj Ali, 'How South Asians sustained the miners' strike', *Tribune*, 29 April 2024, https://www.tribunemag.co.uk/2024/04/how-south-asians-sustained-the-miners-strike (accessed 24 March 2026).
14 Author interview with Nigel Flanagan, 2024. Unless otherwise indicated, all subsequent quotes from Nigel Flanagan in this chapter are taken from this interview.
15 Author interview with Denis Doody, 2024. Unless otherwise indicated, all subsequent quotes from Denis Doody in this chapter are taken from this interview.
16 Author interview with Hardev Dhillon, 2023. Unless otherwise indicated, all subsequent quotes from Hardev Dhillon in this chapter are taken from this interview.
17 Author interview with Nishaharan Vaithilingam, 2024. Unless otherwise indicated, all subsequent quotes from Nishaharan Vaithilingam in this chapter are taken from this interview.
18 Author interview with Mukhtar Dar, 2024.
19 Paul Mackney, quoted in Taj Ali, 'How South Asians Sustained the Miners' Strike'.
20 Paul Mackney, quoted in Taj Ali, 'How South Asians Sustained the Miners' Strike'.

21 Author interview with Mukhtar Dar, 2024.
22 Author interview with Mukhtar Dar, 2024.
23 Author interview with Raj, 2024. Unless otherwise indicated, all subsequent quotes from Raj in this chapter are taken from this interview.
24 Author interview with Asad Rehman, 2024. Unless otherwise indicated, all subsequent quotes from Asad Rehman in this chapter are taken from this interview.
25 Author interview with Pragna Patel, 2025. Unless otherwise indicated, all subsequent quotes from Pragna Patel are taken from this interview.
26 Natalie Thomlinson, *Race, Ethnicity and the Women's Movement in England, 1968–1993* (Basingstoke: Palgrave, 2016), p. 81.
27 Thomlinson, *Race, Ethnicity and the Women's Movement*, p. 81.
28 Author interview with Shirin Housee, 2025. Unless otherwise indicated, all subsequent quotes from Shirin Housee in this chapter are taken from this interview.
29 'Join the sari squad', *Spare Rib*, 11 (1983); 'Asian women bound over', *The Times*, 17 August 1983.
30 'Afia Begum', HC Deb, 11 June 1984, Hansard, vol. 61, cols. 735–42.
31 Author interview with Mukhtar Dar, 2024.
32 Author interview with Mukhtar Dar, 2024.
33 Author interview with Mukhtar Dar, 2020.

11 RUSHDIE, RIOTING AND RELIGIOUS DIVIDES

1 'Afternoon of mayhem', *Telegraph and Argus*, 19 June 1989.
2 Author interview with Mark (pseudonym); 12 October 2025.
3 Author interview with Amrit Wilson, 2025. Unless otherwise indicated, all subsequent quotes from Amrit Wilson in this chapter are taken from this interview.
4 Malcolm Pithers, 'Firebomb attacks on British temples', *Independent*, 8 December 1992, www.independent.co.uk/news/world/fire bomb-attacks-on-british-temples-1562249.html (accessed 4 March 2026).
5 Diana Hinds and Religious Affairs Correspondent, 'Hindu premises targeted in third night of arson', *Independent*, 10 December 1992, www.independent.co.uk/news/uk/hindu-premises-targeted-in-third-night-of-arson-1562688.html (accessed 4 March 2026).
6 Author interview with Asad Rehman, 2025. Unless otherwise indicated, all subsequent quotes from Asad Rehman in this chapter are taken from this interview.

7 Hinds and Religious Affairs Correspondent, 'Hindu premises targeted'.
8 *Evening Standard*, 9 September 1993.
9 *Campaign against Racism and Fascism*, 18, January/February 1994.
10 Author interview with Halima Begum, 2025. Unless otherwise indicated, all subsequent quotes from Halima Begum in this chapter are taken from this interview.
11 *East London Advertiser*, 30 September 1993.
12 'Bradford (Community Relations)', HC Deb, 21 June 1995, Hansard, vol. 262, cols. 281–301.
13 'Bradford (Community Relations): Mr Max Madden', HC Deb, 21 June 1995, Hansard, vol. 262, cols. 291–2.
14 'Bradford (Community Relations): Mr Max Madden', HC Deb, 21 June 1995, Hansard, vol. 262, col. 286.
15 'Bradford (Community Relations): Mr Max Madden', HC Deb, 21 June 1995, Hansard, vol. 262, cols. 287–8.
16 Virinder S. Kalra, *From Textile Mills to Taxi Ranks: Experiences of Migration, Labour and Social Change* (Aldershot: Ashgate, 2000), p. 126.
17 Author interview with Deej Malik Johnson, 2025. Unless otherwise indicated, all subsequent quotes from Deej Malik Johnson in this chapter are taken from this interview.
18 *Campaign against Racism and Fascism*, Feb/Mar 1991.
19 *Oldham Evening Chronicle*, 23 October 1990.
20 *Campaign against Racism and Fascism*, 63, Aug/Sep 2001.
21 Commission for Racial Equality, *Housing Allocations in Oldham* (London: CRE, 1993).
22 Oldham Independent Review, *One Oldham, One Future* (London: HMSO, 2001), p. 96.
23 Institute of Race Relations, *The Politics of Numbers: Police Racism and Crime Figures* (London: IRR, 1999), pp. 6–9.
24 Arun Kundnani, 'From Oldham to Bradford: the violence of the violated', *Institute of Race Relations*, 1 October 2001. Available at: https://irr.org.uk/article/from-oldham-to-bradford-the-violence-of-the-violated/ (accessed 20 May 2026).
25 Kundnani, 'From Oldham to Bradford'.
26 Institute of Race Relations, *The Summer of Rebellion: Special Report* (London: IRR, 1999).
27 Oldham Independent Review, *One Oldham, One Future*, Appendix 5: 'Regeneration Programme Spend by Ward'.
28 Campaign against Racism and Fascism, 'The summer of rebellion: special report by CARF', 1 August 2001.

29 'David Cameron defends Muslim extremism speech', *Sky News online*, 6 February 2011, https://news.sky.com/story/david-cameron-defends-muslim-extremism-speech-10489631 (accessed 24 March 2026).
30 Author interview with Fahim Qureshi, 2019.

EPILOGUE

1 Nabila is a pseudonym.
2 Child Poverty Action Group, 'Written evidence submitted by Child Poverty Action Group (IEDO0013)', December 2024, UK Parliament Work and Pensions Committee, https://committees.parliament.uk/writtenevidence/133080/html/ (accessed 24 March 2026).
3 Fawcett Society, *Double Trouble: The Ethnicity Gender Pay Gap* (2024), https://www.fawcettsociety.org.uk/news/fawcett-society-publish-pay-and-progression-of-women-of-colour-literature-review (accessed 24 March 2026).
4 Author interview with Mukhtar Dar, 2023.
5 Author interview with Fahim Qureshi, 2019.

ACKNOWLEDGEMENTS

'For you I have but one word: write... Believe in yourself, young man. I do.'

Those words were written to me by my English teacher, Helen Fielden, when I left high school. She had taught me for five years, given me extra tuition and treated my writing as something worth taking seriously from an early age.

Growing up, I did not know any authors, historians or journalists. As is the case for many working-class kids, we had no family connections, no informal mentors, no obvious pathways into those worlds, dominated by the wealthy and privileged. That is why I remain deeply grateful for Miss Fielden's encouragement.

Writing this book has been a long and at times exhausting process. It took years of archival research, oral history interviews, endless transcribing, writing and rewriting. There were moments when self-doubt inevitably crept in. But I have been fortunate to have the support and encouragement of many people along the way.

I'm grateful to Ilona Aronovsky for her support with research in Newham; to Liz Fekete and the team at the Institute of Race Relations for their guidance throughout; to Shabna Begum at the Runnymede Trust for her support; and to Suresh Grover of the Monitoring Group for his insight and encouragement. During the writing of this book's early chapters, the Asian and African Studies Reading Room at the British Library became a second home to me. My sincere thanks to the staff for their invaluable assistance. I would like to thank the Royal Society of Literature and the Lipman-Miliband Trust for their generous financial support, which enabled me to take time away from work to research this book.

This book explores how South Asian political activism often crossed religious and cultural divides. One of the most rewarding aspects of the process has been how the people who have supported it most have themselves come from diverse backgrounds. My friend and de-facto line manager Reha Kansara is a Gujarati Hindu with roots in East Africa. She held weekly check-in calls and gave me plenty of useful advice. I want to thank my mentors Aditya Chakrabortty, a Bengali Hindu, and Professor Sukhdev Johal, a Punjabi Sikh, both of whom encouraged me and supported me throughout the process.

I want to thank my immensely talented former colleague Francesca Newton for her feedback on early chapters, John Merrick for his helpful edits and the eagle-eyed Rebecca Durkin for her generous assistance with proofreading.

My thanks also go to my publisher Tom Dark who has been a joy to work with. Thank you for your patience, guidance and steady support throughout.

And finally, I want to thank my family. My dad, whose experiences growing up in Luton in the 1970s and 1980s amid racist violence first sparked my desire to tell these stories. My mum, for always prioritising my wellbeing and mental health above everything else. My siblings, for tolerating laptops on every surface and the dining table becoming a makeshift archive more than once. In particular, my older brother Akmal Ali, for supporting the family. You're a real role model to me and if it wasn't for your success, I doubt I would have had as much freedom to pursue my passions.

And to everyone who shared their stories, encouraged me to write and, crucially, believed in me, thank you.

INDEX

Aberdeen, ix
Acharya, M. P. T., 21, 24, 26
Adams, Rolan, 223
AFA *see* Anti-Fascist Action
Afghanistan, 222, 238
African-American, 54, 107, 132, 135
African People's Revolutionary Party, 216
Ahluwalia, Kiranjit, 211
Ahmed, Muhsin, 239
AITUC, 54
Aiyar, V. V. S., 22–24, 250
Akbar, 13, 40, 43–44, 164
Akhtar, Nasreen, 156
Akhtar, Tasleem, 216
Akram, Tahir, 216, 229
Aldgate, 57, 65, 94
Ali, Aftab, 59
Ali, Ayub, 55, 57, 60
Ali, Ishaque, 142
Ali, Muhammad, 10, 165
Alipore, 21
Ali, Quddus, 224
Ali, Salman, 93
Ali, Surat, 44, 58–60
Ali, Tariq, 85, 215, 255
Ali, Tosir, 91, 94
All-India Muslim League, 10, 26
All-India Seamen's Federation, 58–59
Amalgamated Engineering Union, 194
Amalgamated Union of Foundry Workers, 81
American Negro Labor Congress, 54
Amery, L. S., 41
Amin, Chaturbhuj, 21
Amin, Govind, 24
Amin, Idi, 108
Amritsar, 25, 33, 223
Andaman Islands, 28
Anderson, Lee, ix
Anti-Fascist Action (AFA), 226
anti-imperialist, xi, 29, 45, 52, 171, 196
Anti-Nazi League, 137, 143–144, 166, 234
APEX *see* Association of Professional, Executive, Clerical and Computer Staff
Arab, 2, 48, 52, 58, 141
Arabic, 13
ARCAEL, 106
Archer, John, 53
army, 1–2, 19–21, 32, 51, 64, 99, 166, 197–198

Ashfield, Nigel, 201
Asian youth movements, 154–156, 196, 209, 215, 222, 226, 239, 244
assassination, 8, 26–27, 35, 38
Assembly, London, 236
Association of Professional, Executive, Clerical and Computer Staff (APEX), 119–120, 122–123
Atwal, Parminder, 139
AUFW, 81
Awaz, 126–127
Ayodhya, 221
Aziz, Abdul, 14

Bacon, Francis, 6
Bagh, Jallianwala, 33–34, 40, 42
Bahini, Mukti, 133
Baig, Akhtar Ali, 146–147, 184, 186
Baker, Clarence, 138
Baksh, Khuda, 14
Baldwin, James, xiii
Ballymena, x
Bangladesh, 56, 93, 98–99, 102, 106–107, 133, 143, 213–214, 217
Bangladeshi, xiii, 62, 98–99, 103–106, 143, 196, 200, 217, 225, 228, 230, 233, 238, 243
Bangladeshi Youth Association, 143
Bangladesh Youth Front, 143
Bangladesh Youth League, 143
Bapat, Pandurang Mahadev, 21
Barbados, 62
Barking, 148, 189
Barnet, 139
Barrackpore, 3
Barry, 52
Basra, Thakur Singh, 38, 40, 43
Basra, Ujagar Singh, 38
Battersea, 53
Beackon, Derek, 225
Begum, Afia, 214–215, 263
Begum, Halima, 101, 106, 145, 224–225, 247, 257, 263
Begum, Iqbal, 212
Begum, Julie, 225
Begum, Nasira, 156, 158
Begum, Shabna, 101, 256
Begum, Sufia, 101
Behn, Shardha, 116
Belgium, 51
Bengal, 3, 5–7, 15–16, 21, 41, 47, 54, 58, 77, 99, 104, 249
Bengali, 6, 20, 43, 55–56, 100, 102, 104, 106, 142–144, 225, 256–257
Bengali Housing Action Group, 104
Bengal Mariners' Union, 58
Bengal Renaissance, 5, 7
Benn, Tony, 158
Berber, 21
Bethnal Green, 57, 93, 105, 144–145, 224
BHAG, 104–107
Bharat, Abhinav, 15
Bishop Auckland, vii
Bhujangy, Balbir, 79
Bihar, 19
Birmingham, 38–41, 43–44, 54, 62–63, 77, 83, 85–86, 91, 100, 115, 155, 160, 197, 200–202, 206, 212–213, 216, 221, 238–239, 242, 244, 253–255, 262
Birmingham AYM, 213
Birmingham Black Sisters, 212–213
Birmingham Campaign Against Racism and Fascism, 200
BJP, 28, 249

Black Panthers, 78, 91, 96, 103, 132, 216
Black People's Alliance, 90, 96
Black People Support the Miners, 204
Black Power, 74, 78–79, 85, 87, 89, 91, 93–97, 103, 132
BNP, 220–221, 225–226, 236
Bollywood, 75
Bolshevik, 53
Bolton, 155, 219, 221, 238
bomb, 8, 20–21, 92, 174–175
Bombay, 9, 22, 52–53, 249, 254
Bose, Subhas Chandra, 43
Bosnia, 223
boycott, 7, 51
BPA, 90–91
Bradford, 38, 40–41, 71–73, 151, 160, 170–175, 177–179, 183, 185, 187, 193–194, 197, 199, 204, 216–217, 219–221, 227, 234–235, 239, 242, 260–261, 264
Bradford AYM, 172, 217
Bradley, Ben, 53
Brah, Avtar, 141
Braverman, Suella, ix
Brent, 119, 122, 127
Brexit, 239
Brick Lane, 98–99, 103, 105–106, 143–145, 213, 224–225, 242, 256, 259
Brierfield, 154
Bristol, x
Britain First, 238
British East India Company, 1–2
British Empire, 1, 5, 59, 170, 250
British Guiana, 5
British National Party, 220, 224, 233
British Shipping Act, 58
Brixton, 27, 101, 103, 160, 167–168
Bromley, George, 114
Bromwich, West, 63
Brothers, Kewal, 206
Brussels, 236
Bunsee, Bennie, 111–112, 114, 257
Burke, Edmund, 14
Burnage, 229
Burnley, 72, 151–152, 154, 209, 234–236
Burnsall, 123
Bury Park, 62, 162, 164, 166, 168–169, 237

Calcutta, 3, 5–7, 9, 49, 52
Callaghan, James, 93, 122
Cama, Bhikhaji, 14
Cama, Madame, 30
Cambridge, 16, 19, 248
Camden, 63
Campaign Against Racial Discrimination, 77–78, 254
Canada, 31
Canary Wharf, xiii, 46
Canning Town, 142, 180, 189
Canterbury, 36
CARD, 77–78
Cardiff, 49, 52, 54
Caribbean, 112, 146, 149, 162, 171, 175, 177, 190, 192, 200, 204–205, 218, 259, 261
Carlos, John, 132, 135
Caxton Hall, 26, 34, 36, 50
CCARD, 77–78
central Punjab, 36
Chaggar, Gurdip Singh, 128, 133, 135, 140, 147
Chapekar, Vasudeo, 9
Chapeltown, 160, 177, 198, 205
Chechnyan, 223
Cheema, Charan Singh, 38, 43
Cheema, Karam Singh, 38
Chelsea, 164

Chicago, 30, 35
Chinese, 31, 48, 58, 77, 114, 204
Cirencester, 19
Cohen, Harry, 215
Coleridge, Samuel Taylor, 8
Colonial Seamen's Union, 58
Commonwealth Citizens UK Association, 73
Commonwealth Immigrants Act, 78, 109
Communist Party (CPGB), 52–53, 55, 56, 58, 65–66, 76–77, 80, 96, 114, 135, 203
communists, 40–41, 43, 53, 55, 58
Coneygre, 81
Conservative Party, 41, 176
Corbyn, Jeremy, 215
courts, 19, 22, 25, 50, 96, 139, 148, 174, 179, 215, 250–252
Coventry, 38–45, 255
CPGB *see* Communist Party
Cricklewood, 121
Curzon, 7, 25, 250

Dagenham, 144
Daimler, 39
Dar, Mukhtar, viii, 103, 157, 195–196, 198, 205, 207, 215, 245, 247, 257, 259, 262–263, 265
Darnall, 193, 195
Das, Hemchandra, 21
Datta, Nita, 214
Dayal, Lala Har, 30–31, 244
deindustrialisation, 152, 225, 238
Delhi, 3–4, 87, 248–251
Denham, 36
Deptford, 63
Derbyshire, 63
Derozio, Henry Louis Vivian, 6
Desai, Jayaben, 118, 221
Desai, Unmesh, 149, 184–185, 244, 247
Desh Bhagat Parwar Sahaik Committee, 38
Despard, Charlotte, 12
Detroit, 35
Dewsbury, 155, 219–220
Dhami, Gurdial, 67
Dhillon, Hardev, 203, 247, 262
Dhillon, Parminder, 141
Dhingra, 21, 25–27, 250
Dhingra, Madan Lal, 24, 36
Dhondy, Farrukh, 103–104, 257
diaspora, 5, 7, 29, 31, 37, 108, 223, 251
Ditta, Anwar, 156–157, 209, 259
Doaba, 36
Dominion cinema, 75–76, 128
Doncaster, 44
Doody, Denis, 202, 207, 262
Dorset, 45
Dromey, Jack, 119
Dublin, 17, 27
Duggal, Rohit, 224
Dundee, 40, 49–50, 54, 252
Dunn, Cyril, 76, 254
Duratube and Wire Ltd, 67
Dutt, Clemens Palme, 55
Dutt, Rajani Palme, 55, 58
Dutt, Sukhsagar, 20
Dyer, General, 34

Ealing, 64, 130, 137, 139
Easington, x
East Africa, 5, 37, 108, 113, 117
East African Asians, 108–109
East Ham, 146–147, 149, 180, 259
East India Association, 34
East India Dock, xiii, 46, 56
East London, 49, 142
East London Workers against Racism, 215

Edinburgh, 16, 45, 115, 146, 188, 192
EDL, 236–238
Egypt, 13
Eliot, T. S., 8
Eltham, 224
Essex, x, 160, 212, 240
European Parliament, 215, 236
Evans, Danny, 69

factory, 44, 64–65, 67–71, 73, 79, 82, 106, 109–115, 117–119, 127, 132, 142, 144, 152, 162, 203
Faizi, Ghazala, 214
famine, 12, 15, 41
Farage, Nigel, ix
Fiji, 5
film, 36, 44, 66, 117, 121, 131
Finsbury, 12
First World War, 34, 51, 56
Fitzpatrick, Terry, 104
Fitzwilliam, 203
Flanagan, Nigel, 202, 205, 262
Football Lads Alliance, 238
Forest Gate, 146, 149, 151, 181, 183–184, 190
foundry, 79–81, 193
France, 16, 51, 98, 236
Free Indian Society, 20
Freitas, Michael de, 74
French Revolution, 6

Gaelic American, 14, 17, 27
Gallipoli, 51
Gandhi, 10, 14, 27, 137, 223, 249–250
Ganesh, 24
Garibaldi, 22
Garnett, David, 19, 26, 249
Gate Gourmet, 123, 257
Gaza, ix, 171, 238
Germany, 21, 32, 39, 43, 51, 95
Ghadar, 30–33, 35, 37–38, 41–42, 65, 77, 244, 250–251
Giani, Darshan Singh, 67
Gibraltar, 22
Gipton, 202
Gita, Bhagavad, 9
Glasgow, 40, 49, 52, 59, 253
Glasgow Trades Council, 59, 253
Glodwick, 229–230, 233–234
Greenford, 67
Grover, Suresh, viii, 128, 130, 135, 137, 140, 178, 244, 247, 258
Grunwick, 117–119, 121–123, 200, 257–258
Gujaratis, 55, 108
gurdwara, 51, 135, 179, 182, 184–185
Gurumukhi, 18
Gutzmore, Cecil, 204

Hackney, 101, 142, 144
Handsworth, 160, 198, 202, 206, 213, 242
Harehills, 202, 205
Haringey, 155
Harlem, 84, 133
Hartlepool, vi, vii
Heathrow, 124, 126–127, 141, 214–215
Hernandez, Lupe, 35
Hewit, Eric, 231
Highgate, 8–9, 11, 13, 15–17, 19, 21, 23, 25, 27, 29, 249
High Wycombe, 71
Hillsborough, 208
Hindu, 5–6, 8–9, 18, 28–29, 44, 221–222, 263
Hindus, 3, 20, 45, 68, 221, 233, 242
Hindustani Majlis, 40
Hindutva, 28–29

Hizb ut-Tahrir, 223
Holy Smoke, 134
Hong Kong, 31
Home Rule, 11, 13–14, 17, 24
Hoshiarpur, 36, 65, 77, 110
Houghton Regis, 167
Housee, Shirin 159, 212, 247, 259, 263
Howe, Darcus, 103
Howell, Fred, 69
Huddersfield, 39, 221
Hull, 52
Hume, David, 6
Husayn-Ali-Khan, Matloub, viii, 193, 195, 197, 208, 247, 262
Hussein, Mohammed Fazal, 42
Hyde Park, 95, 143, 160
Hyem, Abdul, 96
Hyndman, Henry, 12, 13

Idrish, Mohammed, 213
Ikram, Muhammad, 164–166, 168, 247, 260
Imperial Institute, 25
imperialism, 40, 96, 250, 260
Imperial Typewriters, 112–113, 115, 124, 257
independence, 3, 18, 45, 89, 250
Independent Labour Party, 40, 53
India House, 8, 12–30, 249
India League, 37, 41
Indian Home Rule Society, 11, 13–14, 17
Indian Mutiny, 3
Indian National Congress, 12, 36–37, 44, 76, 251
Indian Ocean trading network, 2
Indian Progressive Youth Association, 171
Indian Quartermasters' Union, 58
Indian Seamen's Union (ISU), 55–56, 58
Indian Seamen's Welfare League, 60
Indian Sociologist, 10, 14, 17–18, 27, 248–249
Indian Worker, 42
Indian Workers' Association (IWA), 38–45, 65, 66–71, 74–76, 77, 79–81, 85–87, 94, 115, 116, 125, 128, 133, 135, 137, 141, 147, 171, 200–201, 203, 211, 221, 223, 226, 254–255
Industrial Workers of the World Union (IWW), 30, 32
Indus Valley civilisation, 2
inquiry, 16, 111, 116, 139, 166
Institute of Race Relations, 72, 155, 248, 253, 256, 259, 264
Iraq, 51, 238–239
Ireland, 11, 171, 197
Irish, xi, 11–12, 14, 53, 63, 70, 96, 104, 157, 162, 187, 197, 200, 205, 256
Irish republicans, 11
Iron and Steel Workers Confederation, 54
Islamophobia, vii, ix, x, 28, 241
Islington, 101, 137
Israel, 238
ISU *see* Indian Seamen's Union
Italian, 15, 18
IWA *see* Indian Workers' Association
IWW *see* Industrial Workers of the World Union

Jalal, Rajon Uddin, 99, 142, 247, 256, 258–259
Jalandhar, 36, 65
Jamaican, 46, 82
Japanese, 31

Jewish, 78, 98, 162, 200
Jews, 95
Jhansi, Rani Laxmibai of, 19
Jinnah, Muhammad Ali, 10
John, DeWitt, 75, 254
Johnson, Deej Malik, 229, 247, 264
Jones, Claudia, 85
Josephides, Sasha, 77, 254
Joshi, Jagmohan, 77, 85, 87, 94, 200
Jouhl, Avtar Singh, 80, 86, 201, 244, 254

kabaddi, 134, 136
Kadir, Abdul, 101
Kadri, Sibghat, 95
Kanpur Conspiracy Case, 53
Kansara, Reha, 28
Karachi Seamen's Union, 59
Kashmir, 110, 208, 217
Kashmiri, 156, 198, 203, 215
Kaur, Jaswinder, 158
Kehtani, Hasmukh, 114
Kennedy, Helena, 176
Kent, 89, 122, 175, 203, 237
Kent Asian Youth Federation, 89, 175, 237
Kenya, 108–109
Khala, Kalbir Singh, 183
Khaliq, Malik, 73
Khan, Choudhury Akbar, 44
Khankhoje, Pandurang, 32
Khan, Parvaiz, 183, 191
Khan, Rafiq Muhammad, 19
Khan, Sadiq, ix, 237
Khan, Sir Aga, 26
Khomeini, Ayatollah, 219
King, Martin Luther, Jr, 86
Kirklees, 220
Kirtikar, 22–23
Koregaonkar, H.K., 21, 249
Krim, Abdul, 21–22
Ku Klux Klan, 90
Kundnani, Arun 232, 241, 264

Labour, viii, 40, 43, 53, 56, 63, 68, 74, 76, 78, 84, 86–88, 91, 108, 114, 123, 137, 153–154, 172, 194, 201, 215, 217, 236, 239, 251–253, 256, 264
labour, 5, 31–32, 39–40, 46–48, 52, 59–60, 62, 65–67, 71–72, 80–82, 110–111, 113, 122–123, 199, 213, 252–253
Lalcaca, Cawas, 25
Lall, Diwan Chaman, 54
Lancashire, 72, 79, 128, 130, 151, 209, 229, 231, 254
landlord, 262
lascars, xii, 43, 47–52, 54–59
Lascars' Welfare League, 54
Lawrence, Stephen, 224
Leamington Spa, 90
Lee, Bruce, 165
Leech, Kenneth, 95, 256
Leeds, 41, 63, 160, 176, 178, 202, 205, 220, 234
Leicester, 28, 54, 108–112, 115, 124, 137, 204, 242, 257
Liberal Party, 12
Limehouse, 49
Limeside, 230
Lippitt, Eric, 201, 206
Little Ilford, 180, 182, 186–187
Liverpool, 7, 40, 49, 52, 54, 63, 149, 157, 160
Livingstone, Ken, 184
Lokhande, Narayan Meghaji, 52
London, ix, xiii, 8–10, 12, 14–17, 19–20, 22, 24–25, 27, 34–36, 40, 44, 46, 49, 51–52, 54–57, 59–65, 72, 85, 89, 91–93, 95–96, 98–101, 103, 106–107, 109, 116–117, 126–127, 130, 132–133, 138, 142–143, 145,

London (*cont.*)
151, 154–155, 158–160, 168, 173, 180, 184, 190, 202–203, 207, 210, 215, 223–224, 231, 236–237, 248–261, 263–264
Lord Morley, 16
Loughborough, 110–111, 257
Ludhiana, 36, 110
Ludmer, Maurice, 77, 200
Luton, ix, 44, 62, 71, 100, 155, 162, 164–168, 173, 194, 236–239, 245, 260
LYM, 166–169, 178

Maharashtra, 15, 22
Mahasabha, Hindu, 44
Maidenhead, 44
Malaysia, 31
Malik, Masood, 170, 179, 247, 260
Manchester, 7, 16, 39, 41, 54, 62, 85, 155–156, 158, 160, 216, 228, 250
Manningham, 170, 172–173, 198, 227–228
Mann, Kuldeep, 156
Manor Park, 180, 182, 188
Mansfield Hosiery Mills, 110, 257
Mansfield, Michael, 175–176, 187, 260
Maratha, 15, 18
Marathi, 18
Marway, Narinder Singh, 148
Marx, Karl, 199, 262
Master, Ayub Ali, 55, 60
Mathers, Brian, 81
Mauritius, 5, 159
Mazdoor, 44
Mazzini, Giuseppe, 15, 18
Meerut, 3, 53
Mehmood, Tariq, 171, 179, 247, 260
Menon, Krishna, 37
Mexican, 35
Miah, Haji Kona, 57
Miah, Khosru, 106
Mianwali, 35
Middlesbrough, vi, vii
Midland Motor Cylinder Company, 81
Midlands, 38–39, 64, 76–77, 79–85, 90, 94, 109, 200–201, 212, 254–255
migration, 5, 65, 78, 100, 209, 248
Mile End, 127
Milligan, Robert, 46
mills, 31, 52, 54, 62, 72, 79, 113, 152, 228–230
miners, 51, 102, 122–123, 160, 191, 199–207, 209, 213, 262
Mirpuri, 212
Mogul, Shaf, 158
Mohammed, Jan, 40
Morris, Olive, 102
Mosque, vi, ix, x, 93, 143, 146, 154–155, 164, 166–167, 169, 193, 221, 240–241
Moss Side, 160
Movement for Colonial Freedom, 78
Mughal, 3–4, 15, 24
Multan, 35
multiculturalism, 222, 255
Muslim, vi, vii, ix, x, 7, 10, 13, 18, 26, 28, 40, 44, 85, 146, 191, 219–223, 236–238, 240–241, 264
Muslim League, 44
Muswell Hill, 11

Nagra, Kartar Singh, 42–43
Naoroji, Dadabhai, 12
National Association for Freedom, 121

National Council for Civil Liberties, 78
National Front, 102, 105, 109, 111, 115–116, 137, 142, 145, 165–166, 168, 188, 201, 219–220, 224, 229, 233, 236
National Union of Boot and Shoe Operatives, 54
National Union of Hosiery and Knitwear Workers, 111
National Union of Mineworkers (NUM), 121–122, 187, 198, 203, 207
Nation of Islam, 85
Naxalbari, 77
Nazi, 137, 143–144, 150, 165–167, 234
Nelson, 128, 130–132, 154
Newcastle, 39, 41
New Cross, 158–160, 176, 212
Newham, 72, 145, 149, 151, 154–155, 170, 183–187, 189–191, 197, 235, 244, 259, 261
Newham Monitoring Project, 149, 154, 184, 235, 244, 259, 261
Newport, 52
New York, 14, 17, 21, 35, 93, 236, 249, 255
Nicaragua, 216
Northern Ireland, vi, x, 123, 197
North Feltham, 67
Nottingham, 44, 63, 155, 204, 255
Notting Hill, 63, 204
NUM *see* National Union of Mineworkers

Oakland, 30
O'Dwyer, Michael, 34–35
Oldbury, x
Oldham, 100, 216, 221, 228–231, 233–235, 264
Oregon, 31
Orgreave, 191, 198, 205, 208
Overseer, Karam Singh, 43
OWAAD, 102, 127
Oxford, 16, 19, 30, 85, 249–251, 254

Pacific coast, 37
Padosi, 44
Paine, Thomas, 6
Pakistan, 10, 26, 66, 93, 99, 133, 152, 156–157, 171, 191, 209, 216
Pakistani, 62, 66, 71, 73, 78, 81, 85, 93–97, 99, 107, 124, 136, 146, 153, 156, 163–164, 166, 171, 177, 203, 215, 217, 228–230, 238–239, 242–243, 256
Pakistani Welfare Association, 71, 94, 164
Pakistani Workers' Association, 78, 203, 215–217
Pakistani Workers' Union, 94–96, 256
Pal, Bipin Chandra, 20
Palestine, 151, 155, 207, 238
Palestinians, 213, 238
Pal, Niranjan, 20
Pandey, Mangal, 3
Parekh, Palavi, 214
Paris, 14–15, 17–18, 21, 27, 30, 249
Parsi, 53
Pasha, Mustafa Kamel, 13
Patel, N. C., 114
Patel, Pragna, 141, 210, 247, 258, 263
Patnaik, Utsa, 3, 248
Peacehaven, x
Peach, Blair, 138, 140, 258
pedlar, 36
Peirce, Gareth, 179, 185, 191

Pendle, 154–155, 157
Peshwa, Shreemant Nana Saheb, 19
Peterborough, 44
Petticoat Lane, 102, 202
Plaistow, 148, 189
police, 23, 96, 122, 138–139, 158, 161, 177, 195, 208, 238, 258, 264
Polish, 63, 67
political blackness, 85, 140–141, 204, 221
Poplar, 105, 225
Portsmouth, x
Powell, Enoch, 88–89, 95, 109, 162, 255
Pradhan, R. G., 14
Progressive Youth Organisation, 143
Pryce, Eustace, 189
Pryce, Gerald, 189
Pune, 8–9
Punjab, 25, 31, 33–36, 61, 64–66, 75, 77, 79–80, 110, 223
Punjabi, 12, 31–33, 35, 37–39, 41, 43, 45, 60–61, 67–69, 79, 90, 202, 250–251
Purewal, 129–130, 135–136, 138, 140, 161, 247, 258, 260
PWA *see* Pakistani Workers' Association
PWU *see* Pakistani Workers' Union

Qadir, Anwar, 194
Qureshi, Fahim, 166, 178, 237, 245, 247, 260, 264–265
Qureshi, Shah Abdul Majid, 57

Race Today (collective and journal), 67, 103–106, 110, 113, 115–116, 121, 155, 253, 257–258, 260
Racial Adjustment Action Society, 7
Radar, xiii
Rai, Lala Lajpat, 12, 77
Rajan, T. S. S., 22–24
Rana, Balwinder, 89, 175, 178, 237, 247, 255, 260-261
Rana, Sardar Singh, 14
Rand, Walter Charles, 8
Raza, Haider, 14
Reading, 19, 44, 251
Rehman, Asad, 151, 155, 160, 209, 222, 226, 235, 247, 259, 262–263
Rehman, Gulshun, 184
revolution, 4, 9–10, 15–16, 20
Robinson, Tommy, xi, 237
Rochdale, 156–157
Rock Against Racism, 137
Roots, 153
Rose, John, 140, 258
Rotherham, vi, 165, 198
Roy, M. N., 58
Roy, Raja Ram Mohan, 6
RSS, 28
Runnymede Trust, 98, 101, 256
Rushdie, Salman, 219–220
Russia, 21, 40–41, 52–53, 98, 223

Sabha, Atmiya, 6
Sacranie, Iqbal, 221
sailors, 46–48, 50, 52, 55, 60
Saklatvala, Shapurji, 53–55, 58, 252–253
Salafist, 223
Saleem, Mohammed, 239
Salford, 52
Salter, Joseph, 47, 49, 251–252
Saltley, 121, 123
Sandha, Surinder, 140
Sandhu, Tarsem Singh, 86
Sands, Bobby, 157
San Francisco, 35

Sanskrit, 9, 14
Sarabha, Kartar Singh, 33
Sari Squad, 214–215
Sastrya, Vellala Srikantaya, 39, 41–44
Saudi, 222
Savarkar, Vinayak Damodar, 15, 18–29, 249–250
Savile Town, 220
Sawh, Roy, 74
Scargill, Arthur, 122–123, 187, 199, 207, 258
Scotland, 18, 23, 42, 44, 122, 154
Scotland Yard, 23
Scottish, 162
seamen, xiii, 30–31, 44, 48, 51, 56, 58, 252
Second Socialist Congress, 15
Second World War, 59–60, 62, 65, 108
Sen, Mala, 103–106, 113, 115, 257
sepoy, 3
Shah, Bahadur, 4, 13, 19, 24
Shah Jalal restaurant, 57
Shah, Maulvi Ahmadullah, 19
Shah, Zoora, 211
Shaikh, Nilofer, 156
Shanghai, 31
Sharma, Krishna, 211
Sharma, Vishnu Dutt, 66–68, 76, 137, 253
Sheffield, viii, ix, 85, 103, 155, 157, 191, 193–199, 205, 208, 215–217, 219, 261
Sheffield Asian Youth Movement, viii, 103, 193
Sheffield Campaign Against Racism, 194
Sheffield Defence Campaign, 208
Shepherd's Bush, 51
ships, 12, 46–50, 57, 59
Shivaji, 18
Shore, Peter, 93–94
Sikh, x, 19, 38, 40, 51, 61, 82, 87–88, 90, 115, 148, 168, 202, 223, 255
Sikhism, 32–33, 223
Sikhs, 18, 40, 43, 45, 68, 87–88, 179, 221, 223, 233, 237, 254–255
Sikorski, Caroline, 184
Singapore, 32
Singh, Baba Bakhtaura, 202
Singh, Babu Kunwar, 19
Singh, Bhagat, 35, 42, 77
Singh, Gurdev, 68
Singh, Harnam, 19
Singh, Kamaljit, 201
Singh, Kennith, 142, 148
Singh, Maharajah Duleep, 50
Singh, Marsha, 217
Singh, Mukhtiar, 69
Singh, Satnam, 184
Singh, Sophia Duleep, 50, 252
Singh, Udham, 34–36, 38, 42–43, 251
Sinn Féin, 17, 178, 197
Sino-Soviet split, 77
skinheads, 91–93, 95, 131, 146, 160–163, 167–169, 180, 196, 224
Smethwick, 80, 84–86, 123, 254–255
Smith, Tommie, 132, 135
socialism, 53
socialist, 29, 32, 44–45, 95, 135, 158, 172, 251
Socialist Feminist Group, 209
South Africa, 5, 10, 14, 59, 111, 133, 155, 178, 197
Southall, viii, 61–62, 64–67, 72, 74–77, 105, 115, 125, 128–129, 131, 133–135, 137, 139–142, 144–145, 147, 160–163,

Southall (*cont.*)
167–168, 171, 178, 198, 204, 210–211, 213, 244, 253–254, 258–260
Southall Black Sisters, 140–141, 204, 210, 213
Southall Residents Association, 65
Southampton, 36
Southan, Malcolm, 91
South Kensington, 25
Southport, vi
South Shields, 52
South West Africa People's Organisation, 216
Soviet Union, 58, 222
Sparkbrook, 42
Special Patrol Group, 123, 139
Spencer, Herbert, 10
Spitalfields, 98, 101–102, 256–257
Sri Lanka, 133, 156
Staffordshire, 201
Stoke, 233, 238
strike, 24, 32, 49, 51, 54, 67, 69–75, 81–83, 102, 111–116, 119–123, 127, 142, 144, 160, 180, 186, 198, 200–202, 204–206, 209, 213, 254, 257, 262
students, xi, 6, 9–10, 12–13, 16–20, 31, 58, 86, 89, 111, 144, 156, 160, 165, 193, 215, 223
Stuttgart, 15
suffragette, 50
Sufi, 19
Suhrawardy, Abdullah al-Mamun, 13
Sultan, Tipu, 13
Sunak, Rishi, 242
Sunni, 85
Suri, Kalwant, 134
surveillance, xi, 21, 23–24, 33, 38–41, 192, 197, 238
Sussex, x
Swadeshi, 7, 20
Syed, Iram, 186, 247, 261
Sylheti, 55, 98, 252
SYM, 134–138, 140–141, 161

Tamil, 22–23, 156
Tamworth, vi
Tata, Jamsetji, 53
Teare, Parajati, 214
textile, 52, 64, 72, 79, 98, 103, 142, 229
TGWU, 68–69, 71, 73–74, 87, 113–114, 116, 254
Thatcher, Margaret, ix, 168, 172
The Satanic Verses, 219
Tilak, Bal, 9, 11, 15, 249
Tooti Nungs, 134
Tipton, 81
Tower Hamlets, xiii, 92–93, 98, 100, 104, 144, 224
Toxteth, 160, 177, 198
Trades Union Congress (TUC), 52, 54, 66, 120, 123, 200, 258
trade union, 30, 38, 54, 56, 58, 66, 74–75, 79–81, 87, 111, 117, 120–124, 194, 199, 201, 206, 213
Tribune, vii, 37, 252, 261–262
Trinidad, 5
Troops Out, 197, 209
Trotskyist, 39–40, 70, 140, 172
TUC *see* Trades Union Congress
turban, 24, 87, 255
Turkey, 51

Uganda, 35, 108, 130
Ullah, Ahmed Iqbal, 216, 229, 259

union, 53, 56, 58, 66–71, 73, 80–83, 94, 111–114, 116–117, 119–120, 122, 194, 203, 207
Union of Postal Workers, 121–122
United Black Youth League, 173, 217
United States, 30, 35, 54, 74, 78–79, 86, 94
Universal Coloured People's Association, 94
Upton Park, 188
Urdu, 31, 44, 56, 71, 126, 212
Usmani, Shaukat, 53

Vaisakhi, 33
Vaithilingam, 203–204, 206, 247, 262
Varma, Shyamji Krishna, 8–15, 17–18, 24, 27, 249
Vidya Parkash Hansrani, 42
Vietnam, 107, 215
Virk brothers, 147
Visram, Rozina, xi, 16, 249, 251

Wales, 67, 201, 204, 206
Waltham Forest, 159
Wanstead Flats, 188
Ward, George, 121
Washington, 31
Watford, 155, 166
Wembley, 119
West India Dock, 46
West Indian, 48, 58, 63–64, 74, 78, 92, 94, 138, 163, 169, 177, 229, 242
West Indian Gazette, 78
Westwood, 230, 233
Whitechapel, 59, 127, 142, 224
Willesden, 70, 117, 119, 123, 127
Wilson, Amrit, 114, 118, 124, 156, 221, 247, 257–258, 263
Wilson, Harold, 84
Wise, Audrey, 123
Wolverhampton, 39, 81–83, 86–88, 201, 255
Women's Social and Political Union, 50
Women Unite Against Racism (WUAR), 225
Woolfs, 64–65, 67–69, 71
Working People's Party of England, 96
wrestling, 21, 135
WUAR *see* Women Unite Against Racism
WWLI, 53–54

X, Malcolm, 74, 84–86, 132, 151, 153, 255
X, Michael, 74

Yorkshire, 53, 72, 79, 122, 155, 194, 198, 203, 207–209

Zafar, Bahadur Shah, 13
zamindars, 4
Zulu, 14

EU authorised representative for GPSR:
Easy Access System Europe, Mustamäe tee 50,
10621 Tallinn, Estonia
gpsr.requests@easproject.com

www.ingramcontent.com/pod-product-compliance
Lightning Source LLC
LaVergne TN
LVHW030539090926
847673LV00019B/123/J
* 9 7 8 1 5 2 6 1 7 7 5 8 2 *